Urban Regeneration in China

The book examines institutional innovation in urban regeneration in Guangzhou, Shenzhen, and Shanghai, three Chinese cities that have experienced sweeping changes in recent years, providing an ideal guide to the development of urban regeneration practices in China.

As a starting point, the book revisits relevant theoretical developments and the institutional experiences of urban regeneration in some Asian pioneer cities and regions, such as Hong Kong, Taipei, Tokyo, and Singapore. Moving on to the Chinese mainland cities themselves, the core comparative study investigates the institutional systems, key policies, planning formulations, and implementation paths in the urban regeneration processes of the three cities. Gains and losses that have resulted from each city's institutional construction and reform are discussed, as well as the underlying reasons for these. Drawing on these case studies and comparisons, the book puts forward some generic rules for urban regeneration institutional innovation, offering a valuable frame of reference for other cities and regions.

The book will appeal to scholars interested in urban regeneration and renewal, as well as urban planners, architects, policymakers, and urban development administrators.

Yan TANG is an Associate Professor in the School of Architecture at Tsinghua University, China. Her research interests include urban design and planning, urban regeneration, and urban and rural governance.

Dong YANG is an urban planner at the Architectural Design and Research Institute of Tsinghua University, China. His research interests are urban design, urban regeneration, and cultural heritage conservation.

China Perspectives

The *China Perspectives* series focuses on translating and publishing works by leading Chinese scholars, writing about both global topics and China-related themes. It covers Humanities and Social Sciences, Education, Media and Psychology, as well as many interdisciplinary themes.

This is the first time any of these books have been published in English for international readers. The series aims to put forward a Chinese perspective, give insights into cutting-edge academic thinking in China, and inspire researchers globally.

To submit proposals, please contact the Taylor & Francis Publisher for China Publishing Programme, Lian Sun (Lian.Sun@informa.com)

Titles in architecture currently include:

Vertical Urbanism
Designing Compact Cities in China
Zhongjie Lin, José L.S. Gámez

Woven Arch Bridge
Histories of Constructional Thoughts
LIU Yan

Urban Regeneration in China
Institutional Innovation in Guangzhou, Shenzhen, and Shanghai
Yan TANG, Dong YANG

For more information, please visit https://www.routledge.com/China-Perspectives/book-series/CPH

Urban Regeneration in China
Institutional Innovation in Guangzhou, Shenzhen, and Shanghai

Yan TANG and Dong YANG

LONDON AND NEW YORK

First published 2022
by Routledge
2 Park Square, Milton Park, Abingdon, Oxon OX14 4RN

and by Routledge
605 Third Avenue, New York, NY 10158

Routledge is an imprint of the Taylor & Francis Group, an informa business

© 2022 Yan TANG and Dong YANG

The right of Yan TANG and Dong YANG to be identified as authors of this work has been asserted by them in accordance with sections 77 and 78 of the Copyright, Designs and Patents Act 1988.

All rights reserved. No part of this book may be reprinted or reproduced or utilised in any form or by any electronic, mechanical, or other means, now known or hereafter invented, including photocopying and recording, or in any information storage or retrieval system, without permission in writing from the publishers.

Trademark notice: Product or corporate names may be trademarks or registered trademarks, and are used only for identification and explanation without intent to infringe.

British Library Cataloguing-in-Publication Data
A catalogue record for this book is available from the British Library

Library of Congress Cataloging-in-Publication Data
Names: Tang, Yan, 1977- author. | Yang, Dong, 1991- author.
Title: Urban regeneration in China : institutional innovation in Guangzhou, Shenzhen, and Shanghai / Yan Tang, Dong Yang.
Description: 1 Edition. | New York : Routledge, 2021. | Series: China perspectives | Includes bibliographical references and index.
Identifiers: LCCN 2021005566 (print) | LCCN 2021005567 (ebook) | ISBN 9780367704117 (hardback) | ISBN 9780367709112 (paperback) | ISBN 9781003146193 (ebook)
Subjects: LCSH: Urban renewal--China--Case studies. | Urban renewal--Government policy--China--Case studies. | City planning--China--Case studies.
Classification: LCC HT178.C55 T36 2021 (print) | LCC HT178.C55 (ebook) | DDC 307.3/4160951--dc23
LC record available at https://lccn.loc.gov/2021005566
LC ebook record available at https://lccn.loc.gov/2021005567

ISBN: 978-0-367-70411-7 (hbk)
ISBN: 978-0-367-70911-2 (pbk)
ISBN: 978-1-003-14619-3 (ebk)

Typeset in Times New Roman
by SPi Global, India

Contents

List of figures	vi
List of tables	vii
Foreword I	x
Foreword II	xii
Foreword III	xiv
Preface	xvi
Acknowledgements	xvii

1	Introduction: Urban regeneration in China in the modern era	1
2	The institutional innovation of urban regeneration from an Asian perspective	11
3	The evolution of urban regeneration in Guangzhou, Shenzhen, and Shanghai	29
4	Urban regeneration policies and regulations in the three cities	41
5	Development of urban regeneration institutional systems in the three cities	64
6	Spatial management and control of urban regeneration in the three cities	88
7	Urban regeneration implementation paths in the three cities	108
8	Urban regeneration fulfillment and experiences in the three cities	141
9	Critical elements and future development of institutional innovations in urban regeneration in China	172

References	195
Index	200

Figures

1.1	China's City Cluster Plan	4
2.1	Flow Chart of Kowloon Urban Renewal Plan development	15
2.2	Urban Renewal Procedure in Taipei	18
4.1	Structural Framework of the Guangzhou Urban Regeneration Measures	54
4.2	Structural Framework of the Shenzhen Urban Regeneration Measures	55
4.3	Structural Framework of the Shanghai Urban Regeneration Implementation Measures	55
5.1	Institutional System of Urban Regeneration in Guangzhou	64
5.2	Institutional System of Urban Regeneration in Shenzhen	65
5.3	Institutional System of Urban Regeneration in Shanghai	66
5.4	Administrative Procedures for Urban Regeneration Projects involving Comprehensive Renewal in Guangzhou	74
5.5	Administrative Procedures for Urban Regeneration Projects Involving Demolition and Reconstruction in Shenzhen	75
5.6	Administrative Procedures for Urban Regeneration Projects in Shanghai	76
5.7	"1+3+N" Planning System for Urban Regeneration in Guangzhou	78
5.8	Urban Regeneration Planning System in Shenzhen	79
5.9	Flowchart for Urban Regeneration Planning in Shanghai	80
5.10	Distribution of Urban Regeneration Land in Guangzhou	83
5.11	Application Procedure for Urban Renewal Units in Shenzhen	85
6.1	Urban Regeneration and Renovation of Guangzhou: Development Intensity Zones	91
6.2	Zoned Guidance Map for Urban Regeneration in the Shenzhen 13th Five-Year Plan for Urban Regeneration	99
7.1	Major Models of Urban Regeneration in Guangzhou	109
7.2	Land Range (left) and Construction Plan (right) of Yangmei New Village Urban Renewal Unit Plan, Yantian District	123
7.3	Distribution Map of Four Action Plans Projects in Shanghai (12+X, 2016)	128
7.4	Map of Land Use Plan in Xuhui West Bund	136
9.1	Three Critical Areas of Urban Regeneration Institution Innovations	172

Tables

1.1	Ten Dimensions of Urban Regeneration in China	2
1.2	Gross Domestic Product of Guangzhou, Shenzhen, and Shanghai, 2010–2016	7
2.1	Social Impact Assessment of Urban Renewal in Hong Kong	14
2.2	Activities of the Urban Renewal Agency	22
4.1	Urban Regeneration (Implementation) Measures published in Guangzhou, Shenzhen, and Shanghai (2009–2015)	41
4.2	Development of Urban Regeneration Policies in Guangzhou	45
4.3	Comparison of Definition and Approach in the Urban Regeneration (Implementation) Measures in Guangzhou, Shenzhen, and Shanghai	56
4.4	Comparison of Urban Regeneration Annual/Implementation Plans in Guangzhou, Shenzhen, and Shanghai	57
4.5	Regulations on Fund Raising and Funding Allocation in the Urban Regeneration (Implementation) Measures in Guangzhou, Shenzhen, and Shanghai	59
5.1	Urban Regeneration Institutional Innovation in Guangzhou, Shenzhen, and Shanghai compared	66
5.2	Comparison of Institutional Settings in Guangzhou, Shenzhen, and Shanghai	68
5.3	Administrative Responsibilities Delegated from Municipal Level to District Level in Guangzhou	69
5.4	Administration Procedures for Regeneration Projects in Old Towns, Old Villages and Old Industrial Lands in Guangzhou	72
5.5	Urban Regeneration Planning in Guangzhou, Shenzhen, and Shanghai compared	77
5.6	Urban Regeneration/Renewal Units or Districts in Guangzhou, Shenzhen, and Shanghai compared	81
5.7	Disposal of Historical Land in Urban Renewal Projects involving Demolition and Reconstruction in Shenzhen	85
6.1	Function Guidance for Urban Regeneration in Guangzhou	89
6.2	Urban Regeneration of Guangzhou: Development Intensity Classification	90

viii *Tables*

6.3	Classification of Element Guidelines for Micro Renovation of Old Residential Areas in Guangzhou	93
6.4	Compensation Standards for Land Expropriation of Old Factories by the Government	95
6.5	Land Premium Payment for Self-Renewal	95
6.6	Basic Regulations on Intensity Zoning of Urban Construction Land	96
6.7	Floor Area Ratio Guidance for Residential Land	96
6.8	Floor Area Ratio Guidance for Commercial and Services Land	97
6.9	Floor Area Ratio Guidance for Industrial Land	97
6.10	Floor Area Ratio Guidance for Logistics and Storage Land	97
6.11	Floor Area Adjusted for Road Adjacency	98
6.12	Floor Area Adjusted for Metro Stations	98
6.13	Complementary Construction Standards for Innovative Industries Buildings in Shenzhen High-tech Park	100
6.14	Summary of Gratuitously Transferred Public Amenities	101
6.15	Suggestions on Public Elements Lists	105
6.16	Upper Limits of Extra Floor Area for Commercial and Office Buildings	106
6.17	Multiplier Discounting Factor when Exceeding the Requirements of Pertinent Regulations	106
7.1	Complementary Interaction between the Government and the Market in the Urban Regeneration of Guangzhou	110
7.2	City-District-Village Collective Organizational Structure	112
7.3	Urban Renewal Unit Annual Plan of Longgang District in 2018 (Third Batch)	117
7.4	Comparison Between the 2012, 2014, and 2016 Versions of the Provisional Measures in Shenzhen	118
7.5	Typical Examples of Different Urban Regenerations in Shenzhen	119
7.6	Calculation of Land Available for Redevelopment in Yangmei New Village	122
7.7	Four Action Plans of Shanghai Urban Regeneration (12+X, 2016-2017)	126
7.8	Walking in Shanghai - Community Space Minor Renovation Plan (2016, 2017)	129
7.9	Urban Regeneration Unit Public Elements List	132
7.10	Industrial Layout of the West Bund, Shanghai	134
8.1	"Three Olds" Regeneration Projects before the Establishment of Urban Regeneration Bureau (projects till December 2014)	142
8.2	Urban Regeneration Annual Program/Plan of Guangzhou (2015–2018, till the first batch in 2018)	144
8.3	Approved Areas in Urban Regeneration Unit Plans Involving Demolition and Reconstruction in Shenzhen (to the end of 2017)	146
8.4	Annual Program/Plan of Urban Renewal Units in Shenzhen (2010–2017)	147
8.5	Distribution of Urban Renewal Unit Areas in Various Districts during the 13th Five-Year Period in Shenzhen	148

8.6	Land Supply through Urban Regeneration and the Development of New Land in Shenzhen (2010-2015, in hectares)	148
8.7	Shanghai Urban Regeneration Trial Projects (September 2015)	150
8.8	Land-use Proportions after Regeneration of Approved Urban Renewal Units in Shenzhen	162
9.1	Comparison of Policies to Activate Industrial Land across Various Cities (before 2015)	179
9.2	Toolbox for Urban Regeneration Management	187
9.3	Implementation Steps for Urban Regeneration Institution Innovations	193

Foreword I

Cities are living beings: their lives reside in their ever-changing and circulating vitality. Urban regenerations are in turn their metabolism, and are thus an eternal urban theme. However, this metabolism should be more cellular, i.e., small-scale and progressive, rather than large-scale and discrete as is currently the case in China. In an historical exception, rapid mass urban renovation in China has now been going on for more than three decades. Urban construction and development urgently need to get back on track following this exceptional period, moving from extensive incremental development to develop an organic refined inventory. Urban regeneration more often takes on the form of small-scale renovations, continuous optimization of urban functionalities, and the improvement of urban spatial quality. Normally, the expansion development phase aligns with the construction stage of the cities, and the inventory development phase with the maintenance and elevation stage. In the full life-cycle of urban development, expansion development is relatively ephemeral, while inventory development is longer-lasting and the norm.

However, the present urban construction and management institutions in China were established for the purpose of rapid massive construction activities after the reform and opening up. Faced with the rapid transformation in urban development, such existing institutions are manifesting more and more incompatibilities, highlighting the need for the construction of novel institutions.

The authors of this book selected Guangzhou, Shenzhen, and Shanghai to address the latest configuration of urban regenerations in China. The three cities are at the forefront of national urban regeneration and are attempting to solve the current complex institutional dilemma at the heart of urban regeneration – institutional construction. The three cities, having all discovered relatively early the unsustainability of mass expansion, while at the same time faced with the urgent need to further enhance urban functionalities and qualities, took the lead in proposing novel conceptions of urban regeneration addressing their respective realities. A noteworthy phenomenon is that during the last decade all three cities have been raising the relevant institutional construction issues almost simultaneously with their exploration of urban regeneration projects, showing that the difficulties in urban regeneration in China include not only the current institutional obstacles, but also the transformation of development mindsets. Judging from the practices of Guangzhou, Shenzhen, and Shanghai, all three cities have undertaken extremely beneficial exploration. In this regard, this book provides much-needed valuable experience and timely lessons for urban regeneration throughout the nation.

We can also observe that despite the above cities leading the rest of the nation in development attitudes by realizing the need for urgent urban development transformation, and through their timely establishment of corresponding policies and institutions, there remains a possibility that some city officials will interpret urban regeneration as a new catchphrase for a new round of "full-throttle" mass urban construction. Consequently, while some regenerated areas boasting their achievements may present splendid façades but very few public services, the "regeneration" of other vigorous and mature urban areas may generate maximum land revenue, but cause the destruction of the local context and the disappearance of urban vitality. Such pretentious "regenerations" should be clearly opposed. In the institutional construction of urban regeneration, we should encourage new policies and institutions designed to meet actual development and transformation requirements, but oppose "institutional design" that demolishes old neighborhoods, whose residents are unwilling to leave, in the name of urban regeneration. By continuously upgrading urban functionalities and qualities, urban regeneration should improve the life of the average citizen, and ensure the greater integration of cities and citizens.

WU Jiang
Professor of College of Architecture and Urban Planning, Tongji University
Vice President of the Urban Planning Society of China
June, 2019

Foreword II

The importance of urban regeneration in the contemporary urban development of China is growing day by day. After more than three decades of rapid development and expansions of cities, the urbanization of China has shifted from high-speed to mid-to-high-speed, and has entered a new phase of transitional development featuring quality improvement. With the active advance of urban regeneration practices, its implications and connotations are also expanding, in a clearer public recognition that urban regeneration is not only a major strategic issue, but also involves the vital interests of every citizen and all stakeholders. It is not only related to land inventory planning and market operation, but is also closely connected to livelihood projects including shanty-town, urban-village and old residential area renovations, making it a complex social project requiring comprehensive coordination and effective institutional implementation.

Due to the lack of systematic theoretical guidance and top-level institutional designs, urban regeneration in China is currently troubled by a number of recurrent phenomena: (1) driven by economic values, regeneration objectives are mostly beautiful spaces and land revenues, and regeneration methods are mostly demolitions and reconstructions with "apparent" effectiveness, while integrated improvement of urban quality, functions, identities, etc.is neglected; (2) the absence of comprehensive consideration of overall urban function structural adjustments causes individual regeneration projects to deviate from the macroscopic objective of urban regeneration, so that they are incapable of solving the problems of untidy urban layout, severe traffic congestion, low environmental quality, and inefficient transportation, municipal, and public facilities; (3) driven by profits and influenced by misconceptions about cultural heritage preservation, the phenomena of "mass demolitions and constructions", "demolition of the old, and construction of the new", and "demolition of the authentic, and construction of counterfeit" occur, inflicting substantial losses on urban cultural heritage preservation; (4) failing to take account of the rich social lives and stable social networks in the regeneration areas causes problems of distorted interests, profits inequitably distributed, difficulties in the implementation of public welfare projects, and the escalation of social conflicts; and (5) absence of inter-departmental coordination causes the departments of planning, land resource, development and reform, housing, and civil administration to work alone, leading to a lack of organic connection in the relevant supplementary policies on management procedures, permits, the use of reconstruction and resettlement funds, etc.

The following issues have therefore become significant challenges to the urban regeneration of China in the new era: how to strengthen the role of government by utilizing the wisdom of the public to complete the implementation and operation mechanisms of urban regeneration; how to avoid and overcome some disadvantages and negative impacts of the market and safeguard the public interest of the city, while exploiting the active effects of the market by following market rules; and how to establish a normalized institutional platform with multilateral cooperation and mutual participation to strengthen coordination and cooperation between pertinent departments.

Through comparison of and research into the construction of regeneration institutions in recent years in the cities of Guangzhou, Shenzhen, and Shanghai, the young and promising research team of Professor TANG Yan has examined their objectives, pathways, and directions from the perspectives of regeneration organization settings, administrative models, planning formulation, spatial regulation, and policy supplements, applying important academic values and realism to facilitate the sustained and robust development of urban regeneration in China. The following characteristics of this book stand out:

(1) *Wide vision.* The book comprehensively introduces the histories and tendencies of the urban regeneration institutional construction in Hong Kong, Taipei, Tokyo, and Singapore, and interprets China's urban development stages and macroscopic background, laying the foundations for an understanding of the urban regeneration institutions of the three example cities of Guangzhou, Shenzhen, and Shanghai.
(2) *Profound investigations.* Through empirical research into typical cases, this book introduces innovations in the function guidance, development intensity management, public amenity settings, and public element lists of Guangzhou, Shenzhen, and Shanghai, and evaluates the effects of regeneration implementation in the three cities, revealing practical experiences and challenges of their urban regenerations.
(3) *High pertinence.* This book focuses on discussion of the three major elements involved in urban regeneration institutional innovation, namely property rights, function (land use), and volume (development intensity), and suggests future trends in urban regeneration institutional innovation from the perspectives of procedure remaking, subject determination, interest definition, objective guidance, and introduction of diversified mechanisms, etc.

It is hoped that more scholars and departments will be inspired by this book to honest and pragmatic discussion and research on institutional innovation in urban regeneration, thus contributing positively to the standardization and institutionalization of urban regeneration in China.

YANG Jianqiang
Professor of School of Architecture, Southeast University
Chairman of the Urban Regeneration Academic Committee of the Urban Planning Society of China
January, 2019

Foreword III

After the several decades of rapid development in urban construction since the reform and opening up in 1978 in China, the "new-type" urbanization path targeting high-quality development has imposed new requirements on urban planning and construction and social governance. After years of theoretical research and practical exploration, the diverse practices and institutional construction of urban regeneration in China have also entered a new stage. Many Chinese cities, represented by the pioneering cities of Guangzhou, Shenzhen, and Shanghai, have established relatively sound institutional frameworks, although not devoid of deficiencies, to regulate and guide urban regeneration practice. With latecomer cities still in the initial stages of establishing their fundamental institutions, the experiences and lessons from China's pioneering cities are of vital importance.

The naissance of this book is significant in connecting predecessors and successors, examining experiences and lessons from the institutional explorations of the three model cities. The book departs from the locality-specific context of much institutional research to establish a common framework for comparing the fundamental institutions of the three cities, enabling the reader to more clearly identify the formation of different institutions in different cities, tailored to specific local conditions, which will also aid comparisons and mutual references between more cities in this field in the future. Using a fundamental institutional framework, the book further analyzes the different spatial control measures in the urban regeneration of the three cities, ranging from regulations and guidance on regeneration models and development intensities to other special institutional arrangements such as public elements lists, policy-based housing, land-price compensation payments, and floor area ratio transfers, maintaining a logical thread through the fragmented institutions and policies of several decades. The book also analyzes the implementation pathways of the three cities, tracking the entire implementation process for regeneration projects from overall urban regeneration planning through to project completion.

The book goes beyond relevant statistics and numbers, making use of thorough policy and institutional analyses to evaluate the effects of urban regeneration in the three cities. It evaluates the achievement status of policy objectives from various perspectives, and proposes directions for future urban regeneration institution innovations in China. Among its suggestions for future development, the book identifies the three critical elements for successful regeneration as property rights, function, and volume, and proposes a direction for remaking of procedures, subject determination, interest definition, and improvements of mechanisms, as well as advising on the content and stages of institutional construction for governments.

Currently, the urban regeneration transformation of China is in the condition of "time and tide wait for no man", an objective requirement of the current socio-economic development stage of China. Academia must therefore make it its mission to identify deficiencies and make realistic concrete proposals on institutional construction, following theoretical research and discussions. Among the more than 600 cities at varying levels of development in China, only a minority are perfecting their urban regeneration institutions, with the majority still in the exploratory stage, or even earlier. Therefore, fundamental research on urban regeneration institutions is not only theoretically valuable, but also of substantial reference significance for the establishment of scientific and complete institutional systems for China's diverse and growing urban regeneration practices. I believe that *Urban Regeneration in China: Institutional Innovation in Guangzhou, Shenzhen, and Shanghai* will trigger more effective discussions, catalyze the birth of more pragmatic research, and help in the great cause of the construction of China's beautiful future.

BIAN Lanchun
Professor of School of Architecture, Tsinghua University
Executive Director of the Urban Planning Society of China
June, 2019

Preface

This book has taken six years to complete. The Chinese version of the book was officially published by Tsinghua University Press in August 2019, coinciding with the rise of urban regeneration as a significant issue in the urban development of China. In 2020, "implementation of urban regeneration actions" officially became an important national strategy in China; therefore, the Chinese version has attracted a good deal of attention and has been reprinted five times in one and a half years since it came out. We hope that the English version, re-tailored for the international reader, will help the rest of the world to understand the transition in urban planning and construction in China in the new era, to capture the latest policies and practical progress of urban regeneration in China, and to introduce the experiences and lessons of China's urban regeneration institutions more widely.

China's economic growth has been slowing down structurally since the 2010s, which translates into a comprehensive transition of social, political, and spatial developments. In this process, the urban development model of China has gradually shifted from "external expansion" towards "internal improvement", and entered an era of "new-type urbanization" featuring high-quality instead of high-quantity development. Many built-up areas and existing buildings in Chinese cities are awaiting transformation to reach living condition improving, industrial upgrading, environmental optimization, and social progressing.

However, since most of the existing urban institutions in China were established during the era of rapid urbanization, they are incapable of effectively addressing the rising demand for proper regulation of the regeneration of the existing built environment, resulting in an urgent need for urban regeneration institution building. Especially in China's larger cities, there is great pressure on urban construction due to various challenges such as land scarcity, diminishing historical and cultural characteristics, and other increasingly prominent "big city diseases". Since around 2010, in order to fulfill the comprehensive regeneration objectives, some Chinese cities have begun to actively explore and advance urban regeneration management and reform, making substantial progress in the building of urban regeneration institutions that are in urgent need of review.

Thus to reveal the progress and challenges of urban regeneration and relevant planning in China, this book selected the three cities that were on the frontline of urban regeneration institutional reform – Guangzhou, Shenzhen, and Shanghai – as research subjects. The book first recounts the urban regeneration development of the three cities from a historical perspective, and then analyzes the core urban regeneration policies in the three cities in detail, as well as their urban regeneration institution systems, including regeneration organization, planning formulation, implementation mechanisms, and so on. The essence of the book is to reveal the progress, innovation, and potential problems in current construction of the urban regeneration institutions in the three model cities, so as to provide empirical references for solving urban regeneration conundrums, as well as for attracting more cities and regions to embark upon urban regeneration institutional construction in the new era.

During the process of perfecting this book in English, we discovered that reforms and changes to the urban regeneration institutions and their implementation models in Guangzhou, Shenzhen, and Shanghai are occurring on a daily basis, and it outpaced us in updating all the related information in time. In particular, the new round of reforms on urban regeneration administrative organization in the past two years – as a result of the national organizational reform, could not be sufficiently reflected in this book. We hope to fill these gaps in interpretation of the most recent organization and policies in our future research.

TANG Yan and YANG Dong
January, 2021

Acknowledgements

The authors extend gratitude to WANG Xuemei and SUN Wenwei, who have ever held office in the Chaoyang Branch of the Planning and Land Resource Committee of Beijing Municipality. It is them who invited us to undertake a research on experiences and cases of urban regeneration institution construction in China in 2014, out of their astute judgement of the urban regeneration demands and tendencies in China, which provides the footstone for the eventual conception of this book.

The authors also extend gratitude to Professor WANG Shifu of the South China University of Technology, and Dr. SHAO Ting of the Development Research Center of the State Council, with whom the conversations shared during the visit to MIT in 2015 expanded the dimensions and profoundness of this book. The authors also give thanks to Dr. WAN Yong of the Urban and Real-Estate Research Center of the Shanghai Academy of Social Sciences for the firsthand information on the institutional construction and planning of the urban regeneration of Shanghai, given at the Urban Regeneration Saloon organized by him for the journal of *Urban and Rural Planning*. The authors also thank Director WANG Jia of the Urban Regeneration Planning Research Center of the Urban Planning & Design Institute of Shenzhen Ltd., who granted us to use the urban regeneration unit plan formulated by his corporation, which greatly enriched the practical contents of this book.

The authors also extend the gratitude to TANG Jingxian, who helped to accumulate on the comparison framework, and policy and data analysis in the early research. Similar gratitude to Dr. ZHU He of Beijing University of Civil Engineering and Architecture, who supplemented the experiences from other Asian cities and regions, as well as the evolution histories of urban regeneration of the three cities for the Chinese manuscript, which formed the basis of Chapter II and III of this book. Gratitude as well to YUAN Shuang from Tsinghua University, Katrina WANG from University College London, and Dr. FAN Li from University of Kassel, for their great helps in English translation or proofreading of this book.

Gratitude to FENG Ming of the Information Center of the General Office of Beijing Municipal Committee, who invited us to submit the findings of this book to the municipal government of Beijing as references, which was in turn responded and made a contribution to promoting the urban regeneration institution construction in Beijing. Gratitude to Professor WU Jiang, Professor YANG Jianqiang, and Professor BIAN Lanchun from the Urban Regeneration Academic Committee of the Urban Planning Society of China, with whom the continuous academic exchanges are an important motivation for this book. We also hereby thank all other seniors, colleagues and friends, who have given helps, suggestions and encourages to this book at various stages, who we could not enumerate.

1 Introduction
Urban regeneration in China in the modern era

1.1 Urban regeneration as a perennial topic

A city is a living being, vital and in a constant state of change. Urban regeneration, a perennial theme in cities, has existed in various forms since ancient times, ranging from the transformation of urban squares in ancient Rome, the Haussmann renovation of Paris to the regeneration of the ancient capital of Beijing. The concept, practice, and value orientation of urban regeneration may vary dramatically, however, according to era, location, and cultural background.

The conceptual and theoretical development of contemporary urban regeneration can be traced back to the post-World War II era in Europe. In order to solve severe housing shortages and to restore war-torn traditional cities, many European countries actively reconstructed and renovated their old towns, while building new towns on a large scale. Various terms related to regeneration have emerged since then, such as urban renewal, urban redevelopment, urban regeneration, urban renaissance, etc. (Dong, Chen and Wang, 2009). These terms, sometimes used interchangeably, express different focuses of urban transformation under different backgrounds. In this book, the term "urban regeneration" is applied to generally describe the different types of construction activities, including renovation, maintenance, demolition of old to build new, etc., that transform existing built-up areas.

The overall development process of urban regeneration practice after World War II can be briefly summarized as four stages: urban reconstruction, community renewal, old city redevelopment, and organic regeneration (Dong et al. 2009). In the process, the motivation of urban regeneration has changed from solving a single urban problem to achieving comprehensive urban development goals, from large-scale demolition and reconstruction to flexible transformation on various scales. At the same time, the mechanism has evolved from government-led to joint governance and the values have shifted from the improvement of physical structure to sustainable development in social, economic, ecological, historical, and cultural dimensions.

Urban regeneration practice is strongly influenced and shaped by the specific background, in combination with the social, political, economic, and cultural institutions of individual countries. Ten dimensions have been identified as important for understanding contemporary urban regeneration practice in China: strategy, approach, property right, scale, target, actor, activity, urban function, land transfer, and resettlement (Table 1.1). The combination of one or more dimensions helps describe the features of Chinese urban regeneration practice at a specific time in a specific place, further reflecting their institutional background

2 Introduction

Table 1.1 Ten Dimensions of Urban Regeneration in China

Dimension	Elements
Strategy	Physical refurbishment, space creation and supply, land use optimization, historic and cultural conservation, urban functional and structural adjustments, regional revitalization, ecological and environmental remedies, etc.
Approach	Supply oriented (top-down), demand oriented (bottom-up), mixture of both
Property Rights	Public property rights (collectively owned, state owned), private property rights, mixed property rights; single property owner, multiple property owners, etc.
Scale	Single building, group buildings, microscopic spaces, urban areas, etc.
Target	Old cities and towns, old factories, old villages, etc.
Actor	Government, private/state-owned enterprises, property owners, social organizations, planners, scholars, residents, etc.
Activity	Demolition, reconstruction, renovation, preservation, maintenance, etc.
Urban Function	Function maintenance, function implantations, function change, etc.
Land Transfer	Expropriation, leasing, sale, allocation, transfer with compensation, etc.
Resettlement	Resettlement at the original/nearby site, relocation, financial compensation, etc.

Source: Compiled by authors.

and operational environment. For instance, the housing renewal program in Shanghai in the 1990s can be summarized as the type of renewal practice that aims at a top-down government-led approach to housing improvement through the demolition and reconstruction of physical structure while maintaining the original urban functions.

1.2 The rise of China's urban regeneration in the new era of transition

Since the establishment of the People's Republic of China, the focus of urban regeneration has been constantly changing, both in the era of the planned economy and during the transition to a socialist market economy. In the 1950s, due to large-scale urban devastation and limited fiscal ability, the government encouraged the full reuse of the existing urban constructions of old cites to revitalize the economy (Cao and Chu, 1990). The 1960s and 1970s were characterized by political instability along with chaotic demolition, reconstruction and occupation of existing buildings, and urban regeneration was not properly controlled (Xie and Costa, 1993). In the 1980s, Chen Zhanxiang introduced the "theory of metabolism" from Japan and pointed out that the natural law of urban quarters, changing from prosperity to decline, then to prosperity again, should be respected (Zhai and Wu, 2009). In the 1990s, Wu Liangyong suggested the concept of "organic regeneration" which emphasized the conservation and reuse of the historical environment to achieve harmony between the new and the old (Wu, 1994). Meanwhile, Zhang Jie advocated a small-scale incremental approach to urban regeneration (Zhang, 1996, 1999). As the 21st century dawned, given the criticism of large-scale renewal projects in old cities, urban regeneration adopted more small-scale and multi-dimensional approaches, with increasing attention to the conservation and reuse of historic and cultural heritage (Ding and Wu, 2017).

At the end of 1949, the urbanization ratio in China stood at a mere 10.64%, while at the end of 2011, the number had reached a record of 51.3%, increasing to 59.58% by the end of 2018. After more than 30 years of the "Chinese miracle" – as the rapid economic development since the reform and opening up in 1978 became known – economic development has gradually become more stable and transitioned to the "new normal"[1] with medium-to-high growth, bringing with it the comprehensive transformation of society, politics, the economy, culture, and cities (Li, 2014; Wu, 2014). The shortage of land resources has become increasingly obvious in many places. In the city regions of the Yangtze River Delta and Pearl River Delta, around 40–50% of total land has been used for urban construction, leading to a severe shortage of new development land, which calls for urgent land-use reform as well as the development model shifting from external sprawl to internal regeneration, from environmental destruction to environmental protection, from developing manufacturing industries to tertiary industry, and from speed oriented to the pursuit of quality (Tang, 2015). Therefore, in the new era, especially since 2010, a comprehensive and holistic approach to urban regeneration that promotes the reuse of existing urban land and settlement has been key to urban development and construction in China.

In 2013, on the occasion of the National Working Conference on Urbanization, the central government highlighted urban regeneration as an important national development strategy, focusing on "restricting the increase of construction land, revitalizing existing urban areas, restructuring land use and enhancing land use efficiency", as well as "urban development should be shifted from expansion to delimiting the city boundary and optimizing spatial structure". In 2015, the central government again repeatedly emphasized this strategy, including promoting compact urban development, restricting overall construction volume and improving development quality. The former Ministry of Land and Resources[2] also published multiple notices on strict controls of land size for urban development, a policy U-turn that optimized existing land use as opposed to the former urban sprawl. National polices had a direct impact at the local level. First-tier cities, such as Beijing and Shanghai, took the lead and confirmed there would be no increase of construction land in their master plans. The Beijing Urban Master Plan (2016–2035) required that "the decrease of urban and rural built-up areas" be realized by 2020, while the Shanghai Urban Master Plan (2017–2035) stated that land should be used in a more intensive way to realize "negative growth" of land for construction.

Over time, urban regeneration has become an important national strategy to improve the urban environment across the country. Given the different

4 *Introduction*

Figure 1.1 China's City Cluster Plan.

Source: Basic map from the Ministry of Natural Resources of the People's Republic of China, http://bzdt.ch.mnr.gov.cn/browse.html?picId=%22o2 8b062501ad13015501ad2bfc0288%22; city cluster information from the 13th Five-Year Plan for Economic and Social Development of the People's Republic of China (2016–2020).

development stages of cities in China, urban regeneration has been more integrated into the working agenda in the eastern coastal cities than in the cities in other territories (Figure 1.1). In the new era, developed cities and regions have faced major challenges interpreting urban regeneration within the local context and establishing a functional framework to systematically guide regeneration practice. An increasing number of western cities and regions will face the same challenges in the future. Therefore, in October 2020, the CPC Central Committee's Proposals for Formulating the 14th Five-Year Plan for National Economic and Social Development and the Long-Range Objectives Through the Year 2035 announced for the first time the national decision of "implementing urban regeneration action", which promoted a new type of urbanization and pointed the way to innovative modes of urban construction and operation.

1.3 Institutions as crucial challenges and opportunities for urban regeneration in China

D. C. North pointed out that institutions are artificially designed constraints that build interactive relationships in politics, economy, and society, comprising "formal constraints" and "informal constraints". Institutions can therefore be regarded as a collection of behavioral regulations adhered to by the population. At present, the lack of systematic theoretical guidance and top-level institutional designs has hindered the progress of urban regeneration throughout China. Designed to serve rapid large-scale urban expansion, the current urban development and management institutions (formal constraints) have proved to be incompatible with the current urban development stage, and are thus in urgent need of reform. The institutions, especially formal institutions, have therefore become a crucial constraint and an important topic in urban regeneration in China.

In the absence of effective mechanisms, the experimental practice known as "crossing the river by feeling the stones" still dominates urban regeneration in Chinese cities. Constrained by conventional planning and land management systems, the process of urban regeneration, including land acquisition, the relocation and compensation of original residents and enterprises, the functional restructuring of buildings or land, and the demolition and renovation of existing buildings is constantly encountering problems and challenges. Regeneration is often accompanied by challenges such as complicated planning adjustments and ratification procedures, time-consuming and costly negotiations, inequitable distribution of benefits among major stakeholders, and social tension in the neighborhoods. Administratively, inter-departmental collaboration remains inadequate and inefficient in terms of ratification procedures, the allocation of government investment and subsidies, and the management of reconstruction and resettlement. Operating within their respective domains, various departments, including those of urban and rural planning, land resources management, the development and reform commission, and civil affairs have not been sufficiently coordinated. Unless the current institutions are reformed, problems will continue to arise more intensively, with the consequent failure to achieve urban regeneration goals and values.

6 *Introduction*

Specifically, due to the lack of overall integrated urban development guidance, sporadic regeneration projects are usually incapable of solving comprehensive urban problems such as urban function disorders, severe traffic congestion, low environmental quality, and insufficient civil and public amenities. Driven by profit, many urban regeneration projects are excessively focused on physical redevelopment and are aimed at short-term economic benefits through reusing the built-up areas and land value surplus, while overlooking the comprehensive upgrading of urban quality. In particular, ignorance of cultural heritage has led to the loss of cultural value through mass demolition and construction - demolishing the old to construct the new, and even demolishing the authentic and constructing the counterfeit in its place. Further, in some renewal projects, the existing social networks and vibrant social life have been overlooked, with new constructions leading to distortion of social networks, a lack of public services, and the escalation of social tensions.

Thus, around 2010, some large Chinese cities, including Guangzhou, Shenzhen, Shanghai, Nanjing, and Xiamen, began to actively undertake urban regeneration reforms and have made substantial progress in developing a legal framework, establishing agencies, and developing policies and laws. By the end of 2015, three cities, Guangzhou, Shenzhen, and Shanghai, have introduced the Urban Regeneration (Implementation) Measures as legal instruments, stipulating the specific management requirements of various types of urban regeneration projects.

1.4 Guangzhou, Shenzhen, and Shanghai: urban regeneration pioneers and institutional innovators

The Chinese cities of Guangzhou, Shenzhen, and Shanghai have faced challenges of land deficiency and industrial restructuring, and have pioneered institutional innovation in urban regeneration policies and practice. Due to their pioneer status and profound influence on other Chinese cities, the three cities have been chosen as case studies to explore the progress of institutional development in urban regeneration in China.

Urban development in Guangzhou, Shenzhen, and Shanghai has always been strategically significant in China. The GDP of Guangzhou, Shenzhen, and Shanghai ranks among the highest, surpassing one trillion yuan respectively in 2010, 2011, and 2006, with continuing potential for growth (Table 1.2). In 2017, Guangzhou initiated a new urban master plan, which identifies its development goal as an "important central city of China" and "benchmarking global cities". The city of Shenzhen was designated for the first time by the state an "international technology and industrial innovation center" in the 13th Five-Year Plan (2016–2020). Shanghai's new urban master plan was ratified by the State Council in 2017, confirming its objectives of "a national famous historical and cultural city and an international economic, financial, trade, shipping and technological innovation center".

Table 1.2 Gross Domestic Product of Guangzhou, Shenzhen, and Shanghai, 2010–2016 (100 million RMB)

City	2010	2011	2012	2013	2014	2015	2016
Shanghai	17165.98	19195.69	20181.72	21818.15	23567.7	25123.45	28178.65
Guangzhou	10748.3	12423.44	13551.2	15420.14	16706.87	18100.41	19547.44
Shenzhen	9581.5	11505.53	12950.1	14500.23	16001.82	17502.86	19492.6

Source: National Bureau of Statistics, China, 2018.

Given the increasing challenges of land deficiency, environmental protection, and urban problems, the three cities of Guangzhou, Shenzhen, and Shanghai are in urgent need of built-up areas to reuse to achieve their development goals in the new era.

1.4.1 Guangzhou

After more than three decades of rapid urbanization, the problems of inefficient land use and insufficient land supply have become increasingly evident. As of 2015, the economic output of urbanized land in Guangzhou was 1.01 billion RMB per km^2, lower than the 1.65 billion RMB per km^2 of Shenzhen and much lower than the performance of international cities of Hong Kong (5.89 billion RMB/km^2) and Singapore (4.52 billion RMB/km^2), calling for more efficient use of land.[3] Further, the built-up area in Guangzhou already constituted 75% of the available land reserve in 2009, implying an extreme land shortage problem (Tian et al., 2015). In 2015, the total built-up area in Guangzhou reached as much as 1,787.14 km^2, leaving only 161.86 km^2 of new land available for further development, in reference to the overall development land amount defined by the 2020 land-use plan.[4] This fell short of the requirement for 240 km^2 for new development[5] from 2016 to 2020 by around 80 km^2. It is important to balance the deficiency of land supply by optimizing built-up areas with low efficiency. In 2012, the "three olds" areas (old towns, old villages, and old factories/industrial lands) that were inefficiently utilized or even vacant occupied a total of 399.52 km^2 in Guangzhou, roughly one-third of Guangzhou's urbanized land. This sizable land could be reused through urban regeneration to alleviate the land shortage problem (Guangzhou Urban Planning and Design Survey Research Institute, 2012).

1.4.2 Shenzhen

Challenged by the "four unsustainabilities"[6] and initially constrained by land deficiency, the city of Shenzhen has shifted its development approach from speed oriented, known as "Shenzhen speed", to quality oriented or "Shenzhen quality". The Shenzhen Urban Master Plan (2010–2020) confirmed the transition from developing new land towards the reuse of urbanized land. In 2015, the total built-up area in Shenzhen was in excess of 940 km^2, leaving an annual land quota of only 6 km^2 from 2016 and just 30 km^2 in total by 2020. During four decades of urbanization in Shenzhen, the development of affordable housing has lagged far behind the demand. To solve the housing shortage, over a long period informal construction has been spontaneously practiced and tolerated by the local government, creating a large volume of land and buildings with ambiguous property rights. The institutional problems associated with informal development, e.g., ambiguous ownership, illegal status, and a complicated network of stakeholders, have been obstacles to formal redevelopment that call for policy innovation (Song, 2015). According to the 2008 building survey, total floor area in Shenzhen is around 752 million m^2, of which around 400 million m^2 are informally developed. Illegally constructed spaces comprise around 53.19% of the entire floor area in Shenzhen, and around 70% are in the urban villages of Shenzhen (Ma, 2010). Informal settlement has contributed greatly to the rise of Shenzhen, but has also placed serious constraints on its further development.

1.4.3 Shanghai

Like Guangzhou and Shenzhen, Shanghai also underwent rapid urbanization for several decades and recently started to restrict urban expansion. The 13th Five-Year (2016-2020) Shanghai Land Resource Exploitation and Preservation Plan issued in May 2017 by the Shanghai municipal government stipulated that the total amount of land for construction shall not exceed 3,185 km^2 by 2020, and that the proportion of industrial land shall drop from 27% to 17%. Further, the Shanghai Urban Master Plan (2017–2035), published in December 2017, set the limit of total land for construction at 3,200 km^2 by 2035, though in 2015 this figure has already reached as high as 3,145 km^2 (about 45% of the entire land area of the city), almost reaching the limit (Zhuang, 2015a). In Shanghai, the former industrial base of China, the manufacturing sector has contributed greatly to city development. However, as a result of industrial restructuring, there are problems with most of the current industrial land uses, including over proportion, sporadic distribution, low economic output, and inefficient use. In 2011, the economic output per unit of industrial land in Shanghai was 4.09 billion RMB/km^2, a relative underperformance compared to many international cities. The 2013 Implementation Analysis Report on the Shanghai Urban Master Plan (1999-2020) stated that by the end of 2012, industrial land (about 880 km^2) accounted for around 29% of urban land in the municipality, between three and ten times that of its international counterparts. The renewal of industrial land in Shanghai proceeded incrementally due to policy instability, and the regeneration of old residential quarters has also become an increasing challenge.

1.5 Contents and framework of the comparison of urban regeneration institutions in Guangzhou, Shenzhen, and Shanghai

In the eight chapters that follow, this book demonstrates how policy development and institutional reform are tackling problems in the field of urban regeneration by comparing the experiences of three representative Chinese cities. The study illustrates the development progress of urban regeneration practice and related urban planning in China.

The present chapter briefly revisits relevant concepts and urban regeneration theory, exploring the macroscopic background of urban development in China and introducing the three pioneering cities of Guangzhou, Shenzhen, and Shanghai, for the comparative study of their institutional innovation. Chapter 2 introduces institutional development experience in Hong Kong, Taipei, Tokyo, and Singapore from an Asian perspective, and summarizes their trends and characteristics.

Chapters 3 to 6 are the key comparative research chapters on the urban regeneration institutions of the three cities. Chapter 3 examines the evolution of urban regeneration and development in the three cities from a historical perspective. Chapter 4 compares urban regeneration policy systems and analyzes the trends and characteristics of the development process. In particular, the content and structure of the Urban Regeneration (Implementation) Measures in the respective cities are compared. Chapter 5 explores the detailed components of the regeneration institution systems in three cities, including institutional arrangements, project management, regeneration planning, and implementation mechanisms. Chapter 6 discusses measures for spatial management and control in urban regeneration, analyzing innovative instruments to guide urban function restructuring, urban development intensity control, and the development of public infrastructure and amenities in the three cities.

Based on representative practice cases, Chapter 7 demonstrates implementation tools and strategies to apply regeneration institutions in specific environments, including urban regeneration plans, multiple-actor models, regeneration assessments and reviews, and the combination of large-scale renewal and micro regeneration. Chapter 8 examines whether the regeneration assignments and goals have been achieved and the reasons for it, by comparatively reviewing the practical experiences and challenges in the three cities.

Chapter 9 seeks to establish the general principles of urban regeneration in China by summarizing the key elements of institutional innovation in three cities, i.e., property rights, function (land use and building functions) and volume (development intensity). Future directions, strategies, and steps for institutional development in urban regeneration are envisioned.

Notes

1 From 1978 to 2010 China's GDP grew from 364.5 billion RMB to 39.8 trillion RMB with a rapid development average of 9.87% annually. From 2012 to 2013 Chinese economic growth was 7.7% and in 2019, 6.1%.
2 The Ministry of Land and Resources and the Ministry of Housing and Urban-Rural Development mentioned in this book underwent institutional reform in 2018. In March 2018, the Ministry of Natural Resources was established, integrating entirely or in part the responsibilities of the original Ministry of Land and Resources, National Development and Reform Commission, Ministry of Housing and Urban-Rural Development, Ministry of Water Resources, Ministry of Agriculture and Rural Affairs, State Forestry and Grassland Administration, State Oceanic Administration, and the National Administration of Surveying, Mapping, and Geoinformation. The former Ministry of Land and Resources was then dissolved.
3 General Office of People's Government of Guangzhou (2017). The 13th Five-Year Land Use Plan of Guangzhou.
4 According to Guangzhou's Adjustment Scheme of Overall Land Use Plan (2006–2020), construction land should be limited to 1,581 km^2 in 2020, and the overall land scale to 1,949 km^2.
5 General Office of People's Government of Guangzhou (2017). The 13th Five-Year Land Use Plan of Guangzhou.
6 Around 2005, the municipal government summarized the development condition of Shenzhen with the "four unsustainabilities": unsustainable conventional speed model for limited land and spaces; unsustainable energy and water resources; unsustainable population burden, for it needs a bigger labor force to achieve 1 trillion RMB of GDP with the conventional speed development model; and unsustainable environmental capacity that has already been severely overexploited.

2 The institutional innovation of urban regeneration from an Asian perspective

China shares a similar cultural background to many other Asian countries, due to both geographical location and historical interactions. The institutional innovation of urban regeneration in various Asian cities provides a useful reference for the urban regeneration and development of mainland cities in China. Hong Kong, Taipei, Tokyo, and Singapore all went through a period of rapid development in the 20th century, marked by a socio-economic boom, large-scale growth of construction, and urban expansion. In view of land-resource deficiency and historical conservation issues, the task of urban regeneration has become more imperative over time for the governments in these four locations, where a systematic approach and the institutionalization of urban regeneration have gradually developed over several decades. Despite differences in their urban regeneration strategies rooted in their unique cultural traditions, geographical locations, and political and economic systems, they have much in common, including well-designed laws and policies, active public participation, strong public–private cooperation, a combination of inductive and compulsory measures, and special attention to the preservation of historical culture and local identity. These four cases[1] represent effective comparisons for the analysis, understanding, and evaluation of the current institutional innovation of urban regeneration in Guangzhou, Shenzhen, and Shanghai.

2.1 Urban regeneration institutions in Hong Kong

Before the British occupation in 1841, Hong Kong was little more than a fishing port on a barren island. In less than a century, Hong Kong underwent an epic period of rapid urbanization to become a global financial center and one of the most densely populated areas in the world. Meanwhile, the rapid urban sprawl and limited land capacity has made urban regeneration a critical issue for high-density urban development. As its urban regeneration started earlier than that of most other Asian cities, abundant experiences and a relatively well-established system can be found in Hong Kong.

The urban regeneration history of Hong Kong can be roughly divided into three stages: ① from 1841 to the 1980s, in response to the sanitation and environmental crisis caused by the explosive population growth, a non-profit Housing Association was established to assist the government in the renovation of old urban areas; ② from the late 1980s to the beginning of the 21st century, the Land Development Corporation, a semi-public organization, was established by Hong Kong's government to explore sustainable urban renewal approaches, using market mechanisms to cope with the rising house prices and renewal costs during the economic boom; and ③ since the beginning of the 21st century, with the enactment of a series of laws and policies and the establishment of the Urban Renewal Authority, urban renewal in Hong Kong has entered a mature phase, moving towards a comprehensive approach to urban management.

2.1.1 Urban renewal management framework in Hong Kong

In Hong Kong, an Urban Renewal Authority (URA) was established in 2001 to take responsibility for urban renewal activities under the Urban Renewal Authority Ordinance guidelines issued in the same year.[2] Meanwhile, the Hong Kong government also published its Urban Renewal Strategy to provide overall policy guidance for the URA. The key responsibilities of the URA target four strategies: redevelopment, rehabilitation, revitalization, and heritage preservation (Lu and Tang, 2017). Between 2007 and 2009, the government produced a series of policies regarding the renewal of heritage buildings, initiating a review of urban renewal strategies in 2008. Based on the review results, the URA issued supplements to improve the existing urban renewal policies, for example, completing the purchase and compensation standards for tenants, owner occupiers, owners of vacant properties, and owners of non-housing properties (such as car parks) (Yin, 2013). To solve the problems of property acquisition, a Compulsory Sale for Redevelopment of Land (Specification of Lower Percentage) Notice was published in 2010. The Urban Renewal Strategy, the principal guidance document for direction by the URA of urban renewal projects, was updated in 2011, and stated that the social impact of urban renewal projects should be more comprehensively evaluated.

The new version of the Urban Renewal Strategy defines the responsibilities of the URA and administrative procedures relating to urban renewal. First, the Hong Kong government (represented by the Hong Kong Development Bureau) creates a development plan containing the urban renewal goals, and publishes it in the Hong Kong Government Gazette. Following a consultation period, the plan is approved by the Urban Planning Committee (Liu, et al., 2017). On the basis of the plan, the URA further develops a renewal action plan for implementation and takes responsibility for its execution. The URA also submits a Draft Operational Program listing urban renewal projects to be implemented within the next five years, including the list of projects to be implemented in the following year, to the Finance Department for approval. The implementation procedures include the establishment of a consultation platform, a public stakeholder survey, a social impact assessment, negotiations on land acquisition and compensation for property owners, tenants, and entrepreneurs. Only after the completion of all those procedures can urban renewal construction activities start. The Urban Renewal Strategy clearly specifies the provision of financial support for the URA by the higher local authority, including a fund of HK$ 10 billion, price deductions for the land to be renewed and resettled, and preferential loans for renewal projects.

2.1.2 Characteristics of urban renewal institutions in Hong Kong

Establishment of a professional and comprehensive management platform. The URA, the institution responsible for undertaking urban renewal activities, is a semi-public organization that not only plays a traditional administrative role integrating planning, project assessment, and project application and approval, but more importantly, provides a platform for communication among stakeholders. The URA consists of a large number of non-administrative members, such as experts and local representatives, who are in regular contact with academia and the general public. Further, the URA adopts a project-by-project (one project, one discussion) platform for different urban renewal projects, and is responsible for coordinating public and private sectors, i.e., current and future property owners, various government departments, developers, and investors. Subject to the ownership structure, different negotiation strategies are applied by the URA to reach agreement on urban renewal. For instance, if a minority of the property owners own a majority of the properties and are willing to renew and renovate, the URA usually differentiates between them and the other proprietors to facilitate their negotiations. In the case of failed negotiations, the URA would refer to the Land Ordinance on Compulsory Sale for Redevelopment, formulated by the Hong Kong Legislative Council in 1998, and oblige proprietors to sell their property only through public auction to protect their interests (Zhong, 2017). This approach not only takes social equality into consideration, but also solves the dilemmas of property acquisition and avoids negotiation deadlocks, common in many other places, improving the implementation efficiency of urban renewal. In the process, the Land Ordinance on Compulsory Sale for Redevelopment provides strong legal instruments for the practice.

A bottom-up, demand-driven model. The URA has gradually pushed the integration of the top-down approach to urban renewal planning and the bottom-up approach of demand-driven applications. The demand-driven model implies an institutional mechanism for property owners to initiate their urban renewal projects, which will be further assessed by the URA for approval (Lu and Tang, 2017). After a project is approved, the URA may play different roles in the project implementation. In some cases, it acts as project manager, responsible for contracting, resettlement and compensation, design and planning, as well as construction management. Currently, the URA tends to encourage the involvement of the private sector, limiting its own role to that of supervisor, regulator, or facilitator. Further, the URA has established special urban renewal sub-departments, including a consultation platform, an urban renewal trust, and urban renewal intermediary services to provide support on coordination, finance, and technical knowledge. The demand-driven has the advantage that as the project is derived from the interests of property owners, it is easier to reach a consensus between the government and property owners, avoiding administrative enforcement. The model provides an effective balance between top-down urban planning and the demand side on the ground.

A comprehensive system of project impact assessment. After years urban renewal, in 2008 the URA initiated a two-year impact assessment program, the Hong Kong Urban Renewal Strategy Review, which aimed to evaluate completed urban renewal projects and communicate with the public (Yin, 2013). Based on this review program, a systematic assessment mechanism has been established in Hong Kong to evaluate the impact of urban renewal projects, which facilitates the entire process of project implementation and management. The assessment team evaluates not only the economic impact, but also the social impact of the project. As well as cost and revenue balance, the assessment focuses particularly on long-term impact on local and regional society, the scale and structural change of government finance and taxation, the increase in job opportunities, and improvement in income levels. The social impact assessment focuses on whether the renewal project would damage the local social structure or lead to irreversible impacts on specific groups, and further on the continuation of features of urban culture (Lang, Li and Chen, 2017) (Table 2.1).

Shift from physical renewal to urban revitalization. Based on comprehensive social impact assessment and reflection, the Hong Kong government pays extra attention to revitalizing urban areas through the conservation of historic and cultural heritage. In 2016, the Hong Kong SAR government announced government funding of HK$ 500 million via Policy Address to set up the Historic Architecture Conservation Fund, aiming at promoting heritage-led urban renewal. For urban areas of historic and cultural importance, the URA always collaborates with multiple agents, including the Antiques and Monuments Office of the Development Bureau, Advisory Committee on Revitalizing Built Heritage, and the non-government organization Lord Wilson Heritage Trust. On the basis of not affecting the protection of cultural heritage, the Hong Kong government encourages the

Table 2.1 Social Impact Assessment of Urban Renewal in Hong Kong

Phase	Items of Social Impact Assessment
Phase I (before publication of proposed projects)	Demographics, socio-economic background, living conditions, population density, community and welfare amenities, historical background, culture and local features, potential impact on local communities within the border of proposed project area
Phase II (after publication of proposed projects)	Demographics, socio-economic background, tenant resettlement demands, shop relocation demands, willingness to occupy, day-to-day needs, employment conditions, workplace, community network of property owners and tenants, children's education requirements, special requirements of the elderly, the disabled, and single-parent families, potential impact of the proposed project on communities

Source: Hong Kong Development Bureau. (2011). Urban Renewal Strategy. Available at: https://www.ura.org.hk/f/page/1869/4861/URS_eng_2011.pdf [Accessed October 22, 2018].

reuse of historical buildings for multiple purposes, particularly cultural creative industries and commercial activities, in order to conserve their physical structure and maintain their function. The government selects private enterprises through an open market process to undertake project management and operation. In the renewal process, the Development Bureau and the Urban Renewal Agency would host urban design competitions or invite bidding to facilitate spatial quality and highlight local features.

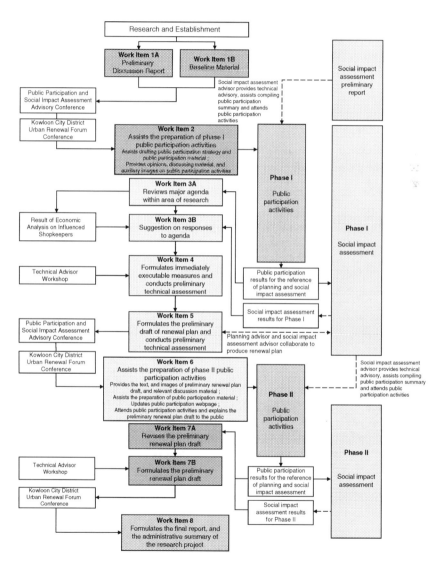

Figure 2.1 Flow Chart of Kowloon Urban Renewal Plan Development.

Redrawn based on relevant sources: Kowloon City District Urban Renewal Forum. (2014). Kowloon City Urban Renewal Plan. Available at: https://www.durf.org.hk/klcity/index.php [Accessed October22, 2018]

Public participation under a legal framework. The latest version of Hong Kong's Urban Renewal Strategy establishes a District Urban Renewal Forum (DURF) to strengthen urban renewal planning at the district level (Hong Kong Development Bureau, 2011). The Hong Kong government established the first trial forum in Kowloon District in June 2011. In Kowloon District, there are numerous worn-out buildings with great potential for renewal projects, but they had seldom been renewed by the URA before. In seeking to promote comprehensive and integrated urban renewal, the Forum undertook the following responsibilities: ① to cooperate with the URA to identify reconstruction and renovation areas and provide conservation and revitalization suggestions to the urban renewal plan; ② to organize and supervise broad public participation, project-related research, and social impact assessment via the Urban Renewal Fund; ③ to supervise the implementation of selected renewal, renovation, conservation and revitalization projects; and ④ to undertake public education and build urban renewal partnership with the local district. The forum started to develop the Kowloon urban renewal plan in May 2012 and finished it 22 months later in February 2014, providing valuable experience for future urban renewal planning and practice (Figure 2.1).

2.2 Urban regeneration institutions in Taipei

The formal development of urban renewal policy in the Taiwan region began in the 1970s with the updating of the Urban Planning Law in 1973 and the publication of specific regulations on renewing old districts. In 1998, the Urban Renewal Ordinance was enacted as a supplement to the Urban Planning Law to clarify relevant procedures. The Urban Renewal Ordinance was updated in 2008 and remains applicable today. The 2009 Loving Taiwan 12 Urban Renewal Promotion Plans established a number of institutions, including the Urban Renewal Fund for local practices, the Urban Renewal Promotion Group and the Urban Renewal Promotion Office (Li and Fang, 2015).

As a central city of the Taiwan region, Taipei has undergone two periods of rapid development in modern times. The first took place at the end of the 1940s, along with the population explosion of 2 million Kuomintang military personnel and civilians that joined the Taiwan region. The second period, between the 1970s and 1980s, was a result of the economic boom. Since then, the issue of urban renewal has been raised in response to economic and demographic changes, leading to the enactment of the Taipei Urban Renewal Implementation Measures in 1983. At that time, urban renewal projects were mostly government dominated. In 1993, the Taipei Urban Renewal Implementation Measures were revised to encourage the involvement of the private sector and promote public–private partnership in urban renewal. Taipei published a succession of documents to regulate urban renewal practice, including the Implementation Measures of Taipei Ordinance on Government-Run Urban Renewal, the Assessment Standards for

Awarding Floor Area in Taipei Urban Renewal Unit Planning and Design, the Taipei Standard Procedures for Defining Urban Renewal Districts, the Taipei Instructions on Self-Designation of Reconstruction Areas in the Renewal Unit, and the Taipei Funding Measures for Promoting Public Engagement in Urban Renewal (Liu et al., 2017).

As early as 1977, the Urban Renewal Department was established in Taipei. Currently, the Urban Renewal Office, the authority responsible for urban renewal, reports to the Taipei Urban Development Bureau. Founded in 2004, the Urban Renewal Office has multiple responsibilities, not only defining urban renewal areas and formulating and supervising the implementation of relevant plans, but also facilitating investment in urban renewal projects by private agencies (Tang, 2013). The other important institution, the Urban Renewal Review Committee, is responsible for reviewing the technical quality and legality of the renewal plan, making decisions on whether the plan is in compliance with government regulations, coordinating stakeholders, and mediating in disputes during the renewal process.

2.2.1 Urban renewal management framework in Taipei

The essential legal instrument for urban renewal in Taipei is the Urban Renewal Ordinance, which sets out a detailed regulatory framework for promoting market-led urban renewal practice. Three main renewal approaches are identified in the ordinance: ① the redevelopment approach, involving demolishing existing buildings and constructing new, changing land-use type or development density, and providing public amenities; ② the renovation approach, which involves renovating existing buildings and providing public amenities; and ③ the maintenance approach, in which public amenities and other elements are maintained by strengthening management. In redevelopment projects, the government acts as the facilitator and supervisor, while in renovation projects, the government also needs to approve the project funding provided by Urban Renewal Fund from the municipal government. Urban renewal districts can be identified in two ways, either defined by the municipal government, or initiated and defined by the citizens. In both cases, the government or land owners can contract private enterprises to develop a renewal plan and initiate renewal. If the private enterprises are contracted by the government, a public assessment and voting procedure must be carried out. In general, urban renewal procedures involve three steps: defining the renewal district, developing an urban renewal plan, and implementing the plan. The urban renewal plan should define the boundary of the renewal areas and the renewal goals and strategies, identify the renewal units or the related standards, describe the status quo of the area, and create land-use plans, overall development plans, project and financial plans, land supply for public amenities and public opinion surveys, etc. (Wang, 2013) (Figure 2.2).

18 *Institutional innovation of urban regeneration*

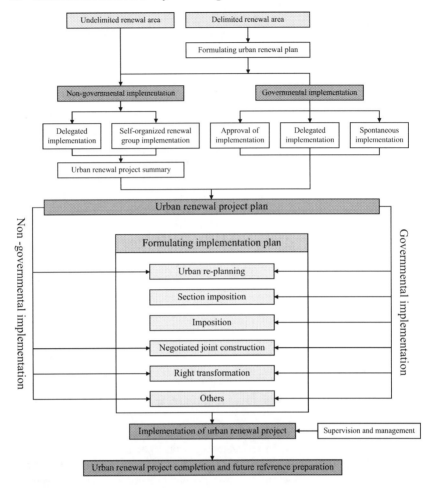

Figure 2.2 Urban Renewal Procedure in Taipei.

Source: Compiled based on relevant materials from the website of Taipei Urban Renewal Office, http://www.uro.taipei.gov.tw/cgi-bin/SM_theme?page=4577d01c.

2.2.2 Pros and cons of FAR transfer

The legal transfer of planned but undeveloped floor space from one site to another is known as Floor Area Ratio (FAR) transfer. This has become the main instrument for attracting investment and covering the cost of urban renewal in Taipei. Through FAR transfer, the cost of urban renewal can be offset, even creating a surplus. A FAR transfer is the government-authorized redistribution of land development rights without changing the land ownership. To encourage land owners to actively undertake urban renewal via FAR transfer, successive laws and regulations enacted include the Implementation Measures on FAR Transfer in Urban Planning, the FAR Transfer Act for Historic Areas and the Assessment Standards for Awarding FAR in Taipei Urban Renewal Unit Planning and

Design (Zhang and Zhang, 2018). Under the legal framework, land from which FAR transfer occurs is mostly designated cultural heritage or public amenities land, which should not be replaced by a high FAR development. The potential FAR can be transferred to residential, commercial, and other public amenity land in the same urban renewal district, thus keeping the overall FAR of the district unchanged. During the transfer process, a value calculation formula is applied as their different locations mean there is usually a difference in value between the reducing FAR and receiving FAR land. Land value should therefore be re-evaluated, rather than simply transferring the same size of floor area. Meanwhile, the transferred quota should not exceed 30% of the floor area of the original land as defined by urban planning (Jin and Dai, 2010).

Despite high land prices and limited land resources in Taipei, private developers and property owners have embraced urban renewal projects facilitated by FAR transfer tools. Since the 1990s, FAR transfer has been regarded as an effective instrument for reducing the cost of urban renewal from the government and for promoting public–private partnerships. However, it has recently been criticized on two grounds. First, public spaces are over-exploited through FAR transfer. Due to skyrocketing housing prices, significant investment has been made in commercial and residential premises, which has consumed the majority of the transferred FAR. Consequently, public spaces have faced more serious difficulties of high renewal costs and low investment returns. Some scholars believe that in the long term, the supply of public services will be even scarcer, which may force the government to redevelop its urban plan and increase urban development density. Second, social justice is challenged due to the strong power of capital investment driven by large profits. Similar to Hong Kong, in the Taiwan region if over two-thirds of the property owners agree with the urban renewal activities, the remaining third should also comply. In practice, developers tend to extend the boundary of the renewal area until a two-thirds consensus is reached. Given the continuous rise in house prices, the developers can always expand project investment, side-stepping the urban renewal issues to ensure a steady profit (Yang, 2013).

2.2.3 *Taipei URS plan*

Known as the Urban Renewal Forward Base in Taipei, the Urban Renewal Station (URS) is a program based on public–private partnership, in which the government provides the right to use public land and buildings for private enterprises or social organizations to promote their participation in urban renewal. It has been a paradigm of public–private partnership in urban renewal, an approach that emphasizes not only renewal of physical structures but also integrated urban revitalization. With the publication of the Taipei URS Promotion Plan in 2010, the Urban Renewal Office managed to collect a number of vacant properties either owned by the Property Bureau or managed by the Urban Renewal Office. Private enterprises and organizations could apply for the free use of these spaces by submitting a renewal plan in accordance with the policy guidance to the Urban

Renewal Office. According to the Subsidy Plan to Promote Urban Renewal Stations in Taipei, a maximum annual subsidy of NT$ 1.2 million is available for an urban renewal plan with positive effects on shaping local features and revitalizing local communities (Ao, 2017). The renewal plan is required to include not only physical space renewal, but also community participation, operational plans, and the organization of activities and events. In practice, the URS plan has already catalyzed a large number of highly distinctive innovation spaces, such as the Art Factory in Dihua Street and the Chung Shan Creative Hub, which have contributed greatly to the overall renovation and revitalization of the neighborhood (Yin and Wang, 2016).

In summary, the urban renewal practice in the Taiwan region has manifested from its early stages a high degree of continuity in developing laws and regulations. From the early government-dominance approach to the active exploration of public–private partnership in the 2000s, the urban renewal approach has been continuously adjusted to adapt to the economic development environment. The legal framework is based on a key instrument, the Urban Renewal Ordinance, supported by other regulations. The government has applied the three renewal strategies of redevelopment, renovation, and maintenance, promoted private investment through FAR transfer, and emphasized cultural heritage conservation, public space supply, and environment coordination via the URS plan. Yet, given the increasing criticism of FAR transfer in recent years, a more sustainable and social justice-oriented approach to urban renewal needs to be explored.

2.3 Urban regeneration policies in Tokyo

Urban renewal in Japan has emphasized the economical use of land. After World War II, Japan underwent a period of rapid economic development, followed by an extended stagnation. During the rapid development era, urban renewal helped to solve land supply problems, while in the stagnation period, it was linked with restructuring of urban space and the stimulation of the urban economy. In 2001, the Urban Regeneration Department (URD), independent of the Ministry of Construction, was established by the Junichiro Koizumi administration to manage and promote nationwide urban renewal (Kong et al., 2018). The Prime Minister at that time, Junichiro Koizumi, served as the first director of the URD and members of the cabinet were URD team members. The URD aims to optimize urban function structures to serve economic, cultural, and residential development and improve the environment (Cabinet Office of Cabinet Public Relations Office, 2004). Thus, urban renewal has been regarded as a national strategy to attract private investment and stimulate economic revival.

In 2014, the Shinzo Abe administration further integrated the URD into a special institution under the Cabinet Secretariat, the Office for Promotion of Regional Revitalization. The Office oversees urban renewal not only within the city boundaries, but also on a larger scale at greater metropolitan and regional levels. Meanwhile, targets for renewal and revitalization have been extended from land and physical space to infrastructure, the ecological environment, human resources, etc., aiming at improving spatial quality in the whole country from a macro level. Both the URD and the Office for Promotion of Regional Revitalization are national-level institutions that coordinate departments, identify principal strategies, and organize funding for urban renewal, while the implementation of specific renewal projects is dominated by local government, making it a process with the participation of multiple actors.

2.3.1 The urban renewal management framework in the Tokyo Metropolitan Region

With its concentration of one-third of Japan's population, the Tokyo Metropolitan Region is one of the economic centers of Japan, contributing nearly 40% of the country's gross national product. Based on the Metropolitan Area Management Law and the Urban Development Law of the Metropolitan Region, the Metropolitan Region Basic Plan has been developed and updated five times, with urban renewal becoming the most important strategy for urban restructuring and development. When the Special Measures for Urban Renaissance were issued in 2002 by the national government, the four cities of Tokyo, Yokohama, Nagoya, and Osaka were designated the "priority regions for urban renaissance". In response, the Greater Tokyo government established the Project Committee on Urban Upgrading to undertake planning and research on urban renewal. In 2005, the Urban Development Bureau of Tokyo started to define renewal districts and develop renewal strategies (Yu and Wen, 2016). Under the Urban and Rural Planning Law, all urban development measures can be categorized into three types: land zoning management, urban redevelopment (urban renaissance), and new development, the first two of which require urban renewal with systematic institutional support (Kidokofio, 2017). The Tokyo Bureau of Urban Development (BUD) is responsible for housing policy, infrastructure development, urban planning and development, land zoning management, and planning and implementation of urban renewal. Land zoning management is a mechanism for altering the existing land-use plan to facilitate urban renewal, so as to integrate land property rights and change the function and quotas of land use. In addition to the reorganization of land, urban renaissance tasks include spatial planning and design, ownership clarification, financial compensation, and construction management. Government-supported semi-public organizations that have contributed greatly to urban renewal include the Urban Renewal Agency, established in 2004 as the successor to the Urban Development Corporation. The activities of the Urban Renewal Agency can be summarized as covering the four main aspects of urban revitalization, improvement of living conditions, disaster recovery, and suburban development (Table 2.2). It is co-financed by central government with a grant of 998.6 billion yen and local government with a 2 billion yen grant. The agency aims to coordinate stakeholders, raise funds, and provide technical and knowledge support to related stakeholders. Currently, the Urban Renewal Agency is participating in around one-tenth of the projects in the Tokyo Metropolitan Region.

22 *Institutional innovation of urban regeneration*

Table 2.2 Activities of the Urban Renewal Agency

Strategies	Targets
Urban Revitalization	Revitalization of "vacant communities" to livable cities
	People, settlement and culture-integrated approach for the new century
	Safe city with earthquake protection and fire protection
	Convenient lifestyle with easy commuting systems
	A modern style for old residential housing
Improvement of Living Conditions	A colorful living space
Disaster Recovery	An anti-disaster urban development
Suburban Development	A new suburban lifestyle

Source: Urban Renewal Agency. Guidelines to Urban Renewal Agency [EB/OL] . (2007-02-01) [2018-05-12]. http://www.uro.taipei.gov.tw/.

2.3.2 Urban renewal model innovation[3]

According to the Urban Development Bureau[4] of the Tokyo Metropolitan Region, there were 230 urban redevelopment projects in total in Greater Tokyo from the 1970s to 2017. Due to the strict protection of private ownership, the implementation of urban renewal projects largely depends on whether a consensus can be reached by the majority of property owners. Thus, the project period tends to be rather long, mostly in the range of 10 years or more. For approved projects, whether initiated by government or property owners, the urban renewal mechanism approach may vary greatly. Although the process is slow, the case-by-case approach has catalyzed innovative solutions, avoiding the problem of using a single solution for dynamic urban issues. The urban renewal project in the Otemachi area in Tokyo, for instance, explored the approach of catalyzing a chain of urban renewal activities through withdrawing state-owned land (Shi, 2018). As early as 1986, the area was identified by the Greater Tokyo government as the "pilot area for urban renewal surrounding Tokyo station" and a preliminary plan was prepared. It was only after 13 years of discussion that in 1999 the Japanese government commissioned the City Planning Research Institute of Japan to establish the Research Committee for the Renewal and Development of Tokyo Station and its Surrounding Area, leading to a further research report which eventually became the guidelines for the renewal of the area. In 2003, government agencies and the local property owners' association organized the Conference on Promoting Urban Renewal in the Otemachi Area, where the renewal chain model was proposed. In the same year, the policy of activating state-owned land for urban renewal was issued by the URD, leading to the withdrawal and relocation of Otemachi Central Joint Office. Occupying an area of 1.3 hectares, the site of the Otemachi Central Joint Office constitutes only a small proportion of the 40 hectares of land for renewal in the whole Otemachi area. The land was subsequently purchased by the Urban Renaissance Agency as a "seed base", and the property owners of the more than 10 surrounding buildings signed contracts and agreed on exchanging property rights with this seed base. These owners could keep using their original buildings while the seed base was under construction. In 2009, the construction of the seed base was completed and the property owners moved in successfully. The seamless connection greatly reduced the relocation costs, and the property owners' original buildings were turned into new seed bases to initiate a new cycle. In 2012, the second group of property owners completed their property exchange. This renewal chain remains ongoing today, and the innovation model has proved to be a sustainable and successful paradigm.

2.3.3 A mature system of land rezoning and reorganization

Unlike other innovative urban regeneration models, the system of land zoning and reorganization has remained quite consistent. In 1888, the Tokyo Urban Renewal Ordinance for the first time identified land rezoning as a legitimate means of urban development. To facilitate rapid urbanization and reconstruction after World War II, the Land Rezoning Law of 1954 regulated related land zoning. The main goal was to protect the interests of land and property owners. Given high land prices and the complicated relationships of stakeholders, the allocation of land, building, or funds after renewal should be based on the provision of land, building, or funds before renewal (Hu, 2000). Currently, over one-third of all urban development projects in Japan have been facilitated with land rezoning and reorganization. Meanwhile, land rezoning and reorganization is also applicable for farmland management, or even mixed management of rural housing and farmland (Gao, 2016). Provided that the land boundary is clearly defined and the consensus of over two-thirds of property owners has been reached, land rezoning can be applied for with the planning authority, irrespective of the size of land to be renewed and whether the renewal is initiated by the original land owner, developers, local government, departments (the Ministry of Construction), or urban investment corporations with government backing. After the application has been approved, property rights will be collected for urban renewal purposes. In the land rezoning plan, a "leverage quota" is usually employed to increase the land development density, so as to not only protect the interests of original property owners, but also provide a reserved small proportion of land for sale, called "cost coverage land", to offset the cost of land reorganization and redevelopment. The website of the Urban Development Bureau of Tokyo Metropolitan Area shows that from 2011 onwards, a total of 414 land rezoning projects involving 13,673.43 hectares of land were completed in the Tokyo Metropolitan Area, with sizes ranging between 0.2 hectare and 394.3 hectares (apart from one special case where the land size is 0.03 hectare).[5]

In general, urban renewal in Tokyo has been facilitated by a legal framework at the national level and supported by the flexible renewal model and sophisticated system of land rezoning at local level. Thus, an effective transmission mechanism has been developed between the central policy and local practice. Although some scholars have criticized the process of urban renewal as not quick enough to follow the rapid space restructuring steps of the Metropolitan Area, the time taken means stable and long-term monitoring from the government, planners and designers, due to the lifetime employment system in Japan for the government and some enterprises. Further, "slow renewal" also helps to avoid some problems or failures in urban renewal such as the extremely high costs, the government monopoly, intensified conflicts between stakeholders, and the updated space not meeting the needs of its users.

2.4 Urban regeneration policies in Singapore

With an area of 719 km^2, the country of Singapore is equivalent to a city, with scarce land resources and dense population. It was not until the 1960s that Singapore became a sovereign nation; later, following arduous economic reforms, it became one of the four "Asian dragons". Along with the dramatic development, the housing shortage and the deterioration of the urban environment called for urgent urban renewal measures. A relatively sound urban planning system was developed, implementing strict management of the limited land resources. In urban renewal, as part of the control of space, strong public intervention can be seen in the form of a legal framework made up of a series of laws and regulations including the Singapore Land Authority Act, the Urban Redevelopment Authority Act, and the Housing and Development Ministry Act (Wang, Sha and Wei, 2012).

2.4.1 The urban renewal management framework in Singapore

Founded by the National Housing and Development Committee in 1964, the Urban Renewal Department (URD) is the first government agency in Singapore responsible for urban renewal. It became the Urban Redevelopment Authority (URA) in 1974 and acquired more functions, including renewal of the old city, and the conservation of monuments and historical buildings. Its functions were further extended in 1989 through a merger with the urban planning, urban research, and statistics authority under the Ministry of National Development. Thus, the new Urban Redevelopment Authority became a big space management department, with full responsibility for coordinating urban planning, urban renewal, historic conservation, land transfer, and infrastructure development (Tang, 2001). Other important organizations related to urban renewal include the Singapore Land Authority and the Housing and Development Board, with the former responsible for collecting land property rights for URA, and the latter for construction and renewal of public rented housing.

2.4.2 A renewal model under public land ownership

Unlike the majority of private land ownership in Hong Kong, Tokyo, and Taipei, more than 90% of the land in Singapore is state owned. Only land-use right (not ownership) can be transferred for a limited period of 30 years, 50 years, 75 years, 99 years, or 999 years according to the urban master plan. When the lease term expires, the government decides if the land-use right can be extended based on land value assessment and urban planning requirements, and sets a price for the extension of the lease. The government also reserves the right of compulsory land acquisition with compensation even if the lease term has not expired, giving it the power to take over land for renewal purposes and avoid the high compensation costs of property rights requisition. Currently, over 85% of Singaporeans reside in public housing managed by the state, with well-developed maintenance systems for regular repainting, rewiring, repair or replacement of elevators, etc. (Huang, 2014). In the case of renewal of large-scale commercial areas and infrastructures, the land-use right will be expropriated by the Land Authority and further leased to private investors through a bidding process under conditions defined by the Urban Redevelopment Authority.

For the remaining 10% of land that is privately owned, the state rarely employs the same incentives as apply in Hong Kong, Tokyo, or Taipei, but rather direct intervention. In Singapore, leasing of privately owned properties is not a completely free market, as the rent may not exceed a standard amount defined by the state. Only after the quality is improved through renovation and rebuilding, can the rent increase be applied by the property owners (Huang, 2007). Meanwhile, it is the owners, rather than the state, that are responsible for renovation based on the strategic plan and the city master plan. For private properties that are severely damaged or do not conform to the safety regulations, the state obliges the property owners to renovate them by applying public renovation funds previously collected from the private owners. If renovation is initiated by the property owners, a consensus of individual property owners must first be reached. At the end of the 20th century, a consensus of all the individual owners had to be reached for urban renewal projects. This requirement was later relaxed so that only 80% of property owners have to agree on the renovation of properties over 10 years old (Liu, 2009).

Successful cases of cultural conservation, such as Chinatown, the Arab District, Little India and the Masjid Abdul Gaffoor, are designated landmarks by the state in the interests of historic conservation and cultural inheritance. Three other projects, the Holland Village, the Jalan Kayu, and the Serangoon Gardens, are designated nodal spaces for development in the updated 2014 master plan.

Singapore's urban renewal system is mainly based on the state ownership of land, which is very different from the previous three cases. However, strong public intervention does not mean ignoring the opinion of social groups. The process of urban renewal seeks to balance public intervention and bottom-up initiatives, since urban renewal in Singapore strictly follows urban planning that involves broad and systematic public participation. The experience of urban renewal in Singapore is highly applicable to China, which shares similar state-led economic development and public land ownership systems.

2.5 Characteristics of urban regeneration institutions in four Asian cities

Urban renewal institutions share many similar features in Hong Kong, Taipei, and Tokyo, while Singapore is an isolated case. Nevertheless, the following institutional characteristics of urban renewal are common to all four places.

2.5.1 Comprehensive policies and laws

Instead of one-step development, it is an incremental process with constant adjustments and improvements to develop comprehensive polices and laws to guide the practice of urban renewal. In all four cases, urban renewal has become an important development strategy and policy priority. Specialist organizations have been established at the highest administrative level of the country or region to supervise overall urban renewal activities including strategy development, coordination of management departments, and funding. Based on the law on urban renewal/regeneration, a series of complementary polices and regulations have been developed to guide urban renewal practice in terms of land transfer, property rights clarification, public participation, and project management. The legal framework integrating laws and regulations at various levels reflects interaction and cooperation between departments at different levels.

2.5.2 Broad public participation

Public participation is embedded in society and is underwritten by laws and regulations at various stages of urban renewal, including participation in renewal plan development, project implementation, and operation feedback. A broad range of institutions and agencies have been involved in organizing the participation process. In Hong Kong, for instance, besides the Urban Renewal Authority, urban renewal trusts and non-governmental organizations also often organize public participation. Active participants include not only the government, property owners and developers, but also scholars, associations, neighboring residents, and the general public. Further, forms of public participation are also becoming more diverse. Besides conventional methods such as meetings and surveys, property owners and neighboring residents are often invited to join the design and planning process directly. Online consultation greatly improves public participation and reduces organizational costs. Slightly different from the three other cities, public participation in Singapore is integrated into the urban planning process, as urban renewal practice is highly dependent on guidelines from urban planning.

2.5.3 Active public–private partnerships

In Singapore, the public-led approach has been more widely adopted than the private-led, but in the three other cities, the private-led approach has been gradually replacing the public-led since the turn of the century. The government has withdrawn the role of project implementer and left it to private developers.

Meanwhile, a demand-oriented bottom-up approach to urban renewal, mainly initiated by the private sector and approved by the government, has developed. Rather than withdrawing completely, the government has shifted its responsibility to serve the private sector and undertaken the tasks of supervision and management, information collection, coordination of different interests, providing legal instruments, funding and financial support, protecting the interests of minority group, historic and cultural conservation, etc. In the case of the URS plan in Taipei, the land-use right of the government-owned land is transferred to the private sector in exchange for offsets in renewal cost, greatly facilitating the revitalization of urban districts. Active public–private partnerships can help to decrease the cost of urban renewal for the government, reducing conflicts between the government and private property owners and avoiding administrative inflexibility, thus enhancing the efficiency of urban renewal. However, given the profit-hungry nature of private investors, the balance between protecting public interest and motivating private investment is not easy to reach in public–private partnerships; therefore, many project plans are decided case by case with frequent supervision and timely adjustments.

2.5.4 A combination of incentives and enforcement

In all four cases, renewal strategies are combined with incentives and enforcement measures. Incentives include subsidies, FAR awards, special funds and loans, etc. The enforcement measures in the four cities such as compulsory sale of property rights and land based on majority rule, which could effectively avoid the "nail-house" phenomenon and improve renewal efficiency, have not yet been officially introduced to mainland China. In the absence of appropriate institutions, land expropriation intensifies social tensions and offends private property rights. On the other hand, institutional arrangements such as freezing investigations on stakeholders, reasonable compensation standards, and the open-market auction of leftover properties can to some extent protect the legal rights of proprietors. However, the majority rule and renewal area rezoning create loopholes that lead to social justice problems that require urgent solutions. This shows that no public policy can be absolutely fair to all and satisfy all stakeholders. In urban renewal projects involving complicated stakeholder relationships, decisions are usually the results of balancing power, efficiency, and equity.

2.5.5 Emphasis on the conservation of history, culture, and local characteristics

In all four cases, the historic and cultural value of urban districts has been damaged during the period of rapid urban development, but has received more and more attention in the later urban renewal process. To create a unique identity has become one of the important tasks of urban renewal. Although the goal of historic and cultural conservation might be hardly coordinated with the economic aims of urban renewal, all four governments realized the positive impacts of historical and cultural conservation, such as the revitalization of the surrounding area and the enhancement of urban competitiveness. In Singapore, the Urban Redevelopment Authority is responsible for both urban renewal and historic conservation. For buildings or areas with historic value, urban plans have been developed by the URA based on systematic assessment under the local context to identify the appropriate renewal strategies, such as holistic conservation, regeneration and reuse, and reconstruction.

Notes

1 Dr ZHU He, lecturer at Beijing University of Civil Engineering and Architecture, contributed the Chinese version of the four cases compared in this chapter in 2019.
2 The Hong Kong Urban Renewal Authority (URA) is a legitimate organization established in May 2001 in accordance with the Urban Renewal Authority Ordinance, to replace the previous Land Development Corporation in undertaking, facilitating, and promoting the urban renewal of Hong Kong. In June 2002, the Financial Committee of Hong Kong's Legislative Council approved an injection by the government of a total of HK$10 billion into the URA over a five-year period, starting from the 2002–2003 fiscal year. The government also subsidizes the URA through other approaches such as allocating land to the URA while waiving the cost. The Hong Kong URA, in accordance with the Urban Renewal Authority Ordinance, should execute urban renewal plans under the principle of cautious financial management.
3 Compiled from: Shi Y (2018), Gearing Type Urban Regeneration Strategy: Case on Otemachi Development in Tokyo, Japan. *Urban Planning International*, 8:132–138.
4 Details refer to http://www.toshiseibi.metro.tokyo.jp/.
5 Ibid.

3 The evolution of urban regeneration in Guangzhou, Shenzhen, and Shanghai

This chapter summarizes the development of urban regeneration in Guangzhou, Shenzhen, and Shanghai from a historical perspective.[1] The practice of urban regeneration in Shanghai can be traced back to before 1949, while the starting point for the study in Guangzhou and Shenzhen is the 1980s and 1990s. Following China's reform and opening up, these decades are the initial period of rapid economic development for Guangzhou and Shenzhen, and also mark an important period for modern urban regeneration activities generally.

3.1 The evolution of urban regeneration in Guangzhou

The development of urban regeneration in Guangzhou has undergone roughly four stages: free-market exploration, government-dominance approach, the "three olds" regeneration movement, and comprehensive urban regeneration. At each stage, various strategies have been developed to tackle the problems that emerged, with reflections on the lessons learnt from past failures. Urban regeneration policies developed in Guangzhou by leapfrog, with drastic differences in policy orientations in various situations, which had the advantage of eliminating abuses of the existing institutional framework, although there were also negative effects. Market players, disorientated by policy inconsistency instead of a stable framework with incremental progress, hence tend to be less motivated.

3.1.1 Exploration of the free market (1980–1999)

This stage began with housing reform, along with China's economic reform and opening up, and ended in 1999, when the Guangzhou government prohibited private developers from participating in the regeneration of old urban areas. At that time, living space in Guangzhou was below 3m^2 per capita, with deteriorating buildings and poor living conditions in the old city. Lacking both experience and funding, the government was incapable of undertaking urban regeneration alone, and thus left the task of urban upgrading to the private sector. With the gradual ending of welfare housing after the reform and opening up in 1978, state policy turned towards development of commercialized housing, encouraging private enterprises to enter the real-estate market. In 1981, the first commercial housing residential district, Donghu New Village, was completed in Guangzhou after two years of negotiation and construction, setting an important example for urban regeneration in Guangzhou and even the whole of China. Located in Dashatou, Dongshan District (later merged into Yuexiu District), the project was at the center of the historical town of Guangzhou, close to the Pearl River. In

1979, the Guangzhou government officially introduced investment from Hong Kong for urban regeneration, on condition that the newly constructed housing be partly used as resettlement housing beyond commodity housing. This laid the foundations of the Guangzhou urban regeneration model, in which the government would attract private investment by supplying land while reserving a proportion of the new housing for resettlement (Wang, Bouhouch and Wu, 2017). Later on in the free-market exploration, a 40–60 split model was established as a conventional consensus, i.e., the developers would take 60% of the regenerated floor area for profit, and the government would get the remaining 40% for resettlement and compensation. Substantially relieving the financial burden on the government, this model has been frequently applied in contemporary projects in Guangzhou, including the Wuyang New Town and Jiangnan New Village real-estate projects, as well as the commercial Liwan Square project. However, the model also has its negative impacts. First, the price of the newly constructed commercial housing was too high to be affordable given the average income level at that time. The Donghu village, for example, was sold at 700 RMB/m^2, when the average monthly income of Guangzhou residents was a mere 40 RMB. The commercial housing thus essentially failed in its purpose of improving the living conditions of residents in Guangzhou, as they ended up becoming residences for Hong Kong and foreign businessmen. Second, regeneration projects typically lacked management and development control, and took a mass demolition and construction approach. At that time, the local government was in an absolutely dominant position in the distribution of land-use right. Having witnessed the "low cost, short cycle, and quick results" (*duan, ping, kuai*) effect of this project model, the government was eager to involve further private capital to extend this type of regeneration based on mass demolition and new construction. The transformation of old urban areas with a low floor area ratio into new districts with high-rise buildings, while appealing to the government, overlooked the integrated approach to neighborhood development. The public amenities in the neighborhood areas encountered capacity problems and the historical landscape was largely damaged by the new construction.

3.1.2 Government-dominance approach (1999–2009)

Due to its negative effects, property-led urban regeneration was abandoned by the municipal government in 1999 (private developers were prohibited from participating in regeneration projects) and replaced by the government-dominance approach till the launch of the urban regeneration movement, marked by the Guangzhou government's 2009 publication of Opinions on Facilitating "Three Olds" Regeneration. Thus, the government took full responsibility for project management including investment, relocation, resettlement, and construction. This approach was feasible for several reasons. First, rapid economic development and land sales income in the 1990s enlarged government revenue. Second, the previous cooperation with private enterprises provided abundant project management and financing experience for the government. Funded by district and municipal governments, as well as property owners, the regeneration projects were implemented as not-for-profit or low profit, without much change to the density and FAR of the area after transformation. In 2000, a fund of 5 billion RMB was allocated by Guangzhou municipal government specifically for regenerating seven urban villages. Further, the 2002 Opinions on the Regeneration of Urban Villages identified property owners as the principal investors and beneficiaries of regeneration, which implied that construction costs would be levied from the property owners based on size and the deficit would be covered by the government. With the publication of Industrial Land Disposal Measures for Withdrawing Secondary Industry and Promoting Tertiary Industry in Guangzhou (2008), which defined the area of the secondary industries to be withdrawn, industrial enterprises could apply for compensation for their land expropriated by the government for land reserve, or transform their business into any type of tertiary industry (except real estate) on the condition of retaining formal land-use type and ownership (Yao and Tian, 2017). The government-dominated regeneration, guided by detailed policies and regulations for renewal of old towns, old villages, or old factories (industrial lands), aimed at protecting the public interest. In practice, however, due to the many old areas in Guangzhou, the government was overwhelmed by the residents' high expectation of resettlement benefits that had been consistently promoted by the property-led mass new construction model since the 1990s. To balance the cost, the ratio of demolition to new construction increased in the later stages to 1:1.2, or even 1:1.5. In 2008, the ratio reached as high as 1:2.65 in the renewal of Liede Village, with enormous relocation compensation (Wang, Bouhouch and Wu, 2017).

3.1.3 "Three olds" regeneration movement (2009–2015)

The "three olds" regeneration movement started in 2009 with the publication of the Opinions on Facilitating "Three Olds" Regeneration and the establishment of the Three Olds Regeneration Office, and ended in 2015 with the founding of the first Urban Regeneration Bureau in China. Within a short period of five years (2010-2015), many policy documents were issued, including the Guangzhou Old Urban Area Regeneration and Renovation Plan, the Guangzhou Old Industrial Buildings Renovation Special Plan, and the Supplementary Opinions on Facilitating "Three Olds" Regeneration, aimed at developing a comprehensive renewal system and collectively termed a "movement". A thorough investigation of overall land with renewal potential showed that by the end of 2014, inefficiently used land constituted one-third of all land built on, creating great potential for renewal (Wang and Shen, 2015). Thus, the Guangzhou "Three Olds" Regeneration Plan (2010-2020) was developed, which comprehensively coordinated and identified the regeneration of three old spaces – old towns, old villages, and old factories (industrial lands), followed by the launch of a large-scale regeneration program to massively accelerate urban regeneration. In the "three olds" regeneration movement, private investors were allowed to rejoin renewal activities under certain conditions. Distinct from the profit-oriented model in the free-market exploration period, the principle of "mutual benefit and moderate profit" was formulated by the government. As well as the positive effect of more efficient land use through introducing new uses for old industrial lands, known as "emptying cages and changing the birds" (*teng long huan niao*), the "three olds" regeneration movement also solved the legitimacy problems of illegally used land by integrating them into the urban renewal program and legalizing the *de facto* land-use type after renewal. However, the "three olds" regeneration movement also had negative effects. First, the model of "massive new construction" with extremely high floor area ratios resurfaced on a large scale. Second, regeneration practices that were initiated by the Guangdong provincial government and the Ministry of Land and Resources in order to reform land management were not properly coordinated with the urban planning department. Aiming at improving land-use efficiency and increasing the economic output of the land, the "three olds" regeneration movement emphasized regulations and control of land-use quotas, while overlooking spatial control from the perspective of urban planning. The chronology and range of regeneration failed to reflect the development strategy defined by urban planning, which is as important as "the head of a dragon". Further, new land use after renewal and development quota control in the long term were not sufficiently taken into consideration.

3.1.4 Comprehensive urban regeneration (2015-present)

This period started in 2015, when the provisional Three Olds Regeneration Office was replaced by the permanent Urban Regeneration Bureau. With the enactment of the Guangzhou Urban Regeneration Measures in 2016, urban regeneration in Guangzhou has shifted from land-use change to comprehensive urban spatial regeneration, and from massive demolition, construction, and individual property unit regeneration to a combination of comprehensive macro- and micro-level renewal. According to the Urban Regeneration Bureau in Guangzhou,[2] seven key tasks have been identified: ① the expropriation, purchasing, and reorganization of land within the area of urban regeneration; ② management of the application and approval process for land ownership change from collectively owned to state owned; ③ the preparation of administrative procedures for legalizing illegally used land; ④ the approval of plans for urban regeneration projects; ⑤ the coordination and allocation of resettlement housing; ⑥ the supervision of funds for reconstruction and resettlement; and ⑦ the supervision of the implementation of urban regeneration projects. Thus, the Urban Regeneration Bureau's responsibilities are designed to tackle the problems reflected in the previous stages of urban regeneration and to meet the current demands. Led by the Urban Regeneration Bureau, the Guangzhou Overall Urban Regeneration Plan(2015–2020) was developed, identifying a long-term and effective plan for a comprehensive urban regeneration system by 2020, supported by stable policies and standardized procedures. In recent years, five supplementary guidelines and technical standards have been produced, including Guidance on Application Procedures for Urban Regeneration Projects in Guangzhou, and Guidance on Development of District Urban Regeneration Plans in Guangzhou. The Guangzhou Urban Regeneration Ordinance was included in the list of preparatory legislation in 2018, to be approved by the People's Congress in the coming years. As a trans-unit organization, the Urban Regeneration Bureau coordinated the three key departments of land use, urban planning and urban construction, and functioned as a platform for exchange, representing a milestone in institutional development for urban regeneration nationwide. The Guangzhou Urban Regeneration Bureau operated until the reform of state institutions in 2018, and was abolished in 2019 because of the promotion of large ministries in China. The newly established Ministry of Natural Resources took on total or partial responsibilities of several original ministries.

3.2 The evolution of urban regeneration in Shenzhen

Urban regeneration in Shenzhen went through roughly three periods: spontaneous scattered regeneration, government-led special regeneration, and the establishment of key institutions. Shenzhen and Guangzhou are both located in Guangdong Province and share some similarities in their urban regeneration evolution: urban regeneration strategies have shifted from "three olds" regeneration to comprehensive and integrated urban regeneration. However, unlike Guangzhou, which witnessed leapfrogging of urban regeneration policies in terms of main actors, the policies in Shenzhen have been more consistent. With only 40 years of urban development since the reform and opening up, the young city of Shenzhen does not have many historical areas, so its urban regeneration practice started later than that of the other two cities. The motivation for urban regeneration in Shenzhen is more individual than in the other two cities, deriving from restructuring urban functions and renewing the informal settlement of urban villages.

3.2.1 Spontaneous scattered regeneration period (1990s–2004)

Starting with the establishment of the Shenzhen Special Economic Zone in 1980, the first stage of urban regeneration was spontaneous and scattered, until the publication of a series of regeneration policies relating to urban villages and old industrial areas in 2004. For the first two decades, urban development in Shenzhen was focused on developing new land rather than improving built-up areas. The main regeneration activities at that time took place on collectively owned village land; informal, sporadic, and spontaneous, it was led by individual property owners. Due to rapid urban expansion, the original rural villages on the margins of the city were quickly transformed into urban fringe villages or urban villages to accommodate the influx of working population. Theoretically, all urban village land has been nationalized in Shenzhen and collectively owned land abolished (Geng, 2015). But in reality, the villages were not urbanized, and the villagers have not become urban employees. Consequently, "urban villages" remained outside the development scheme and construction supervised by the government. Informal profit-driven regeneration in urban villages proved rather active, transforming village houses into informal high-density, low-quality cheap housing for the transient low-income population. The other type of spontaneous informal regeneration involved the reuse of old industrial buildings in industrial areas, such as Bagualing and Shangbu, as wholesale markets to serve labor-intensive manufacturing industries. Instead of being prohibited by the government, informal spontaneous regeneration was tolerated in the early stages, which facilitated urban development through space production for special social groups, but left several problems to be tackled by later generations.

3.2.2 Government-led special regeneration program (2004–2009)

The government-led special regeneration program was launched with the publication of Provisional Measures on Urban Villages (Old Villages) Regeneration in Shenzhen in 2004, and continued until the enactment of Shenzhen Urban Regeneration Measures in 2009. From the late 1990s, aware of the deficiency of land resources and the unsustainability of urban sprawl, the government had begun to limit new land development and strengthen control over illegal construction. Yet, the strict controls over the increase in construction land were not facilitated by appropriate regeneration of built-up areas, indirectly leading to an increase in housing and land prices. Finally, the publication of the Provisional Measures on Urban Villages (Old Villages) Regeneration in Shenzhen in 2004 marked the launch of government-led organized large-scale urban regeneration in Shenzhen. Under these measures, land transfer for the purpose of urban renewal can be exempt from auction. The regeneration procedures have been simplified and relaxed to allow negotiation-based land transfer, effectively motivating the private sector to practice urban regeneration. In the same year, the enactment of the Decision on Investigation of and Penalties for Illegal Building and Land Use to some extent put a stop to the practice of acquiring extra relocation compensation through illegal construction in urban villages. Henceforth, policies and regulations such as Overall Plan for Urban Village (Old Villages) Regeneration in Shenzhen (2005–2010) and Technical Regulations on Developing Regeneration Plans for Urban Villages (Old Villages) in Shenzhen promoted the practice of urban regeneration in urban villages. With the publication of Opinions on the Upgrading and Renovation of Industrial Districts in 2007, the regeneration of old industrial areas has become an important industrial restructuring strategy in Shenzhen. The Work Program on Accelerating Upgrading and Renovation of Old Industrial Districts in Shenzhen (2008) stipulated four categories of industrial districts to be renewed, defined strategies for industrial land renewal and outlined 12 trial projects. The four categories were: industrial areas that are incompatible with industrial restructuring plans and modern industry requirements; areas incompatible with production safety and environmental protection requirements; areas with low building floor area ratios and inefficient land use; and areas with unreasonable internal planning, insufficient infrastructure and low-quality construction. The government issued Outlines of Overall Planning of the Upgrading and Renovation of Old Industrial Districts in Shenzhen (2007–2020) based on the Work Program. Focusing on urban villages and old industrial areas, a series of regeneration projects took place in Shenzhen, including Yunong Village, Gangsha Village, and Shuiku New Village. Most projects involved mass demolition and construction, yet some projects could not be pursued due to problems with relocation compensation and land transfer, which called for more systematic regeneration institutions and long-term strategies from the government.

3.2.3 Establishment of key institutions (2009-present)

To facilitate the "three olds" regeneration trial projects promoted by the Ministry of Land and Resources and the Guangdong provincial government, the Shenzhen Urban Regeneration Measures were enacted in 2009, becoming the first local government legislation to provide specific guidance for urban regeneration in China. In 2012, when the area of renewed construction land exceeded that of the increased new land for the first time, the Detailed Implementation Regulations for Urban Regeneration Measures in Shenzhen were enacted. In the same year, the Shenzhen Land Acquisition and Relocation Office was upgraded to a standing quasi-bureau organization, the Shenzhen Land Organization Bureau, directed by the deputy chairman of the Municipal Planning and Land Resources Committee, which was upgraded to the Urban Regeneration (Land Organization) Bureau in 2015. The Urban Regeneration Unit has been developed as a key management tool in urban planning and three types of strategies have been identified in practice: demolition and reconstruction, change of use, and comprehensive renovation. The targets of urban regeneration have been extended beyond old villages, old towns, and old industrial lands. Legislation, policies, technical standards, and regulations have all been consistently developed and appropriately adjusted based on the Shenzhen Urban Regeneration Measures (Zou, 2017. The Provisional Measures for Strengthening and Improving the Implementation of Urban Regeneration, for instance, was revised in 2012, 2014, and 2016, to take account of land price valuation, small-scale regeneration, development of urban regeneration plans, etc. Problems remained in the practice of urban regeneration in Shenzhen, including steadily increasing FAR, the dominance of profit-driven real estate and commercial development, and insufficient land for public facilities. To tackle the problems of high density, in 2013 the new version of the Urban Planning Standards and Rules came into effect, stipulating development density standards for urban renewal projects. In general, the government-led model became a "government-induced, market-led" model, where the government is mainly responsible for managing surveys on regeneration willingness, project application and approval, formulation of planning in the early stages and supervision of project implementation in the later stages. This has ensured the integration of top-down planning and guidance with bottom-up demand-driven project initiatives.

3.3 The evolution of urban regeneration in Shanghai

As one of the largest and the most advanced cities in China, and as the birthplace of modern urban planning in China, Shanghai has been consistently undergoing modern urban regeneration ever since the port opened in 1843. Unlike the spontaneous practices observed in Guangzhou and Shenzhen, planned urban regeneration in Shanghai can be traced back to the 1840s. After the reform and opening up, urban regeneration practice in Shanghai started with solving the housing problem and developing an overall urban development strategy. In general, urban regeneration in Shanghai can be divided into five periods: from port opening to liberation; the planned economy era; the improvement of living conditions and functional restructuring; the conceptual transition period; and the comprehensive strategy.

3.3.1 From port opening to liberation (1840s–1949)

Transformed from a feudal-era city to a modern metropolis after port opening in the 1840s, Shanghai gradually rose to the position of a global city, with advanced industry, commerce and transportation. In the early stage, reconstruction and new construction were independently practiced in different concessions[3] without much demarcation coordination. Most of the new spaces in the concessions for shops, modern factories, warehouses and docks were created through demolition of old buildings and reconstruction of new. The population in Shanghai exceeded 1 million in 1880, was over 3 million in 1930, and reached a historical peak at 6 million in 1945. The economic development and population increase led to large-scale spontaneous renewal that changed the traditional one-story courtyard housing into dense town houses. Urban development master plans in this period included the Shanghai Region Development Plan (1924), the Great Shanghai Plan (1931), and the New Construction Plan of the Metropolis (1937). After World War II, the Greater Shanghai Metropolitan Plan, developed by the Kuomintang government, identified the problems of over-density and deterioration of buildings in the inner city, and correspondingly introduced the concepts of "satellite cities" and "organic decentralization" to integrate the renewal of old towns and the construction of new areas at the macroscopic level.

3.3.2 The planned economy era (1949–1978)

This period started in 1949 with the foundation of the People's Republic of China and continued until the reform and opening up in 1978. After the liberation, urban development strategies were identified as "gradually renovating the old urban areas, strictly controlling suburban industrial areas, and developing satellite cities" (Su, 2017), as stated in the Shanghai Master Plan (1953) and the Shanghai Overall Plan (1959). In the Third Five-Year Plan, issued in 1963, urban regeneration tasks were identified as "improving featured areas, demolishing and reconstructing housing settlement, renewing buildings with additional stories, connecting and reconstructing roads, improving crossroads and expanding civil infrastructure". Due to budget constraints, not many urban regeneration projects were actually implemented, and those that were, were mostly projects for public spaces, such as the People's Square and the People's Park, as well as a few social housing projects upgrading slums. In this period, urban regeneration was undertaken through compulsory administrative orders. Problems that were frequently observed in the later stages of urban regeneration, such as stakeholder conflicts and relocation compensation, did not yet arise in the planned economy era.

3.3.3 Improvement of living conditions and functional restructuring period (1978–2000)

In 1978, the Central Urban Housing Construction Conference marked the beginning of nationwide housing reform, followed by a working conference on housing construction by Shanghai Municipal Government in 1980, which stated that low living space and poor living conditions would be improved through combining "housing construction and urban development, new area construction and old area regeneration, and construction of new housing and renovation of old housing". Meanwhile, the government stipulated that old area regeneration should adhere to the principle of "selecting concentrated areas of slums for contiguous areas of renewal". In response to this appeal, a massive housing improvement movement took effect over nearly 20 years. In 1987, the Shanghai government published the Paid Transfer of Land-Use Rights Measures, paving the way for the private sector to undertake urban renewal projects. In 1991, the "365 slum clearances program", aimed at the demolition and reconstruction of slum areas across the city, rapidly and substantially transformed the appearance of the old town of Shanghai, dramatically resolving the housing shortage (Kuang, 2017). In 1993, the government document, Notice Approving the Municipal Construction Committee's "Request for Streamlining Administration and Delegating Authorities, and Improving Two-Tier Management of Land Leasing" enabled subordinate districts of Shanghai to retain revenues acquired through land leasing, strongly motivating the district governments to participate in urban regeneration. So far, a sophisticated approach developed, in which the government was responsible for relocation, resettlement, land acquisition, land preparation, land assessment and leasing, and the developers were allowed to invest and redevelop the land, mostly by way of mass demolition and construction. Moreover, the Shanghai Urban Master Plan (1986) stated that Shanghai should transform itself from a single industrial manufacturing center into China's outward-facing multifunctional economic center (Su, 2017). Under the Master Plan, urban functions were to be restructured based on urban economic development planning, and the city center would be transformed from a single administrative district to a comprehensive commercial, cultural, and entertainment center. To realize the new functions in the inner city, the large area of industrial land where factories were mostly relocated or closed down could provide potential land resources. Mostly state owned, the industrial land could be easily taken back by the state through relocation and resettlement procedures facilitated by internal negotiations among government departments, paving the way for the expansion of the urban transformation.

3.3.4 Conceptual transition period (2000–2014)

Based on the self-examination of the previous practice, urban regeneration in this period experienced three transitions: ① strengthening of urban planning guidance; ② critiquing review of the mass demolition and construction; and ③ increased attention to historical and cultural conservation. In 2000, with the completion of the Shanghai Master Plan (1999-2020) and full coverage of regulatory planning (zoning) for each block in Shanghai, urban regeneration was guided and regulated by multiple urban planning guidance, including the urban master plan, the district plan, and in particular the regulatory plans. Meanwhile, based on a critical review of the "365 slum clearances" scheme, a new round of old area regeneration was launched in 2002, suggesting four strategies of urban regeneration-demolition, renovation, conservation, and repair-with more emphasis on conservation. "Demolition" applies to old neighborhoods with shabby structures and poor living conditions, while buildings with well-maintained structure but poor functional structures should be renovated. District, buildings, garden residences and new-style neighborhoods with historic and cultural value should be "conserved", and partially damaged physical structures should be "repaired" (Ge, Guan and Nie, 2017). An approach that combined "sporadic regeneration" with "contiguous areas renewal" was proposed in the Opinions on Further Promoting Old Area Regeneration in Shanghai, published in 2009. In the same year, the Opinions on Pre-Consultation of Old Area Regeneration encouraged residents to become involved by proposing bottom-up initiatives for renewal projects. Only when a certain proportion of property owners had agreed on a relocation and compensation plan after two rounds of consultation, could the resettlement plan be approved. In terms of historical conservation, a series of individual projects involving historical and cultural conservation were initiated in the late 1990s, such as Xintiandi and Tianzifang, but it was not until the early 2000s that the government started to pay more attention to historical preservation. Enacted in 2003, the Ordinance for Protection of Historical and Cultural Districts and Outstanding Historical Buildings in Shanghai provided a legal instrument for historical conservation. The Notice on Further Strengthening Protection of Historical and Cultural Districts and Outstanding Historical Buildings in Shanghai (2004) paid special attention to conservation of historical architecture and urban landscape. Around 2005, conservation plans for historical districts were developed in Shanghai, based on a thorough investigation of "all the areas that have to be conserved". Thus, historical protection has been closely linked with urban regeneration and urban revitalization. In general, urban regeneration in Shanghai underwent a significant transition from a narrow economic indicator-oriented approach to integrated and comprehensive overall urban regeneration.

3.3.5 The comprehensive strategy period (2014-present)

In 2014, on the occasion of the Sixth Working Conference on Planning and Land Resources Management in Shanghai, the significance of urban regeneration, beyond its practical function of providing land for new forms of economic activity, was highlighted as a comprehensive strategy to improve the quality of the urban environment of Shanghai. In the conference, the Communist Party Secretary, Han Zheng, requested that "the planned size of construction land in Shanghai should target negative growth", and mayor Yang Xiong responded with "promoting urban transformation through changing land use model". Zhuang Shaoqin, the Shanghai Party Secretary and Director of the Bureau of Planning and Land Resources believed that Shanghai had reached the stage of "reverse growth", with more orientation towards quality and vitality (Zhuang, 2015a).

In 2015, the Shanghai Urban Regeneration Implementation Measures were published, followed by a series of complementary regulations, including the Detailed Land Regulations on Implementation of Urban Regeneration Planning, the Operational Regulations on Management of Urban Regeneration Planning and the Standards of Regional Assessment Reports of Urban Regeneration, marking the preliminary establishment of a legal framework for urban regeneration in Shanghai. In the process, more urban regeneration strategies have been identified. First, the practice of urban regeneration should be guided by urban planning and promoted step by step to achieve dynamic, sustainable and organic regeneration. Second, based primarily on the assessment of current public amenities and the principle of public interest, the urban regeneration plan should integrate upgrading urban functions and improving urban quality. Third, a coordination platform should be developed to encourage multiple actors, including the private sector, the public, and experts, to achieve a win–win effect by participating in the urban regeneration process. Thus, the model of mass demolition and new construction has been replaced by a comprehensive regeneration approach of improving existing spatial quality and urban function. Under the guidance of these strategies, Shanghai launched a "four actions plan" in 2016, identifying the key target areas of urban regeneration as shared communities, innovation parks, charming landscape, and entertainment networks. Under the four actions plan, 12 pilot projects have been identified and planned for implementation within three years, ranging from micro regeneration, industrial upgrading, historical and cultural conservation to leisure space shaping. The Shanghai Urban Master Plan (2017-2035), published in 2017, further strengthened the comprehensive urban regeneration approach. First, in the inner city the former principle of demolition first, and renovation and conservation second, should be replaced by conservation and renovation first, followed by demolition. As well as listed monuments, more valuable objects should be included within the scope of conservation. Second, as well as community revitalization and historical inheritance, more attention should be paid to optimizing urban function, improving spatial quality, enhancing regional coordination, and promoting compact and mixed land use to achieve low-carbon and highly efficient urban development. Though relevant institutions are still under development in Shanghai, urban regeneration has already been positioned as the supreme development strategy to comprehensively improve living conditions.

3.4 Conclusions

Various operational features and implementation models in different development stages can be observed according to the different development levels, the various local institutional systems, conceptual differences, and the changing roles of government and the private sector. In the case of Guangzhou, market mechanisms were introduced at an early stage, but were abandoned and replaced by the government-dominance approach due to their negative profit-oriented effect, high redevelopment intensity, and failure to consider public amenities. Given the unsustainability of both approaches, a middle way was eventually settled on a government-led approach with multiple actor participation. In the younger city of Shenzhen, it was not until the beginning of the 21st century that urban regeneration policies began to be actively explored and developed. At the forefront of reform and opening up, Shenzhen expanded most rapidly, causing land resources to be used up within two short decades by the end of the 20th century. Forced to reuse built-up areas, Shenzhen was the first of the three cities to develop a legal instrument for urban regeneration, the Shenzhen Urban Regeneration Measures, and the first to establish a unique organization for urban renewal management, the Land Integration and Preparation Bureau. In the case of Shanghai, the practice of urban regeneration started early, but policy development lagged behind. The "365 slum clearances" scheme in the 1990s remained practical progress rather than policy development. In the 21st century, inspired by Guangzhou and Shenzhen, where urban regeneration was regarded as a strategy for optimizing land use along with the "three olds" regeneration movement, Shanghai has moved forward to explore the effects of urban regeneration polices through trial projects for improving the quality of the urban environment and promoting historical, cultural, and ecological conservation.

Despite dramatic differences between the three cities in the evolution of their urban renewal policies, five common issues exist: ① the main actors have changed from taking the government as the sole actor to multiple players including the private and public sectors; ② the strategies have shifted from mass demolition and construction towards more diverse measures, including demolition, renovation, conservation, repair, and maintenance; ③ the approach has changed from a government-led top-down approach to mutual approaches supporting bottom-up initiatives; ④ the regeneration goals have shifted from improving housing conditions and optimizing land use to promoting comprehensive and sustainable urban development; and ⑤ based on the Urban Regeneration (Implementation) Measures issued in the respective cities, more laws and regulations have been developed step by step as legal instruments.

Notes

1 Dr ZHU He, lecturer at Beijing University of Civil Engineering and Architecture, contributed the Chinese version of the history study on urban regeneration in the three cities of this chapter in 2019.
2 http://www.gdzwfw.gov.cn/portal/affairs-public-duty-list?region=440100&deptCode=550590033.
3 The foreign concessions in Shanghai were the earliest, the longest and the largest, which has a profound influence on the modern history of China. On November 29, 1845, the local governor of Shanghai and the British Consul signed the Shanghai Land Regulations in accordance with the Nanjing Treaty, confirming the establishment of the British Concession in Shanghai. Thereafter, the American Concession and the French Concession were established. The county of Shanghai (Huajie) under the jurisdiction of China, together with the self-governing concessions by foreign parties, constituted together the entire Shanghai of that period.

4 Urban regeneration policies and regulations in the three cities

4.1 The development of urban regeneration policies in Guangzhou, Shenzhen, and Shanghai

Between 2009 and 2015, the Urban Regeneration (Implementation) Measures were published successively in Shenzhen, Shanghai, and Guangzhou, marking a milestone in the institutional development of urban regeneration in the three cities (Table 4.1). The standardized urban regeneration procedures developed in Guangzhou and Shenzhen were facilitated by the trial of policy reform in Guangdong province to promote more intensified and efficient land use, initiated by the Ministry of Land Resources in 2008. During the trial and the subsequent "three olds" regeneration movement,[1] a series of land policy reforms paved the way for further urban regeneration practice. Regulations on land circulation and land-use quotas were developed. The negotiated transfer of land-use rights in respect of profit-making land was permitted instead of auction,[2] and revenues generated from the land transfer could be returned to the original land owners of village collectives to develop their economy. In the case of Shanghai, urban regeneration relied more on accumulated experience, formal regulation and documents, and trial projects, rather than on aggressive land reform policy. The timeline for the Urban Regeneration (Implementation) Measures in the three cities is shown in Table 4.1.

Table 4.1 Urban Regeneration (Implementation) Measures published in Guangzhou, Shenzhen, and Shanghai (2009–2015)

	Legal instrument	Goals of regeneration	Date of issue	Date of enforcement
Guangzhou	Guangzhou Urban Regeneration Measures	Promoting plan-based utilization of urban land, improving urban functions and living conditions, preserving history and culture, optimizing industrial structure, coordinating urban and rural development, enhancing land-use efficiency, and protecting public interests	December 1, 2015	January 1, 2016

(*Continued*)

Table 4.1 (Continued)

	Legal instrument	Goals of regeneration	Date of issue	Date of enforcement
Shenzhen	Shenzhen Urban Regeneration Measures	Improving urban function, optimizing industrial structure, improving living conditions, promoting sustainable social and economic development, and facilitating the economical and intensified use of land, energy, and resources	October 22, 2009	December 1, 2009
Shanghai	Shanghai Urban Regeneration Implementation Measures	Upgrading urban function, stimulating urban vitality, improving living conditions, strengthening urban attraction, and facilitating economical and intensified use of urban built-up land	May 15, 2015	June 1, 2015

Sources: Secretariat of the General Office of the People's Government of Guangzhou (2015), Urban Regeneration Measures; Shenzhen Municipal Government (2016), Shenzhen Urban Regeneration Measures; Shanghai Municipal Government (2015), Shanghai Urban Regeneration Implementation Measures.

4.1.1 Guangzhou

With the economic reform and opening up, Guangdong province witnessed an opening up in all aspects of life, including rapid urbanization. In the new era, challenged by the shortage of new land for urban development, the Ministry of Land Resources of China, in cooperation with Guangdong Provincial Government, issued the Opinions on Promoting Economical and Integsified Use of Land[3] to promote the regeneration of old towns, old villages, and old factories/industrial lands ("three olds" regeneration), aiming at exploring a model of reusing built-up land to solve land shortages. In the same year, the Guangzhou Municipal Government issued the Opinions on Facilitating "Three Olds" Regeneration, with specific regulations on urban regeneration in the local context, marking the official launch of the "three olds" trial regeneration program in Guangzhou. With the deepening of economic transition in Guangzhou, new situations and problems continued to arise during the "three olds" regeneration practice, resulting in the issue of the Supplementary Opinions on Facilitating "Three Olds" Regeneration in 2012 to tackle the unresolved problems. Great achievements were made in terms of the restructuring of industries, enhanced land-use efficiency, and improved living conditions. Further, in December 2015, with the issue of Guangzhou Urban Regeneration Measures and its supplementary documents, Regeneration Implementation Measures, for old towns, old villages, and old industrial lands respectively, the "three olds" regeneration has been upgraded from a trial program to a long-term comprehensive urban regeneration program.

4.1.2 Shenzhen

Driven by the urgent need for efficient land use or reuse to solve the land shortage problems, the Shenzhen Urban Regeneration Measures were published in October 2009, followed by the supplementary document, Implementation Details of Shenzhen Urban Regeneration Measures, in January 2012. Thus, a legal framework on urban regeneration was established in Shenzhen. Further, the amended version of the 2009 Shenzhen Urban Regeneration Measures was re-issued in 2016. In the same year, an urban regeneration plan for the whole city, the 13th Five-Year Plan for Urban Regeneration in Shenzhen (2016–2020), was published.

4.1.3 Shanghai

Before the publication of the Shanghai Urban Regeneration Implementation Measures, several policies had already been issued to address specific industrial restructuring and old town regeneration tasks, such as Implementation Measures for Revitalizing Existing Industrial Land in Shanghai (Trial) (2014). Yet, the policy fluctuated between strict and lenient measures and called for a more stable and systematic legal framework. Eventually, along with a series of supplementary documents, in May 2015 the Shanghai Urban Regeneration Implementation Measures were published, becoming the core legal instrument to provide guidance for urban regeneration practice. By mid-2018, around 50 urban regeneration pilot projects had been launched to drive the overall urban regeneration practice forward. For instance, 17 Urban Renewal Plans were initiated in Shanghai in 2015, and pilot projects, followed by four Urban Regeneration Action Plans, also known as "12+X" actions, in 12 trial areas were launched in 2016. As well as the top-down approach, a bottom-up approach has been promoted by the district governments to encourage the participation of the local community in micro-regeneration, such as the Colorful Community program facilitated by the Community Planner system developed for urban renewal initiatives at the grassroots level.

4.2 Comparison of urban regeneration policies in the three cities

In the three cities, the significance of stable policies and strong legal instruments had been recognized by the authorities. Based on previous experiences of urban renewal practice, constant efforts and innovations have been made to develop and update the related legal framework step by step, and to adapt it to the local context.

4.2.1 Guangzhou: "1+3+N" policy system[4]

After some years of policy and practice experimentation, a "1+3+N" policy framework has been developed in Guangzhou: "1" represents the core document, which is the Guangzhou Urban Regeneration Measures ; "3" stands for the three supplementary documents, which are Regeneration Implementation Measures for old towns, old villages, and old industrial lands respectively; and "N" denotes other detailed regulations. The urban regeneration policy orientation in Guangzhou has undergone many revisions and adjustments. Since the launch of the "three olds" regeneration in 2009, the main actor of urban renewal practice has changed from the private sector (in the early stages) to the government, along with tighter regulation and stronger public intervention. More emphasis has also been placed on project management details and project outcomes.

4.2.2 Shenzhen: "1+1+N" policy system

The "1+1+N" policy framework developed in Shenzhen is based on the experience in policy development and urban renewal practice since 2009: the two "1s" represents the two key legal instruments, the Urban Regeneration Measures and the Implementation Details of Urban Regeneration Measures respectively, while the "N" refers to a series of supplementary documents on policies, regulations, technical standards, and practical guidelines. One of the important, regularly amended supplementary documents, the Provisional Measures on Strengthening and Improving Implementation of Urban Regeneration, stipulates detailed regulations on urban renewal practice. Facilitated by the two key legal instruments and multiple supplementary documents, various problems in the urban regeneration process in Shenzhen can be solved in a flexible way.

4.2.3 Shanghai: "1+N" policy system

The Shanghai framework is based on "1+N", in which "1" represents Shanghai Urban Regeneration Measures issued in 2015, and "N" stands for a series of supplementary documents and regulations, including the Implementation Details of Land Use Planning for Urban Regeneration in Shanghai (amended and published in November 2017), Management and Operational Regulations of Urban Regeneration Planning in Shanghai and Outcome Specifications of Regional Assessment Reports of Urban Regeneration in Shanghai, all published by the Planning and Land Resources Bureau of Shanghai. It should be noted that that the scope of the Urban Regeneration Implementation Measures in Shanghai is narrower than that of its counterparts in Guangzhou and Shenzhen, and it applies mainly to projects initiated by property owners or led by the government. That is to say, unlike Guangzhou and Shenzhen, the Shanghai Urban Regeneration Implementation Measures do not apply to renewals such as large-scale redevelopment of old industrial or residential areas by developers, which still conform to the specific policies and regulations issued prior to the Urban Regeneration Implementation Measures.

4.2.4 Summary

In general, the policy frameworks in Guangzhou, Shenzhen, and Shanghai all consist of a core legal instrument, Urban Regeneration (Implementation) Measures, and multiple sets of supplementary documents to guide and regulate urban regeneration matters, but with some differences in the three respective cities. In Guangzhou, uniquely among the three cities, and largely as a legacy of the "three olds" regeneration program, the legal framework includes three individual implementation documents developed for old towns, old villages, and old industrial land. In the case of Shenzhen, the policy framework consists of the key instrument, Urban Regeneration Measures, and supplementary documents containing detailed regulations, such as Implementation Details and Provisional Measures. In Shanghai, more attention is given to project implementation, and these processes are covered by Urban Regeneration Implementation Measures as the core instrument, and multiple supplementary documents such as the Implementation Details of Land-Use Planning for Urban Regeneration, Management and Operational Regulations of Urban Regeneration Planning, and Outcome Specifications of Regional Assessment Reports of Urban Regeneration.

4.3 The evolution of core urban regeneration policies in the three cities

4.3.1 Guangzhou: from market oriented to government led

From 2009, the main trend of urban regeneration policies in Guangzhou began to turn from market oriented towards government led, from the free-market approach (Document 56) to strengthening government dominance (Document 20), supporting the approach of integrating the market and the government and encouraging government-led cooperation with the private sector (Document 134) (Table 4.2). Documents 56, 20, and 134 (Guangzhou Urban Regeneration Measures) show the policy changes in different periods.

Table 4.2 Development of Urban Regeneration Policies in Guangzhou

	Document 56 (2009) Opinions on Facilitating "Three Olds" Regeneration	Document 20 (2012) Supplementary Opinions on Facilitating "Three Olds" Regeneration	Document 134 (2015) Guangzhou Urban Regeneration Measures
Approach	Led by private sector under market mechanism	Government-dominance with private-sector participation	Government-led partnership with private sector
Actor	Initiated by private sector under market mechanisms	Multiple actors coordinated by the government	Public and private sectors

(*Continued*)

Table 4.2 (Continued)

	Document 56 (2009) Opinions on Facilitating "Three Olds" Regeneration	Document 20 (2012) Supplementary Opinions on Facilitating "Three Olds" Regeneration	Document 134 (2015) Guangzhou Urban Regeneration Measures
Scale	Large-scale urban renewal	Encouraging continuous area renewal	Comprehensive renewal and micro-regeneration
Main land policy	Compulsory expropriation for public interest (with compensation), land transfer through public bidding or negotiation, etc.	Land expropriated and reserved by the government first, then transferred for private projects	Multiple approaches of land expropriation and reserve, self-renovation, collaborative renewal, etc.
Impact	Strong motivation for private sector; urban regeneration projects booming	Pursuit of profit constrained; regeneration practice slowing down and stagnating	Upgrading of "three olds" regeneration to comprehensive urban regeneration; slowing down of large-scale regeneration projects; increase of micro-regeneration

Source: Edited by authors.

4.3.1.1 *"Three olds" regeneration trial period (Document 56)*

Issued in 2009, Opinions on Facilitating "Three Olds" Regeneration, also known as Document 56, greatly motivated the private sector to undertake renewal projects, leading to the rapid progress of "three olds" regeneration. To promote the involvement of private investors and property owners, the government allowed the private sector to share the revenues generated from land. Meanwhile, renewal projects in land with ambiguous property rights could be included in the "three olds" regeneration program following procedures to clarify ownership (Tian et al., 2015). Document 56 stated that the government should "adhere to the guidelines of market operations for a win–win situation, to create attractive economic and policy environment through tax deductions and refunds within the scope of the municipal authority, to broaden financial channels land resources, to attract private investors in 'three olds' regeneration, to carefully select development enterprises with social responsibilities, reputation, capability, and experiences to participate in the'three olds'regeneration, and to allow original land users to initiate projects through cooperation or joint-ventures under certain conditions". "Three olds" regeneration was embraced by the private sector and implemented successfully, with a total area of 19.48 km^2 of land renewed between 2009 and 2012. Within three years, 25 old village renewal projects had been approved, proceeding much more rapidly than the government-dominated approach that had preceded the "three olds" regeneration policy (Lai and Wu, 2013). By the end of 2012, over 220 renewal projects of state-owned industrial land had been approved. At the time, old factories on state-owned land could be renewed in two ways: in the conventional approach, the government organized the land transfer and then shared the revenue generated with the state-owned enterprise, the original user of the land, as compensation; in the alternative approach, the state-owned enterprise was allowed to undertake renewal activities themselves after paying a land premium to the government for changing the land-use type from industrial to other uses, in most cases commercial and real-estate purposes. In the case of renewing old villages on collectively owned land, either through land transfer by negotiation or renewal by village collectives themselves,land-use type and development intensity can be changed after the renewal process. Empowered to organize regeneration activities, village collectives were allowed to retain land development rights.[5] Thus, the main actor in old village renewal has shifted from the government to village collectives. Subject to their economic power and management capability, village collectives can choose various approaches to renewal including village-collective led, private-sector led or a mixture of both (Yang et al., 2012).

4.3.1.2 "Three olds" regeneration adjustment period (Document 20)

Through Document 56, the private sector was empowered to undertake renewal projects and benefit from land value capture, and the income of property owners from the renewal also increased. However, the overall "three olds" regeneration goals have been affected by the profit-oriented approach of urban renewal. Due to clear property rights and a large potential land value surplus, state-owned manufacturing land has been favored by private investors, but the transformation from industrial to non-industrial use, in most cases for commercial purposes, has contributed little to the provision or improvement of public amenities and public spaces, and has led to an over-supply of commercial and business space. The large scale of the renewal also failed to promote the development of modern service and high-tech industries. For the same reasons, in the case of old village renewal, old factories rather than old residential areas have been favored by the developers. Due to complicated and ambiguous property rights, old residential village properties, particularly villages with relatively unfavorable locations, inefficient use and poor environment quality, hardly made it onto the urban renewal agenda. Therefore, in the later stages of "three olds" regeneration, a consensus was reached that urban regeneration practice should not "completely follow market mechanisms" and be "directly done by the developers".[6] Government intervention needed to be strengthened to regulate the market and balance costs and profits. This led to the promulgation in 2012 of Document 20, Supplementary Opinions on Facilitating "Three Olds" Regeneration, which shifted the direction of "three olds" regeneration from the market-dominant and efficiency-oriented approach to the government-dominance approach and tightened control of "three olds" regeneration. By highlighting the principle of "government-dominant, market supplemented, promoting 'contiguous area' renewal instead of scattered renewal, and with planning in advance", Document 20 imposed new "three olds" regeneration requirements. First, land banking should be strengthened, particularly in areas with favorable locations and potential land value surplus, "to expropriate all land that should be expropriated". Second, the cherry picking of selected profitable areas for sporadic renewal, and the ignoring of others, should be prevented and replaced by a holistic scale. Further, the "contiguous area" urban renewal target should be shifted towards state-owned industrial lands and their surrounding areas. Third, in the case of renewal of state-owned industrial lands, the revenue generated from land value surplus should be re-distributed and the land premium standard adjusted. Fourth, in the case of village renewal, a higher consensus should be reached (more than 90% of the villagers), and collective properties and old factories should be bundled with old residential areas for renewal projects (Yao and Tian, 2017). Following this 2012 policy tightening, "three olds" regeneration in Guangzhou immediately slowed down to stagnation point. Consequently, the period between 2013 and 2015 is regarded as the "three olds" regeneration adjustment phase in Guangzhou. Land banking activities continued, with listed state-owned factory land withdrawn from secondary industry still purchased and stored by the Guangzhou Land Development Center (Yao and Tian, 2017).

4.3.1.3 Transition from "three olds" regeneration to holistic urban regeneration (Document 134)

Under the "three olds" regeneration framework, from 2009 to 2015, policies targeting specific areas had been developed but were not sufficiently integrated to tackle comprehensive urban problems. In the new era, urban regeneration called for a more holistic approach. To promote comprehensive urban regeneration in the entire city, the Guangzhou Urban Regeneration Bureau,[7] a special department in charge of overall regeneration, was established in 2015. Later that year, the Guangzhou Urban Regeneration Measures, or Document 134, along with its three supplementary documents, the Regeneration Implementation Measures for old towns, for old villages, and for old industrial lands respectively, were published. In the "1+3" policy package, the general term "three olds regeneration" was replaced by "urban regeneration". Two scales and strengths of regeneration were also defined: "comprehensive renewal" and "micro-regeneration".[8] The new policy package integrates existing documents on various types of regeneration practice, such as policies on "three olds", dilapidated buildings, and slums, respectively, into a fundamental framework for guiding urban regeneration-related activities, such as developing regeneration plans and programs, regulating land use, fund raising, and project supervision and management. In 2016, with further appeals for more intensified use of land, the Ministry of Land Resources and the Guangdong Provincial Government were required to accelerate "three olds" regeneration and also improve practice,[9] which led to a policy relaxation with the issue of the Implementation Opinions of Guangzhou on Improving Urban Regeneration Quality and Promoting Economical and Intensified Land Use (Document 6) in 2017. The 2017 Opinions motivated property owners to undertake regeneration projects by providing preferential policies, encouraged "contiguous area" regeneration, and promoted a holistic approach to urban regeneration to facilitate industrial restructuring and upgrading, encourage the integration of industry and urban development, and strengthen land banking. Altogether, the sporadic "three olds" renewal practice was to be transformed into a systematic, interlinked, and diversified urban regeneration approach. Document 134 identifies the different management methods for comprehensive renewal and micro-regeneration, the former involving more complicated interest groups, higher cost, longer duration, and greater difficulties than the latter. By integrating the two renewal scales, urban regeneration targeted multiple goals of improving living conditions and reusing urban land (Yao and Tian, 2017; Wang and Shen, 2015). Further, as stipulated in Document 20, in the case of old village renewal, the collective properties and old factories are bundled with old residential areas for joint regeneration through a shared FAR, aiming at integrated renewal of the whole village (Yang et al., 2012). However, the idea encountered difficulties in practice, as the renewal of old factories and collective properties has stagnated due to the difficulties in renewing the residential space in the village. This requirement was therefore relaxed in Document 134 and Document 6, allowing old factories and rural collective properties to be renewed first without being bundled with old residential areas for the purposes of investment invitation from the government, deduction of reserved land quota, and free transfer of certain property areas to the government, etc. Beyond other regulations on urban regeneration procedures, the two documents intend to revitalize urban renewal practice and promote new forms of practice, particularly micro-regeneration. But in general, the pace of urban regeneration can still be regarded as slow.

4.3.2 Shenzhen: from government led to government facilitated

Compared with the other two cities, urban regeneration policy in Shenzhen proved to be relative stable. The main transition point, in 2009, consisted of a change from the government-led to government-facilitated and private sector-led approach. Under a public–private partnership, the government plays the role of regulator, while the private sector plays the main role of improving spatial quality and promoting industrial upgrading.

4.3.2.1 Early stage of urban regeneration (Document 211)

In the light of the "three olds" regeneration movement in Guangdong province, Shenzhen explored regulating urban renewal practice by issuing China's first legal instrument for urban renewal in 2009, Shenzhen Urban Regeneration Measures (Document 211). Urban regeneration is clearly defined in Document 211 – applicable to all old areas in the built-up area throughout Shenzhen – as demolition and reconstruction, function change and comprehensive renovation activities undertaken by eligible actors in specific built-up areas in a particular situation conforming to the regulations in the Measures and urban planning procedures. The Measures also stipulated that the fundamental principles and *modus operandi* of urban regeneration are "government-facilitated, market operation,

50 *Urban regeneration policies and regulations*

planning and coordination, economical and intensified (land use), right and interest protection, and public participation". The Urban Regeneration Unit was introduced in the Measures as a planning instrument.[10] Property owners as well as developers and investors were eligible to undertake urban renewal of their own properties under the Measures.

4.3.2.2 Urban regeneration policies consolidation (Document 1)

The 2009 Urban Regeneration Measures, along with their Implementation Details (Document 1) issued in 2012, constitute the two essential legal instruments for urban regeneration in Shenzhen. Based on Document 211, Document 1 provides detailed regulations on urban regeneration-related activities, such as re-distribution of the responsibilities of different parties, and the requirements to develop regeneration plans and programs. The document also stipulates various implementation regulations for demolition and reconstruction, function change and comprehensive renovation. An orderly and long-term effective institutional system for urban regeneration that is adapted to the local context has thus been established in Shenzhen, facilitating economical and intensified use of urban spatial resources, tackling historical land-use problems, and restructuring urban industry. Furthermore, to address new problems and social needs that emerged during the process, Shenzhen made timely improvements and supplements to consolidate the legal framework, such as the promulgation of the 2012 and 2014 versions of Provisional Measures on Strengthening and Improving Implementation of Urban Regeneration.

4.3.2.3 Further development of urban regeneration policies
(Document 290 and Document 38)

In 2016, urban regeneration in Shenzhen was in full swing. In the space of one year, a record number of 97 Urban Regeneration Unit plans were released in six batches, and 2.39 km² of built-up area was released as redeveloped land through urban renewal. From January to November 2016, total investment in urban regeneration projects reached 58.9 billion RMB (*Shenzhen Special Zone Daily*, 2017). Published in November 2016, the 13th Five-Year Plan for Urban Regeneration in Shenzhen (2016–2020) identified the overall objectives and development strategies of urban regeneration in Shenzhen during the period. The Urban Regeneration Measures were amended in December 2016 (and renamed Document 290) seven years after their enactment. Two main reforms resulted from reflections and from problems identified in practice. First, in line with the decentralization policy in Shenzhen, the new institutional arrangements can be reformed when needed, such as the re-distribution of responsibilities between the municipal and district government, and the devolution of administrative and approval authority for urban regeneration. Second, the land price system is simplified. The land premium regulations stipulated in Document 211 were removed and replaced by the land price standards of the Provisional Measures on Strengthening and Improving Implementation of Urban Regeneration. The latest version of these measures, issued in December 2016, also known as Document 38, upgraded the regulations in regard to innovation of implementation mechanisms, simplification of the land price system, improvement of public service amenities, expansion of channels to develop affordable housing, and pilot Urban Regeneration Unit projects designed to improve efficiency of urban regeneration practice.

4.3.3 Shanghai: government-led approach, quality rather than quantity oriented, and pilot projects

By the end of the 20th century, urban regeneration had become widespread in old industrial and residential areas in Shanghai. In the new century, in response to the lessons learned from the negative effects of mass demolition and construction, such as the "365 slum clearance" scheme of the 1990s, the single demolition and reconstruction approach was replaced by a multi-dimensional approach integrating public participation and historical preservation in at scale in many types of regeneration area. Highlighting the roles of both government and market, the new policies stressed quality over quantity and the significance of pilot projects. Document 38 excludes the developer-led approach of renewal under market mechanisms, and encourages practice initiated by property owners. Thus, small steps and slow pace became the pattern adopted in Shanghai to explore policy innovation and institutional construction.

4.3.3.1 Exploring policies for urban regeneration through pilot projects

The urban regeneration of Shanghai can be traced back to the time of the port opening; later, reform and opening up were followed by active renewal of old residential buildings and industrial sites. The Implementation Measures for Revitalizing Existing Industrial Land in Shanghai (2014) provide guideline for formal renewal of industrial areas. By the end of 2015, a total of 73 million m^2 of dilapidated housing and old buildings had been demolished to improve the living condition of around 1.2 million families. However, many problems emerged during design of a systematic approach to urban regeneration. First, there were no policies on the regeneration of commercial and office space. Second, policies on regeneration of industrial land were inconsistent, fluctuating between loose and tight. Third, the practice of regenerating residential space suffered from insufficient funding. Meanwhile, various types of regeneration activities lacked policy coordination. This called for urgent institutional reform to foster urban regeneration practice.[11] Around 2012, with quality, not quantity, in mind, Shanghai wanted to explore new urban regeneration institutions by launching pilot projects, which laid the foundations for the forthcoming Urban Regeneration Implementation Measures. Multiple goals, particularly the improvement of urban land use and public service amenities, were integrated into the pilot projects.[12] The case of the transformation of the West Asia Hotel in Xujiahui to high-level office buildings illustrates how partial land-use change, increase in building height and FAR were achieved without demolishing the existing building. The property owner funded not only building-related regeneration activities, but also the improvement of public amenities, including public car parks, public open spaces, and public service facilities; in return, they were granted extra FAR and partial land-use change. The improvement of spatial quality is the other goal of urban regeneration. In one of the pilot projects, the regeneration of the neighborhood in the Xujiahui Catholic Church, the land-use mixture, including the church, the meteorology square, and the archives, was restructured to reduce office space, increase cultural facilities, and integrate and optimize the surrounding open space. The spatial quality in the area has thus been improved. The third goal is to increase public green space, such as is the case in the North Square area regeneration of Shanghai Railway Station in Jing'an District. Besides the increase of public space and community facilities, public green spaces increased by around 9,000 m^2 in this project. The fourth goal is preservation of historic buildings, such as the regeneration of East Siwenli in Jing'an District. After a systematic investigation and assessment of historical buildings, a group of valuable buildings was listed for conservation and excluded from the development volume control.

Other innovative institutions have been initiated and explored by the district governments in urban renewal practice (Information Office of Shanghai Municipality, 2015). One example is the establishment of a coordination institute between the government and the private sector. In Caojiadu area, located at the intersection of three districts (Jing'an District, Putuo District, and Changning District), the Caojiadu Business Association was established to strengthen communication and collaboration among enterprises in the three districts, and to cooperate with the government to promote urban regeneration in the area. Another innovation is joint renewal planning. In Xuhui District, the integration of different types of regeneration areas, including the conservation area and the planned renewal area, has been planned to balance costs and benefits, such as transferring the development quota from one renewal area to the other as compensation. The third innovation concerns funding mechanisms. In Jing'an District, an Urban Regeneration Investment Fund was established to facilitate urban regeneration practice: not only to broaden financial channels, but more importantly to give full play to the operational advantages of fund management companies, financial market advantages, development advantages of the enterprise, and the management advantage of professional agencies for implementing urban regeneration.

4.3.3.2 Consolidation period of urban regeneration policies (Document 20): institutional construction and pilot projects in parallel

The publication of Urban Regeneration Implementation Measures in May 2015 marks a new era in the development of a legal framework for urban regeneration in Shanghai. Detailed working procedures, technical requirements and other regulations were specified by Shanghai Planning and Land Resources Bureau. A series of supporting documents, including Implementation Details of Urban Regeneration Implementation Measures, provided guidance on urban planning, land use, construction management, property right and so on. Since the enactment of the Measures, pilot projects have been undertaken to promote the transition of urban spatial development models and urban governance mechanisms, and to promote the constant improvement of land-use functions and service facilities. By April 2018, around 50 important urban regeneration projects had been planned and practiced in Shanghai (Chen, 2018). In 2015, 17 pilot projects were selected in the ten districts of inner Shanghai, including the regeneration of Xujiahui business district, the renewal of the area along Handan Road in Dabaishu, and the renovation of the Xinzhuang Grand Hotel. In the "Four Action Plans" launched in 2016, i.e., the shared community plan, the innovation park plan, the charming appearance plan and the entertainment network plan, 12 key projects were selected based on the principles of representativeness, innovation, publicity and feasibility, to explore institutional innovation and explore the integration of urban regeneration into all urban planning and land management procedures. Micro-regeneration was actively promoted and generated strong community concerns and responses. For instance, in a 2017 pilot project exploring a new model of community involvement, 49 projects in nine categories[13] were selected for "colorful community" micro-regeneration in the five sub-districts (Weifang, Yangjing, Lujiazui, Tangqiao, and Huamu) of Pudong District. As well as the positive effects of improving living conditions, optimizing urban land-use function and contributing to the transport infrastructure, the practice of micro-regeneration strengthened a sense of belonging and added a human touch. A new understanding of urban regeneration of old districts began at the start of 2017. First, in regard to existing buildings, the "demolition-dominated approach, supplemented by renovation and preservation" was to be replaced by "preservation-dominated, supplemented by renovation and demolition". The change in the order of the three words symbolized a major shift in urban regeneration ideology in Shanghai, showing real consideration for historical consideration as an integral part of practice. Second, besides more attention towards the conservation and preservation of existing buildings, new strategies were to be developed to improve the living conditions of residents in old areas and to preserve the historical context and cultural legacies of Shanghai.[14]

4.4 Comparison of Urban Regeneration (Implementation) Measures in the three cities

4.4.1 Structure of Urban Regeneration (Implementation) Measures

Comparison of the Measures in the three cities exposes significant differences. The Urban Regeneration Measures in Guangzhou and Shenzhen are organized into chapters and articles, while the Urban Regeneration Implementation Measures of Shanghai are only in articles without being structured in chapters. The administration of urban regeneration projects is based on implementation procedures and land-use categories in Guangzhou, and in Shenzhen on the scale and approaches of urban regeneration projects. In Shanghai, management by contract based on regional assessment reports and implementation plans from the government plays the key role in the administration system.

54 Urban regeneration policies and regulations

There are three main parts to the seven chapters and 57 articles of Guangzhou Urban Regeneration Measures. Part One, also the first chapter, stipulates the goals, connotations, principles, and organization of urban regeneration practice in Guangzhou. Part Two, in Chapters 2–4, covers general regulations, regulations on regeneration planning and schemes, regulations on land disposal, and so on. The general regulations include requirements for defining regeneration areas, identifying strategies and actors, investigation and data collection, expert evaluation, public advisory committees, and the disposal of historically illegally used land. Regeneration planning and schemes refers to planning-related activities, including medium- and long-term plans, designation of renewal districts, drafting and review of planning schemes, Annual Programs for regeneration, and so on. Regulations on land disposal stipulate measures for resolving historical illegal or informal land-use problems. Part Three, in Chapters 5–7, covers the regulations on raising and allocation of funds for urban regeneration, project supervision and management, and so on. (Figure 4.1).

The Shenzhen Urban Regeneration Measures consists of four main parts containing seven chapters and 48 articles. Part One defines the goals, connotations, principles, actors, funds, and institutions of urban regeneration in Shenzhen. Part Two provides two levels of planning for urban regeneration in Shenzhen, a special urban regeneration plan for the whole municipality, and an Urban Regeneration Unit plan for a specific renewal area, in line with statutory plans. Part Two also stipulates Urban Regeneration Unit plan-related activities, including application procedures, drawing up plans, the approval schedule, and so on. The third part regulates urban regeneration in detail, including comprehensive renovation, function change, and demolition and reconstruction. The fourth part provides links to other legal instruments, project supervision and management, and other supplementary regulations. (Figure 4.2).

The Shanghai Urban Regeneration Implementation Measures are in three parts. The first part, in Articles 1 to 7, specifies general urban regeneration requirements for Shanghai, and stipulates the objectives, connotation, principles, and institutions of urban regeneration. The second part, in Articles 8 to 16, regulates project

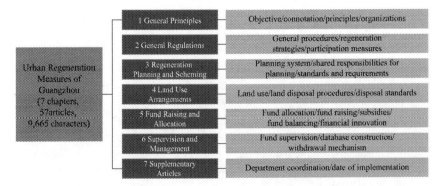

Figure 4.1 Structural Framework of the Guangzhou Urban Regeneration Measures.
Source: Drawn by authors.

Urban regeneration policies and regulations 55

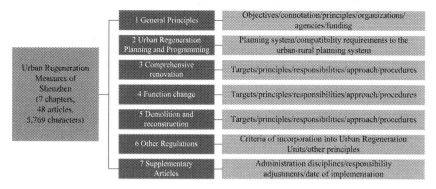

Figure 4.2 Structural Framework of the Shenzhen Urban Regeneration Measures.
Source: Drawn by authors.

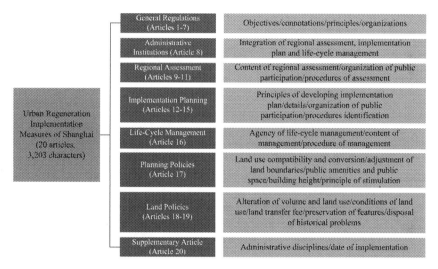

Figure 4.3 Structural Framework of the Shanghai Urban Regeneration Implementation Measures.
Source: Drawn by authors.

management procedures and measures in urban regeneration practice, including regional assessment, implementation planning, and life-cycle management. Part Three, Articles 17 to 20, includes detailed regulations on planning and land use for urban regeneration (Figure 4.3).

4.4.2 Definition and approach to urban regeneration

A definition of urban regeneration helps us to understand the scope and the strategies of urban regeneration activities. In Article 2 of the respective Urban Regeneration (Implementation) Measures for Guangzhou, Shenzhen, and Shanghai (Table 4.3), the targets and the scope of urban regeneration are defined in detail.

Table 4.3 Comparison of Definition and Approach in the Urban Regeneration (Implementation) Measures in Guangzhou, Shenzhen, and Shanghai

City	Definition	Scope	Approaches
Guangzhou	Construction activities to revitalize and utilize inefficiently used land in "three olds" areas, and renovation, improvement, and reconstruction activities and the revitalization of dangerous, dilapidated and old buildings, which are undertaken by government, property owners, or other eligible parties in accordance with respective policies and urban regeneration plan	"Three olds", shanty towns, dilapidated buildings, etc.*	Comprehensive renewal Micro-regeneration
Shenzhen	Comprehensive renovation activities, functional change, or demolition and reconstruction in built-up urban areas in accordance with legal procedures, and undertaken by eligible parties	Old industrial areas, old commercial areas, old residential areas, urban villages, and old villages	Comprehensive renovation Functional change Demolition and reconstruction
Shanghai	Construction activities to improve spatial qualities and urban functions in built-up urban areas	Regeneration districts in built-up areas designated by the municipal government according to stipulated procedures	–

Sources: Secretariat of the General Office of the People's Government of Guangzhou (2015), *Guangzhou Urban Regeneration Measures*; Shenzhen Municipal Government (2015), *Shenzhen Urban Regeneration Measures*; Shanghai Municipal Government (2015), *Shanghai Urban Regeneration Implementation Measures*.
* For details, refer to: article explanations in *Guangzhou Urban Regeneration Measures*, http://www.gz.gov.cn/gzscsgxj/zcjd/201612/beeea7801fa6429aaf6d407890f6e6f0.shtml

Despite slight distinctions, urban regeneration shares the same goals in all three cities, including revitalizing and utilizing inefficiently used land, improving urban land use, enhancing urban spatial quality, increasing public amenities, and stimulating the vitality of the city to achieve overall socio-economic development. Further, the scope of urban regeneration in the three cities varies between the respective Measures. The urban regeneration approach in Guangzhou is derived from the "three olds" regeneration movement, as stipulated in the Guangzhou Measures, and covers not only built-up urban areas, but also eligible rural villages, while the Shenzhen Measures refer to all deteriorated spaces in built-up areas. The Shanghai Measures are not applicable to all regeneration areas, since certain old urban areas, industrial transformation areas or urban villages designated by the government are obliged to adhere to other regulations.

In addition, different strategies are specified in the three Measures. In the Guangzhou Measures, two urban regeneration strategies, comprehensive renewal and micro-regeneration (Article 34, Guangzhou Urban Regeneration Measures), are regulated, while in the Shenzhen Measures, the three types of strategies stipulated are comprehensive renovation, function change, and demolition and reconstruction (Article 2, Shenzhen Urban Regeneration Measures). The Shanghai Measures do not provide similar regulations on urban regeneration practice.

4.4.3 Planning and programming of urban regeneration

Planning and programming regulations, which form the core components of the Urban Regeneration (Implementation) Measures in the three cities, focus on urban regeneration planning, urban regeneration programs, and implementation strategies (Table 4.4). Both in Guangzhou and in Shenzhen, urban regeneration

Table 4.4 Comparison of Urban Regeneration Annual/Implementation Plans in Guangzhou, Shenzhen, and Shanghai

Items	Guangzhou	Shenzhen	Shanghai
Plan guidance at the municipal level	Medium- to long-term urban regeneration planning	Special urban regeneration planning	–
Basis of planning	Urban regeneration demands and implementation conditions, and planning scheme of urban regeneration areas	Urban regeneration projects based on demands and implementation conditions	Regional Assessment Report and property owners' commitment
Planning instrument	Urban Regeneration District	Urban Regeneration Unit	Urban Regeneration Unit
Contents of a plan	Renewal projects, project implementation plans, and funding plans	Urban Regeneration Unit planning schemes, and list of projects to be implemented and their funding sources	Construction scheme, project implementation plan, eligible parties, rights and responsibilities of the stakeholders, and the requirements of the schedules
Applicants	Government departments, enterprises, public institutions, and property owners	Government departments, enterprises, and public institutions	District and county governments

Compiled from relevant sources: Secretariat of the General Office of the People's Government of Guangzhou (2015), Guangzhou Urban Regeneration Measures; Shenzhen Municipal Government (2015), Shenzhen Urban Regeneration Measures; Shanghai Municipal Government (2015), Shanghai Urban Regeneration Implementation Measures.

areas are defined based on an overall urban regeneration plan at the municipal level. Selected urban regeneration areas are incorporated into the Annual Program for implementation. In Shanghai, the designation of urban regeneration areas as Urban Regeneration Units derives directly from regulatory plans, which define the areas to be renewed after careful evaluation.

4.4.3.1 Guangzhou: urban regeneration planning and Annual Program (Chapter 2, Guangzhou Urban Regeneration Measures)

In Guangzhou, Urban Regeneration Districts are defined by the medium- to long-term urban regeneration plans at the municipal level developed by Guangzhou Urban Regeneration Bureau (Article 20 and Article 21). A planning scheme for individual Urban Regeneration Districts is used for application for Annual Program Projects (Article 23). Each year the municipal urban regeneration authority develops the following year's Annual Program after examination and approval of projects applied for by the end of June, which include renewal projects, project implementation plans, and funding plans (Article 27).

4.4.3.2 Shenzhen: Urban Renewal Unit planning and Annual Program (Chapter 2, Shenzhen Urban Regeneration Measures).

In Shenzhen, the special urban regeneration plan at the municipal level, developed based on the urban master plan (Article 9), roughly defines the key areas of urban regeneration, and regulates its orientation, goals, sequence, scale, and strategies. Urban Renewal Units are designated based on the municipal special urban regeneration plan. A statutory plan is prepared for each Urban Renewal Unit (Article 11), which stipulates planning guidance and the scope of regeneration, such as the scale of infrastructure and public services (Article 10). Urban Renewal Unit applications from district governments are approved by the municipal urban planning and land resources authority and incorporated into the Annual Program (Article 15), which lays down the Urban Renewal Units planning scheme, the list of projects to be implemented, and the sources of funding (Article 14).

4.4.3.3 Shanghai: implementation plan based on Urban Regeneration Unit (Articles 9–15 Shanghai Urban Regeneration Implementation Measures).

In contrast with Guangzhou and Shenzhen, where an urban regeneration plan at the municipal level plays an important role in defining urban regeneration areas, in Shanghai an Urban Regeneration Unit is defined based on Regional Assessment Reports derived from regulatory plans (Article 9). A detailed implementation plan for Urban Regeneration Units, taking account of the level of property owners' commitment to regeneration, is formulated to identify specific projects, construction schemes, project implementation plans, eligible parties, rights and responsibilities of the stakeholders, and the requirements of the schedules (Article 12 and Article 13).

4.4.4 Fund raising and fund allocation for urban regeneration

As the success of projects depends heavily on funding, raising and allocation of funds are regulated by the Urban Regeneration (Implementation) Measures in the three cities. In Guangzhou, the regulations on funding are rather detailed (Chapter 5, Guangzhou Urban Regeneration Measures), covering financial sources and channels, fund allocation, and preferential policies to acquire funding (Articles 43, 44, and 45). Particular attention is paid to finance channels. Community associations and the private sector are encouraged to provide funds for urban regeneration and to apply for national funding to implement it. Financial institutions are encouraged to explore innovative financial products and new models for granting and securing loans under public–private partnerships (Article 46). In Shenzhen and Shanghai, with less attention to fund raising and allocation, regulations on the payment and allocation of land transfer fees generated from urban renewal are stipulated (Article 6, Chapter 1, Shenzhen Urban Regeneration Measures; Article 18, Shanghai Urban Regeneration Implementation Measures). In all three cities, preferential financial policies are provided for urban regeneration projects to relieve financial pressure and facilitate project implementation (Table 4.5).

Table 4.5 Regulations on Fund Raising and Funding Allocation in the Urban Regeneration (Implementation) Measures in Guangzhou, Shenzhen, and Shanghai

Items	Guangzhou	Shenzhen	Shanghai
Fund raising	State funding, credit funds, land transfer fee, market investment, and self-financing	State funding, land transfer fee, and self-financing	State funding and land transfer fee
Fund allocation	Planning and programming, foundation survey and data collection, database construction, land acquisition and pooling, project subsidy, and research on theory and technical standards	Organization and implementation of urban renewal projects, and construction of infrastructure and public service amenities	Organization and implementation of urban renewal projects, and infrastructure construction
Application of preferential policies	Relocation and resettlement housing, etc.	–	Urban regeneration projects, etc.

Compiled from relevant sources: Secretariat of the General Office of the People's Government of Guangzhou (2015), Guangzhou Urban Regeneration Measures; Shenzhen Municipal Government (2015), Shenzhen Urban Regeneration Measures; Shanghai Municipal Government (2015), Shanghai Urban Regeneration Implementation Measures.

4.4.5 Public participation in urban regeneration

An important component of the renewal regeneration process is that public participation can effectively facilitate the supervision of urban regeneration projects, and protect and safeguard individual and public interests. Various approaches to promoting public participation are adopted in the Urban Regeneration (Implementation) Measures in Guangzhou, Shenzhen, and Shanghai. In Guangzhou, establishment of a coordination agency in the form of a committee or a council is proposed to protect the legal rights and interests of the public and resolve problems of urban regeneration practice through internal negotiations. In Shenzhen, different participation models are adopted to target different types of renewal projects, such as multi-party negotiation and public opinion surveys. In Shanghai, government-led public participation is practiced by collecting public opinion.

4.4.5.1 Guangzhou: public consultancy committee/villager council

When important livelihood issues are at stake, public consultancy committees may be established in old town regeneration, and villager councils in old village regeneration, to balance differences of opinion, coordinate disputes, and resolve conflicts during the urban regeneration process, thus protecting the legal rights of stakeholders and promoting the smooth execution of urban regeneration projects (Article 18, Guangzhou Urban Regeneration Measures). Meanwhile, urban regeneration should take into account the interests of all parties, protect the rights and interests of landowners, and encourage relevant stakeholders to actively participate in regeneration, and to achieve win–win results and the sharing of benefits (Article 9).

4.4.5.2 Shenzhen: different participation models

Following the principle of "public participation" (Article 3), various forms of participation are suggested according to the type of regeneration strategy – comprehensive renovation, function change, and demolition and reconstruction. In the case of comprehensive renovation, decisions are settled by multi-party negotiation (Article 22). In the case of function change, consent of all the stakeholders is required (Article 25). In the case of demolition and reconstruction, the consent of over 2/3 of the property owners, who own more than 2/3 of the total construction area is required.

4.4.5.3 Shanghai: public participation in developing Regional Assessment Plan and implementation plan

The Shanghai Urban Regeneration Implementation Measures require public participation in the development of Regional Assessment Plans and implementation plans. For Regional Assessment Plans, the general public, stakeholders, and administrative departments at municipal, district, and county levels should be involved. For implementation plans, opinions from the general public, stakeholders, and administrative departments at municipal, district, and county levels should be collected, and citizens and experts are encouraged to participate in the planning process (Article 10 and Article 14, Shanghai Urban Regeneration Implementation Measures).

4.4.6 Project supervision and management

Project supervision and management can not only facilitate the achievement of the expected goals of urban regeneration, but can also help to protect the interests of stakeholders. In the three cities, regulations dealing with acts that are violations of the law or rules are stipulated. Particularly in Guangzhou, the Measures regulate the supervision and management of funding, project withdrawal, protection of public interest, and so on, in great detail.

4.4.6.1 Project supervision and management in Guangzhou.

In the Guangzhou Urban Regeneration Measures, an entire chapter (Chapter 6) is devoted to regulations on project supervision and management in regard to five issues: reconstruction and relocation of funds for old village renewal, urban regeneration database, project withdrawal, protection of public interest, and dealing with the violation of laws and rules. First, the allocation of reconstruction and relocation funds for old village renewal should be supervised through a tripartite contract signed by the urban regeneration department, the owner of the reconstruction, and the bank of the escrow account for relocation funds (Article 48). Second, standardized drawings and documents on regeneration project review, project implementation and completion acceptance should be stored in the urban regeneration database for real-time supervision of the project life-cycle. Regular assessments and reports on the implementation and construction status of key regeneration projects are required, so that the working mechanisms, fund allocation, completion status, and project supervision, etc., can be checked (Article 49). Third, time management of urban regeneration projects should be strengthened, and regeneration projects not completed on schedule should be withdrawn or re-approved (Article 50). Fourth, to protect the public interest at project launch, other construction activities are not allowed to start until the specified procedures, such as resettlement before demolition, and prioritization of constructing public services, have been completed(Article 51 and 52). Fifth, measures to be handled by relevant departments are stipulated in regard to violation of rules and laws. Illegal activities are reported to and handled by the judiciary (Articles 54 and 55).

4.4.6.2 Project supervision and management in Shenzhen

Government departments and personnel involved in breach of rules in project management should be held accountable (Article 46, Shenzhen Urban Regeneration Measures).

4.4.6.3 Project supervision and management in Shanghai

Government departments, government personnel and property owners involved in breaches of project management rules should be held to account (Article 26, Shanghai Urban Regeneration Implementation Measures).

4.5 Summary

In summary, the Urban Regeneration (Implementation) Measures in Guangzhou, Shenzhen, and Shanghai stipulate a number of common aspects regarding planning and programming, with some subtle distinctions in project implementation procedures, contents, and schedule. The Measures provide specific regulations on key aspects of urban regeneration practice, including regeneration measures, eligible parties, working procedures, public participation, and fund raising.

Notes

1 In 2008, the Ministry of Land Resources of China and Guangdong Provincial Government decided to jointly develop Guangdong as a pilot and demonstration province for resource-saving and intensive land use, in accordance with the important instructions from the then Premier Wen Jiabao, who hoped Guangdong would be a nationwide example achieving intensified and efficient land use.
2 In China, all urban land is owned by the state, but land-use rights can be transferred. In order to prevent rent seeking and interest loss in land transfer, the state stipulates that profit-making land can only be transferred through market means, such as bidding, auctions, and listing. Land policy reform in Guangdong province has achieved a major breakthrough by changing the rules and making land transfer easier and more freely achievable.
3 Department of Land Resources of Guangdong Province (2009), Some Opinions on Advancing Three Olds Regeneration and Promoting Economical and Intensified Use of Land.
4 Lai S, Wu J (2013), Speed and Effect: Policy Exploration of Guangzhou "Sanjiu" Redevelopment under New Urbanization. *Planners*, 29(5): 36–41.
5 Land development right usually refers to the right of capturing land value through land-use change or increased development intensity.
6 In the topic-based consultancy conference of the Standing Committee of Guangzhou People's Congress, then standing deputy mayor of Guangzhou, Chen Rugui, emphasized that urban regeneration should be led, coordinated, and implemented by the government, rather than by developers.
7 The Urban Regeneration Bureau was dissolved in 2019 during the reform of state institutions that began in 2018. Its main functions are now discharged by the newly established Planning and Natural Resources Bureau of Guangzhou.
8 Micro-regeneration refers to regeneration strategies that make little change to the existing pattern of the built-up environment, such as partial demolition and construction, function alteration, preservation and repair of buildings, and the renovation, protection, revitalization, and improvement of infrastructure. It is mostly applicable to land parcels within the built-up area that have little influence on the overall pattern inf the city, but have functional contradictions with district development, low land-use efficiency, and unfavorable living condition.

9 In September, 2016, in order to facilitate "three olds" regeneration and improve "three olds" regeneration levels, Guangdong Provincial Government issued the Guangdong Province Notice on Improving "Three Olds" Regeneration Levels and Promoting Intensified and Economical Land Use.
10 Urban Regeneration Unit planning is a comprehensive regulatory planning system for regeneration projects involving definition of boundaries, spatial control, the balance of interests, and implementation plans, etc.
11 Ge, Y. (2018), From "Limited Participation" to "Mutual Decision": Social Justice and Community Governance in Urban Regeneration of Shanghai. 2018 Annual Conference (Report) of Urban Regeneration Academic Committee of the Urban Planning Society of China. Chongqing, December 20–21, 2018.
12 Press conferences on Shanghai Urban Regeneration Implementation Measures (2015). Available at: http://www.scio.gov.cn/xwfbh/gssxwfbh/fbh/Document/1432931/1432931.htm [Accessed March 22, 2018].
13 Nine elements closely related to residents' daily lives: lively streets, small parks, footpaths, facility composites, art spaces, shaded boulevards, sports facilities, breaks in walls, and corner spaces.
14 https://www.jfdaily.com/news/detail?id=43931.

5 Development of urban regeneration institutional systems in the three cities

A comprehensive institutional system of urban regeneration contains urban regeneration policies and regulations, the establishment of administrative organizations, urban regeneration planning, decision-making mechanisms, negotiation mechanisms, the implementation requirements of regeneration projects, etc. The previous chapter on the evolution of urban regeneration policies in Guangzhou, Shenzhen and Shanghai, and the comparison of their respective Urban Regeneration (Implementation) Measures, provided a brief outline of the institutional system of urban regeneration in the three cities. Through establishing a universal framework of institutional systems, this chapter further compares and analyzes the constitution and characteristics of the institutional systems in Guangzhou, Shenzhen, and Shanghai.

5.1 Urban regeneration institutional systems in the three cities

In Guangzhou, the administrative or responsible institution for urban regeneration is the Urban Regeneration Bureau at the municipal level. The "1+3+N" system has been developed as a policy and planning framework that has changed from market led to government led, integrating policies and the programs targeting the three regeneration categories of old towns, old villages, and old industrial lands. Under this system, the Guangzhou Urban Regeneration Master Plan has overall control of urban regeneration, and a project plan is developed for each regeneration district to guide regeneration practice. Regeneration projects, either for comprehensive renewal or micro-regeneration, are applied for by different actors, and further reviewed and approved by the authority (Figure 5.1). To achieve orderly implementation of regeneration activities in practice, innovative strategies have been applied, including construction of a database for regeneration areas, expert evaluation, and negotiation and review mechanisms.

Figure 5.1 Institutional System of Urban Regeneration in Guangzhou.
Source: Drawn by authors.

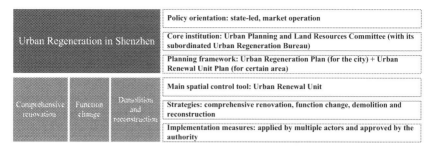

Figure 5.2 Institutional System of Urban Regeneration in Shenzhen.
Source: Drawn by authors.

In Shenzhen, the Urban Planning and Land Resources Committee, along with its subordinate agency the Urban Regeneration Bureau at the municipal level, is the core administrative institution responsible for urban regeneration. Highlighting law-based control and market-based practice, urban regeneration policies emphasize the "government-led and market operation" approach. Three types of renewal strategies are identified: comprehensive renovation, change of use, and demolition and reconstruction. Planning controls are based on the Special Urban Regeneration Plan at the municipal level and the Urban Renewal Unit[1] Plan for the respective district. Project management follows the principle of "applied for by multi-actors and approved by the authority" to actively mobilize various forces to promote urban regeneration (Figure 5.2).

In Shanghai, the Planning and Land Resources Bureau, along with its subordinate office, the Urban Regeneration Office, is the core administrative institution for urban regeneration. The policies on urban regeneration highlight "reducing quantity, increasing efficiency and encouraging pilot projects" led by the government. Similar to Shenzhen, the Urban Regeneration Unit in Shanghai is an important planning instrument and administrative tool. Project implementation follows the procedures of regional assessment, project plan (land life-cycle management), and project implementation. The principle of "prioritizing public interest and participation of multiple actors" has been highlighted as the principle of urban regeneration practice in Shanghai, implying three strategies. First, requirements to provide or improve public amenities, otherwise known as a planned public element list, should be stated in the Regional Assessment Report. Second, public participation has to be sought in regional assessments and the drafting of implementation plans. Third, the provision of open public spaces and public amenities via FAR award and FAR transfer is encouraged (Figure 5.3).

The three cities share some similarities in their urban regeneration institutional systems (Table 5.1), such as the issuing of Urban Regeneration (Implementation) Measures, establishment of administrative institutions for urban regeneration, differentiation of regeneration project types, and reform and innovation of planning tools and instruments to adapt to conventional urban planning systems. In terms of project implementation, the government plays a more dominant role in

66 *Development of urban regeneration*

Urban Regeneration in Shanghai	Policy orientation: reduce quantity and increase efficiency guided by the government
	Core institution: Planning and Land Resources Bureau (with its subordinated Urban Regeneration Office)
	Planning instrument: Urban Regeneration Unit
Urban Regeneration Area designated according to regulated procedures by the authority	Strategies: Regional Assessment+ Implementation plan + Urban Regeneration Unit
	Principles: plan-based, quality-oriented, orderly progress, prioritization of public interest, multiple participants
	Implementation measures: social participation and effective motivation

Figure 5.3 Institutional System of Urban Regeneration in Shanghai.
Source: Drawn by authors.

Table 5.1 Urban Regeneration Institutional Innovation in Guangzhou, Shenzhen, and Shanghai compared

Items	Guangzhou	Shenzhen	Shanghai
Responsible organization	Urban Regeneration Bureau	Urban Planning and Land Resource Committee (with subordinated Urban Regeneration Bureau)	Planning and Land Resource Bureau (with subordinated Urban Regeneration Office)
Legal instrument	Urban Regeneration Measures	Urban Regeneration Measures	Urban Regeneration Implementation Measures
Targets and strategies	Old towns, old villages, and old industrial lands	Demolition and reconstruction, change of use, and comprehensive renovation	Urban regeneration areas designated by the authority according to stipulated procedures
Planning tools and framework	"1+3+N" system	Special Urban Regeneration Plan and Urban Renewal Unit Plan	Urban Regeneration Unit Plan
Approach	Government led, market operation	Government-guided, market operation	Government led, mutual approaches by the government and the market, and trials and pilot projects
Procedure	Applied by multiple actors, and examined and approved by the authority	Applied by multiple actors, and examined and approved by the authority	Priority of pilot projects, and projects examined and approved by the authority
Features and Innovations	Data collection and investigation (Regeneration Database), expert evaluation, negotiation and review, etc.	Emphasis on affordable housing, public amenities, buildings for creative industries, land for public welfare, etc.	Land-use change, list of public elements, community planner, micro-regeneration, etc.

Source: Edited by authors.

Guangzhou, the market is dominant in Shenzhen, and both the government and the market are equally important in Shanghai. All projects must be examined and approved by the government before implementation.

5.2 Institutional settings for urban regeneration

Special administrative institutions for urban regeneration have been set up in Guangzhou, Shenzhen, and Shanghai, but the hierarchy, authority, responsibilities, administrative forms, and division of tasks remain different (Table 5.2). In Guangzhou, an independent administrative institution was established at the municipal level, called the Urban Regeneration Bureau, which is responsible for all aspects of urban regeneration, including policy development, fund raising and allocation, land pooling, project preparation, project examination and approval, construction supervision, and so on. In both Shenzhen and Shanghai, the urban planning authority is the department responsible for urban regeneration. In Shenzhen, the Urban Planning and Land Resources Committee at municipal level, along with its subordinated Urban Regeneration Bureau, is responsible for the overall coordination of urban regeneration affairs, and the district governments are in charge of the administration of urban regeneration projects. In Shanghai, the Urban Regeneration Office at municipal level, which reports to Shanghai Planning and Land Resources Bureau, is responsible for overall coordination, and the district governments are responsible for the administration of urban regeneration practice.

Table 5.2 Comparison of Institutional Settings in Guangzhou, Shenzhen, and Shanghai

	Guangzhou	*Shenzhen*	*Shanghai*
Higher-level supervision (municipal level)	Leading Group of Urban Regeneration	Leading Group of Urban Regeneration and Supervision of Illegal Construction	Leading Group of Urban Regeneration
Institution at municipal level	Urban Regeneration Bureau	Committee of Urban Planning and Land Resources (with its subordinated Urban Regeneration Bureau)	Planning and Land Resources Bureau (with its subordinated Urban Regeneration Office)
Main function of the institution at municipal level	Organizing approval and implementation, development of policies and regulations, and research on institutional innovation	Organization and coordination of urban regeneration affairs, development of policies and regulations, and development of regeneration planning	Development of policies and regulations, organization and coordination of urban regeneration affairs, and publicity for regeneration policy

(*Continued*)

68 Development of urban regeneration

Table 5.2 (Continued)

	Guangzhou	Shenzhen	Shanghai
Institution at district level	District governments Urban regeneration institutions at district and country level	District governments Urban regeneration institutions at district and country level	District governments Urban regeneration institutions at district and country level
Main function of the institution at district level	Review and approval of regeneration projects	Administrative review and approval, project confirmation, project management service, project supervision and investigation, etc.	Development of Area Assessment Reports and Implementation Plans

Source: Edited by authors.

5.2.1 Guangzhou: Urban regeneration Bureau

Under the institutional reform in Guangzhou, the Urban Regeneration Bureau was established in 2015 to integrate the responsibilities of the previous Three Olds Office for improving urban and rural living conditions. The transition from the Three Olds Office to the Urban Regeneration Bureau implies more than just a transition of hierarchy and mindset, but rather symbolizes a new institutional innovation. The Three Olds Office enjoyed the power of developing and approving plans for "three olds" projects, and allocating special funds for project implementation. Even when approved by the Three Olds Office, "three olds" project plan development quotas were often incompatible with existing urban planning requirements, leading to incompatibilities between the Three Olds Office and the Urban Planning Bureau, the latter having the authority to examine and approve project construction. The establishment of the Urban Regeneration Bureau with integrated approval power was an innovative institutional solution to adjust the previous distribution of responsibilities and power, though a certain level of contradictions and conflicts remains.[2]

As the main administrative institution for urban regeneration, the Urban Regeneration Bureau is responsible for the development of policies and regulations, research on administrative management measures, and the coordination of urban regeneration affairs. Reporting to the Leading Group of Urban Regeneration, the Urban Regeneration Bureau is the key administration organization for urban regeneration in Guangzhou, in cooperation with other relevant departments, particularly the Planning and Land Resources department. Under the Urban Regeneration Bureau, one General Office and six divisional offices were established – the Office for Policies and Regulations, Planning and Funding, Land Pooling, Preliminary Work, Project Approval, and Construction Supervision – covering the whole process of urban regeneration practice. The Urban Regeneration Bureau also has four affiliated institutions, the Urban Regeneration Project Construction Office, the Urban Regeneration Planning Research Institute, the Urban Regeneration Land Pooling Center, and the Urban Regeneration Data Center, to provide various kinds of support for urban regeneration activities.

In 2016, in response to decentralization reforms, 26 urban regeneration pilot projects were selected to experiment with the transfer of project review and approval authority from the municipal level to the district level, which served to strengthen the role of the district government as the primary responsible department. The decentralization reform was formally launched in August 2017 with publication of the Notice on Further Decentralization Reform in Guangzhou, which specified the scope and guidelines of decentralization, as well as its tasks and schedules. In February 2018, in adherence to the requirements of Decisions on Devolution of Administrative Power from the Guangzhou Municipal Level to the District Level, the municipal Urban Regeneration Bureau delegated the four administrative authorities, stated in Document 157, to district-level administration and the Administrative Committee of Guangzhou Airport Economic Zone. First, authority to review and approve regeneration project implementation plans in Urban Regeneration Districts was delegated to the district level. The second delegated administrative power was to develop the Annual Regeneration Program/Plan, which listed all the projects approved for implementation in each year. Third, the implementation plan for projects for the regeneration of village-level industrial parks and old factories that involved demolition and reconstruction, developed in compliance with binding regulatory plans and municipal industrial development plan, can be reviewed and approved by the district level rather than the municipal level. The fourth authority was to review and approve program planning and implementation planning of renewal projects involving adjustment of regulatory plans (Table 5.3).[3]

Table 5.3 Administrative Responsibilities Delegated from Municipal Level to District Level in Guangzhou

Sequence number in Document 157	Items to be reviewed and approved	Detailed devolved regulations
140	Concept plan and implementation plan of regeneration programs and projects in Urban Regeneration Districts	1. The administrative authority to review and approve the concept plan and implementation plan of the Urban Regeneration District is delegated to the district level. Plan-related activities include boundary delimitation, collection of stakeholder opinions, investigation and verification of basic data, organization of plan development, organization of expert evaluation, and collection of comments from the member institutions of the Leading Group of Urban Regeneration. 2. Implementation plans of regeneration projects in Huangpu District, Nansha District, Zengcheng District and Guangzhou Airport Economic Zone should be reviewed and approved by the respective district governments.

(*Continued*)

70 Development of urban regeneration

Table 5.3 (Continued)

Sequence number in Document 157	Items to be reviewed and approved	Detailed devolved regulations
141	Annual Program/ Plan of Regeneration	Devolved to the districts and the Guangzhou Airport Economic District for implementation
142	Projects for the regeneration of village-level industrial parks and old factories that involve demolition and reconstruction, in compliance with binding regulatory plans and municipal industrial development plan	Devolved to the districts and the Guangzhou Airport Economic District for implementation
143	Programs and implementation plans of projects in Urban Regeneration Districts involving the adjustment of regulatory plans	Devolved to the Huangpu District, Nansha District, Zengcheng District, and the Guangzhou Airport Economic Zone for implementation, consistent with the administrative authority regulatory planning arrangements in Guangzhou

Sources: Urban Regeneration Bureau in Guangzhou, Notice of the Urban Regeneration Bureau of Guangzhou to Transfer Municipal Administrative Authorities to the Districts [EB/OL]. (2018-02-27) [2018-10-12] http://www.gz.gov.cn/gzscsgxj/tzgg/201803/d1b03b6ac8e84fcabad370940f979f22.shtml.

5.2.2 Shenzhen: Planning and land resources committee

As the department with full authority over urban regeneration in Shenzhen, the Planning and Land Resources Committee coordinates urban regeneration planning and conventional urban planning, to avoid conflicts between the two and reduce delays in project approval due to inefficient communication between the various authorities. In response to the decentralization reform in Shenzhen,[4] the reform in urban regeneration affairs was kicked off at the beginning of 2016 in Luohu District with an experimental institutional reform of spatial planning under a decentralized system.[5] After approximately one year of reform trials in Luohu District, the urban regeneration goals had been more than fulfilled. Altogether 12.2 billion RMB of fixed capital investment was completed, with year-on-year growth of 122%. The rate of urban regeneration project implementation increased from 29% in 2015 to 36% in 2016. In addition, 0.147 km^2 of land was renewed during this period and 0.096 km^2 of land was pooled (Fan, 2017). In October 2016, a decision was made to expand the experience of reform in Luohu

District to the entire municipality, and the relevant administrative authority was delegated to the districts with the publication of Decision on Implementing Urban Regeneration Reform in Shenzhen, which claimed three aspects for the future reform. First, the administrative authority for urban regeneration was delegated from the Planning and Land Resources Committee and its affiliated agencies to the district level. Second, the authority to review and approve urban regeneration plans was transferred from the municipal government to the district governments. Third, policies between the old and the new should be time-coordinated.

Following overall implementation of decentralization reform in Shenzhen, the focus of the municipal Planning and Land Resources Committee mainly shifted to the organization and coordination of urban regeneration affairs, developing the Special Urban Regeneration Plan, and the development of policies and regulations, such as technical standards and codes, and administrative regulations. The administrative authorities exercised at the district level are focused on the five aspects of administrative approval, administrative service, and project supervision and inspection. First, the review, approval, and inspection of the Urban Renewal Unit is done by district-level authorities. Second, investigation of buildings and clarification of land tenure, including the disposal of historically illegally used land, become the responsibilities of the district authorities. The third category of administrative obligations includes the approval of building plots for renewal projects, the review of Land Use Permits, land price accounting, and signing contracts transferring state-owned land. The fourth concerns the issue of Land Use Permits and Land Construction Permits for regeneration projects, and the verification and acceptance of construction projects. Finally, the administrative authority for supervision and inspection of urban regeneration projects is delegated to the district level.

With decentralization, urban renewal practice was more efficient and effective, as the districts were allowed to operate urban regeneration taking account of their specific needs and feasibility. Yet, it has also triggered some problems. District governments, driven by pro-growth development, failed to control development density and volume. So many policies and documents to cope with various problems were issued by the respective district governments that the system became over-complex, causing difficulties in administration. In addition, increased capacity is urgently needed for administrative and technical personnel at the district level.

5.2.3 Shanghai: Leading group for urban regeneration

Under the Shanghai Municipal Government, the Leading Group for Urban Regeneration is responsible for taking a lead in city-wide urban regeneration affairs in Shanghai and for decision-making on important issues of regeneration. Further, the Urban Regeneration Office, reporting to the municipal Planning and Land Resources Bureau, is in charge of routine administration of urban regeneration affairs, such as the formulation of technical standards and administrative regulations, the organization and coordination of projects, inspection and supervision of projects, and publicity for urban regeneration policies. The district governments are responsible for urban regeneration affairs under their respective jurisdiction,

72 *Development of urban regeneration*

including the development of Regional Assessment Reports and Implementation Plans of urban regeneration projects.

5.3 Procedures and stages for administrative management of urban regeneration

5.3.1 Guangzhou: phase-based administration system

In Guangzhou, urban regeneration targets are divided into the three categories of old towns, old villages, and old industrial lands for differential administration, yet the basic procedure of the three types of practice is mostly identical, with only minor distinctions in terms of the process of opinion collection and the main actors of urban renewal (Table 5.4). In the case of comprehensive renewal, the types of projects include comprehensive renewal of old villages, self-renewal of old factories, land reserve of old factories by the government, mixed strategies of integrating land reserve of old factories by the government and self-renewal, comprehensive renewal of old towns, and renewal of industrial parks at village level. For those types of projects, the procedures can be divided into five phases – project application, plan formulation, project review, project approval, and project implementation.

In the project application phase, all land conforming to the requirements of urban regeneration should be incorporated into the Regeneration Database ("drawings and information database"), from which Urban Regeneration Districts should be selected for Annual Program applications. In the plan formulation phase, a plan for the implementation of urban regeneration projects is formulated. In case the binding regulatory plan needs to be adjusted, a planning scheme should

Table 5.4 Administration Procedures for Regeneration Projects in Old Towns, Old Villages, and Old Industrial Lands in Guangzhou

Phase	Issue	Old Towns	Old Villages	Old Industrial Lands
Application	Willingness for renewal	Agreed by over 90% of households	Attendance of over 2/3 of representatives, and approved by over 2/3 attendees	Applied by property owners (authorizing one body to apply in case of multiple property ownership)
Formulation	Agencies responsible for developing a planning scheme	District governments	District governments	Property owners of the old factories

Table 5.4 (Continued)

Phase	Issue	Old Towns	Old Villages	Old Industrial Lands
	Agencies responsible for developing an implementation plan	District government or district urban regeneration institutions	District governments	Property owners of the old factories
Implementation	Project management	Organized by the district government	Managed by village collectives under guidance from district governments or district urban regeneration institutions	Self-renewal, land reserve by the state, or combination of both
	Renewal approach	Land acquisition and further transfer by the state	Self-renewal, cooperative regeneration, or land reserve by the state	Self-renewal, land reserve by the state, or combination of both

Source: Compiled from relevant sources: Urban Regeneration Bureau of Guangzhou Prefecture, Declaration Guidance on Comprehensive Renewal and Regeneration Projects of Old Towns, Declaration Guidance on Projects Combined Government Expropriation and Inventory (Preparation) and Spontaneous Renovations of Old Factories, Declaration Guidance on Government Expropriation and Inventory (Preparation) Projects of Old Factories, Declaration Guidance of Spontaneous Renovations Projects of Old Factories, Declaration Guidance of Comprehensive Renewal and Regeneration Projects of Old Villages, http://www.gzuro.gov.cn/csgxj/bszn/list.shtml.

be developed first for the Urban Regeneration District, followed by adjustments to the regulatory plan in accordance with the regulated procedures. In the project review phase, urban regeneration plans are reviewed and examined by the Urban Regeneration Bureau. Then, in the project approval phase, the Urban Regeneration Bureau processes the submitted application for approval. If an implementation plan needs to be revised, social risk assessments are conducted after its revision. In the final phase of project implementation, the urban regeneration institution provides guidance on implementation and carries out inspection upon completion. In addition, where historically illegally used lands are involved, the situation must be reported for rights validation in the project review phase, and all these "historical lands" have to be legally registered after the regeneration is complete (Figure 5.4). In line with comprehensive renewal, micro-regeneration procedures in old villages and old towns in Guangzhou are similarly divided into the five phases of plan application, formulation, review, approval, and implementation, but without involving the adjustment of regulatory plans.

74 *Development of urban regeneration*

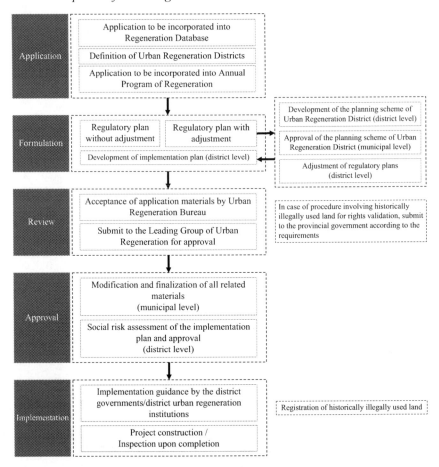

Figure 5.4 Administrative Procedures for Urban Regeneration Projects involving Comprehensive Renewal in Guangzhou.
(Note: After decentralization, review and approval authority was transferred to the district governments.).
Source: Drawn by authors.

5.3.2 Shenzhen: strategy-based administrative management

In Shenzhen, the implementation of urban regeneration projects is guided by the Urban Master Plan, Land Use Plan, and Special Plan for Urban Regeneration in accordance with the periodic national Five-Year Plans. For the three strategies of implementation, including demolition and reconstruction, change of use, and comprehensive renewal, different procedures are required. In the case of demolition and reconstruction, the three phases of application, formulation, and implementation are required to strictly follow the Urban Renewal Unit Plans and the Annual Program of Regeneration. In the application phase, Urban Renewal Units are defined and applications made for their incorporation in the Annual Regeneration Program. In the latter phase of formulation, which usually takes 1-2 years, a plan for an Urban Renewal Unit is approved after certain procedures, including

Development of urban regeneration 75

investigation of land and buildings, formulation of Urban Renewal Unit Plans and submission for approval, review by the authorities and correlation with the binding statutory plans, whose requirements are the basis for developing Urban Renewal Unit Plans. In the final implementation phase, Land Grant Contracts and Land Use Permits are issued after the identification of a single implementation agency, the completion of the Urban Renewal Unit implementation plan, and the submission of the land premium to the local government (Figure 5.5). In the case of the second strategy of function change, a series of procedures should be followed. Applications for change of land use are submitted by property owners for approval by the authorities. Further, a Land Grant Contract or a Supplementary Agreement of Land Grant Contract should be signed to complete the planning and land-use procedures before project implementation. In the case of comprehensive renewal, projects should be submitted by the implementing agency and approved by the authorities before implementation.

Plans for Urban Renewal Units should be formulated in accordance with the binding requirements defined in the statutory plans. In practice, an approved Urban Renewal Unit Plan is allowed to function as an updated statutory plan, which means that the modification of an Urban Renewal Unit Plan will lead to the corresponding changes in the statutory plans. Thus, Urban Renewal Unit planning fits into the conventional planning systems well, enabling rapid approval under the existing planning framework, so as to reduce time and manpower costs and improve planning efficiency. However, this practice tends to create frequent

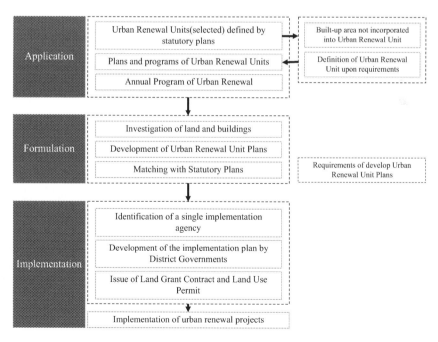

Figure 5.5 Administrative Procedures for Urban Regeneration Projects Involving Demolition and Reconstruction in Shenzhen.

Source: Drawn by authors.

alterations to statutory plans and undermines the position of the statutory plan as a legal instrument. It is therefore argued that the statutory plans should be more respected, and any changes to them should be dealt with more carefully, particularly in the case of altering binding regulations.

5.3.3 Shanghai: assessment and program management

A life-cycle management process that highlights the integration of "regional assessment and implementation programs" has been adopted for urban regeneration projects in Shanghai. In the Land Grant Contract, as well as development procedures and progress schedules, project requirements are clearly stipulated in regard to land use, operational management, supporting amenities, period of land use, and energy saving and environmental protection. Implementation of urban regeneration projects includes three main procedures (Figure 5.6). First, in the regional assessment phase, the Urban Regeneration Units and the list of public amenities are defined by the authorities based on the assessment of certain regions. A thorough investigation should be undertaken in the Urban Regeneration Units to prepare for further urban regeneration activities, such as a demand for public

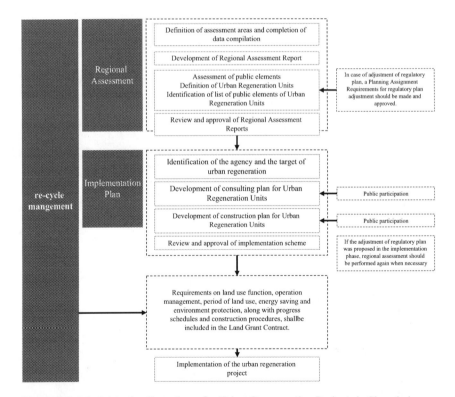

Figure 5.6 Administrative Procedures for Urban Regeneration Projects in Shanghai.
Compiled from relevant sources: Government of Shanghai (2015), Shanghai Urban Regeneration Implementation Measures

services and current capacity. In the plan implementation phase, a draft Urban Regeneration Unit Plan should be developed by a single agency for public consultation, based on which a formal Urban Regeneration Unit Plan will be finalized after public participation. Before the submission of the Urban Regeneration Unit Plan for approval, the binding regulatory plans together with related modifications and supplements should be approved. In the final phase, plan implementation, construction activities will be carried out in sequence. For many urban regeneration projects, not only should a complete procedure to develop the Urban Regeneration Unit Plan be followed, but regulatory plans and detailed plans should also be adjusted in parallel, which usually takes between six and twelve months. The long procedure, and thus the high cost of plan development, tends to discourage investors and property owners from participating in urban regeneration projects.

5.4 Urban regeneration planning systems in the three cities

In Guangzhou, Shenzhen, and Shanghai, urban regeneration planning has been reformed to adapt to conventional statutory planning. The urban regeneration planning framework in Guangzhou, which consists of the Urban Regeneration Master Plan, Three Olds Regeneration Planning, and Urban Regeneration District Plan, is linked to the "1+3+N" policy, and the conventional planning system of master plan and regulatory plans. In Shenzhen, the Special Urban Regeneration Plan is the Urban Master Plan and regional plan, while Urban Renewal Unit Plans fulfil the requirements of binding statutory plans. Further, the Key Districts Coordination Plan is explored to fill in the planning gap between Special Urban Regeneration Plan and Urban Renewal Unit Plan. In Shanghai, either the Urban Regeneration Unit Plan should conform to the requirements of regulatory plans or the regulatory plans should be adjusted to be in line with the Urban Regeneration Unit Plan (Table 5.5).

Table 5.5 Urban Regeneration Planning in Guangzhou, Shenzhen, and Shanghai compared

Items	Guangzhou	Shenzhen	Shanghai
Planning system	1+3+N	Special Urban Regeneration planning and Urban Renewal Unit Planning	Urban Regeneration Unit Planning
Planning at municipal level	Urban Regeneration Master Plan in Guangzhou	Special Urban Regeneration Plan in Shenzhen	–
Area-based planning	Urban Regeneration District planning	Urban Renewal Unit planning	Urban Regeneration Unit planning
Related planning instrument	Regulatory planning	Statutory planning	Regulatory planning

Source: Edited by authors.

78 Development of urban regeneration

5.4.1 Guangzhou: "1+3+N" planning system

In Guangzhou, a "1+3+N" framework has been developed by integrating it with the previous "three olds" planning system (Figure 5.7).[6] The "1" refers to the Guangzhou Urban Regeneration Master Plan, the "3" refers to the "three olds" special regeneration planning, and "N" stands for the programs and projects on the "three olds" renewal land. This structure corresponds to the conventional planning and policy systems at three levels. First, relating to Guangzhou Urban Master Plan and Guangzhou Land Use Master Plan, the "1" Urban Regeneration Master Plan regulates the goals, principles, strategies, missions, scope, density and approaches of urban regeneration, as well as infrastructure improvement at the municipal level. Second, in line with general regulatory plans, the "3" types of special urban renewal planning include binding regulations – land use, development volume and density – reflecting the goals and requirements of urban regeneration at the meso-level. Third, linked with the plot regulatory plans, the "N" functions as the implementation plans for urban regeneration projects with details of project implementation.

5.4.2 Shenzhen: Special Urban Regeneration planning and Urban Renewal Unit planning systems

In Shenzhen, a planning system that integrates special regeneration planning and Urban Renewal Unit planning has been developed for urban regeneration (Figure 5.8). At the macro level, Special Urban Regeneration planning,[7] which covers both the municipality and the districts, serves as comprehensive guidance for urban regeneration, and regulates the principles, goals, and spatial control of urban regeneration. It also specifies the short-term requirements of the implementation plan, such as the priority areas for demolition and reconstruction, the areas for integrating comprehensive renovation with demolition and reconstruction,

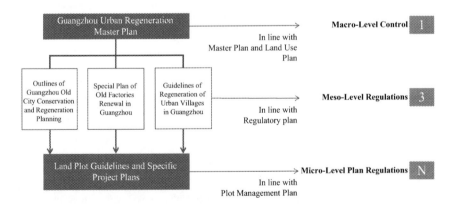

Figure 5.7 "1+3+N" Planning System for Urban Regeneration in Guangzhou.

Redrawn from relevant sources: Lai and Wu (2013). Speed and Benefit: Guangzhou "Sanjiu" Redevelopment Strategies for New Urbanization. Planners, 29(5):36-41.

Development of urban regeneration 79

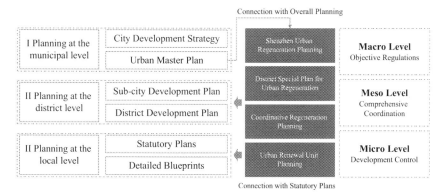

Figure 5.8 Urban Regeneration Planning System in Shenzhen.
Source: Drawn by authors.

the areas restricted from demolition and reconstruction, basic ecological control lines, and the boundaries of the approved Urban Renewal Units. In accordance with the statutory plan, the Urban Renewal Unit Plan is formulated to define the goals, strategies, and binding requirements of urban regeneration projects, as well as infrastructure improvement, public services, and urban design guidance. Further, in the Urban Renewal Unit Plan, the boundaries of land for demolition, for reserve and for development are defined. To improve the planning feasibility, implementation plans are required to be developed to support Urban Renewal Unit Plans, including phased implementation plans, deadlines for implementation, and the responsibilities of the implementation agencies, such as responsibility for demolition and transfer of land and facilities.

In 2016, the 13th Five-Year Plan of Urban Regeneration in Shenzhen proposed the concept of "Coordination Planning for Key Regeneration Areas", based on the existing planning framework, to define the development capacity of regeneration areas, and the layout and the scale of public amenities and open space. Given the gaps between sporadic regeneration projects and the overall urban regeneration goals, the Coordination Planning for Key Regeneration Areas aims at strengthening public intervention to coordinate various plans, balance benefits in different areas, and improve the supply of public infrastructure.

In order to standardize the formulation of Urban Renewal Unit Plans and bridge the gap between plan and project implementation, the Technical Regulations on the Formulation of Urban Renewal Unit Plans (Trial), published in 2011, established the Urban Renewal Unit as the fundamental instrument to administrate urban regeneration projects involving demolition and reconstruction. Further, the Technical Regulations on the Formulation of Urban Renewal Unit Plans with Demolition and Reconstruction (Draft for Opinion Collection), published in 2014, symbolizes the transition of urban regeneration strategies from speed oriented to quality oriented. In September 2018, the Technical Regulations on the Formulation of Urban Renewal Unit Plans with Demolition and Reconstruction was formally published and distributed, which links to the regulations on the

80 Development of urban regeneration

review and approval of Urban Renewal Unit Plans, as well as the upper-level requirements from the master plan, statutory plans, and the regeneration units program. It also imposed administrative approval requirements in the next phase. The delivery of Urban Renewal Unit Plans includes technical documents, such as planning research reports, monographic/specific study and technical drawings, and administrative documents, such as texts, figures, and approved planning documents. The specific study focuses on topics such as urban design, "sponge city", ecological remediation, and historical and cultural preservation.

5.4.3 Shanghai: project-based urban planning

The main task of urban regeneration planning in Shanghai is to develop plans for Urban Regeneration Units. Unlike Guangzhou and Shenzhen, in Shanghai, there is no regeneration master plan at the municipal level to provide overall guidance. Instead, in reference to the requirements of binding regulatory plans, Urban Regeneration Unit Plans are developed to provide guidance for urban regeneration (Figure 5.9). Through this process, a procedure of "assessment before planning" has been adopted.[8] First, facilitated by a Regional Assessment Report, Urban Regeneration Units are defined based on the assessment of urban problems, particularly in the provision of public services. Where a regulatory plan is adjusted, the urban planning and land resources authorities at district or county level need to prepare Planning Assignment Requirements based on the requirements stated in the Regional Assessment Report, and report to urban planning and land resources authorities at the municipal level. After the Regional Assessment Report is approved by the district or county governments and is reported to the Leading Group of Urban Regeneration at the municipal level, the Planning Assignment Requirements are completed and reviewed in parallel by the urban planning and land resources authority at the municipal level to launch the adjustment of the regulatory plan. In the next step, the draft plan for the Urban Regeneration Unit is developed, and awaits finalization. If adjustments to a regulatory plan are required after the launch of the project implementation plan, a new round of regional assessment needs to be carried out.

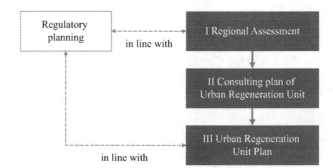

Figure 5.9 Flowchart for Urban Regeneration Planning in Shanghai.
Source: Drawn by authors.

In March 2017, Changning District published the Urban Regeneration Plan for Changning District 2017–2021 and the Urban Regeneration Action Plan for Changning District 2017–2018. Regarded as the first comprehensive urban regeneration plan in Shanghai, Urban Regeneration Plan for Changning District 2017–2021 defined the key areas as developing a vibrant community, new business districts, historical district, low-carbon ecological district, and underground space. Urban regeneration planning at the municipal and district level has since been launched in Shanghai.

5.5 Definition of an Urban Regeneration/Renewal Unit or District

As a planning instrument, the Urban Regeneration/Renewal Unit or District links urban regeneration to the statutory plans and provides guidance for project implementation. Consisting of one or multiple renewal projects, the Urban Regeneration/Renewal Unit or District concept is similar in Guangzhou, Shanghai, and Shenzhen. Defining an Urban Regeneration/Renewal Unit or District is facilitated by a Regeneration Database ("drawings and information database") in Guangzhou, based on the statutory plans or multiple applications by multiple actors in Shenzhen, and based on the Regional Assessment Report in Shanghai. The scale of an Urban Renewal Unit is specified in Shenzhen by land size, but is not regulated in the other two cities. Subject to urban problems and regeneration goals, the details regulated in the Urban Regeneration/Renewal Unit or District may vary (Table 5.6). In Shenzhen, Urban Renewal Unit categories have increased from one to three: including the General Renewal Unit, Microscale Renewal Unit ,and Key Renewal Unit. Further, with the issue of Report on the Status of Urban Regeneration in Shenzhen by the Urban Planning and Land Resources Committee in April 2018, abolition of the Small-plot Renewal Unit[9] was suggested due to the problem of piecemeal spaces and insufficient public amenity supply.

Table 5.6 Urban Regeneration/Renewal Units or Districts in Guangzhou, Shenzhen, and Shanghai compared

City	Category	Scale	Reference	Selection criteria
Guangzhou	Urban Regeneration District	–	Regeneration Database ("drawings and information database")	① With some infrastructure and public service amenities ② Natural boundaries and property right ③ In continuous areas and conforming to general rules

(*Continued*)

82 *Development of urban regeneration*

Table 5.3 (Continued)

City	Category	Scale	Reference	Selection criteria
Shenzhen	General Renewal Unit Key Renewal Unit Small-plot Renewal Unit	≥10,000 m² ≥3,000 m²	Statutory Plans, and application from multiple actors	① Public service amenities in urgent need of improvement ② Poor environmental conditions or potential safety risks ③ Not conforming to socio-economic development, and with negative impact on urban planning implementation
Shanghai	Urban Regeneration Unit	One neighborhood block as the basic unit	Regional Assessment Report	① Areas with poor living conditions or low building quality, in urgent need of upgrading and improved public services ② Areas in urgent need of public amenities based on assessment ③ Areas where construction would be feasible in the near future

Sources: compiled by the author.

5.5.1 Guangzhou: defining an Urban Regeneration District based on the Regeneration Database[10]

Since 2009, in order to facilitate the "three olds" regeneration movement, a Regeneration Database("drawings and information database") has been developed to collect detailed land-use information for "three olds" projects and monitor the regeneration process in real time. The information collected in the database includes locations, scope, size, tenures, and existing conditions of the plots (Figure 5.10). Recently, in response to a call to strengthen general surveys in Guangzhou,[11] the Regeneration Database information has been extended to include demographic data, economic industries, public amenities, cultural heritage, land data, building data, and fundamental survey results. The Regeneration Database is an important source for defining an Urban Regeneration District.

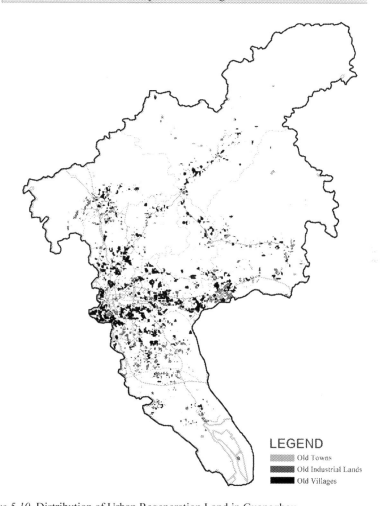

Figure 5.10 Distribution of Urban Regeneration Land in Guangzhou.

Redrawn from relevant sources: Guangzhou Urban Regeneration Bureau (2017), Land Use Plan for Urban Regeneration (2015–2020). Available at: http://www.gzuro.gov.cn/gzsgxj/gxj/u/cms/www/201709/18090336bw0u.pdf [Accessed October 22, 2018].

Except in the case of micro-regeneration projects, only land plots listed in the database are eligible to undertake urban regeneration activities and enjoy preferential policies. The micro-regeneration type, defined in the Guangzhou Urban Regeneration Measures, is exempt from inclusion in the database, as it does not belong to the "three olds" regeneration program, but still proves a significant regeneration type. Updated twice a year, the Regeneration Database is established through a standard procedure. First, the application agent, which can be the government at either sub-district or county level, state-owned enterprises, or privately owned enterprises, collects information on the plot and reports to the district urban regeneration authorities for initial approval. The information is then reviewed by the municipal Urban Regeneration Bureau in accordance with the requirements regulated by the land resources authority at the provincial level, and further reported to the provincial land resources authority for final approval and release. According to statistics, up till October 2016, the total area of land for urban regeneration in Guangzhou stood at approximately 589.58 km^2, of which 360.78 km^2 were included in implementation plans before 2020.[12]

5.5.2 Shenzhen: defining an Urban Renewal Unit based on statutory plans and applications

In Shenzhen, an Urban Regeneration Unit is defined based on statutory plans and applications by the implementation agencies. Designated based on statutory plans in many cases, an Urban Regeneration Unit should meet the requirements of the Special Urban Regeneration Plan in Shenzhen and its economic, social, and cultural impacts assessed. Although an Urban Regeneration Unit is derived from the statutory plan, proposals have often been made to break through the binding regulations of the statutory plans, as there tends to be an inadequate response by the statutory plan to urban problems, particularly demand for public space and public amenities, due to its long development process. An Urban Regeneration Unit can be applied for by multiple agencies, including property owners (such as village collectives), a single developer or the enterprise contracted by the property owners, or a government department. Before the application for an Urban Regeneration Unit, a survey has to be conducted to collect the opinions of stakeholders. An Urban Regeneration Unit regulated in Special Urban Regeneration Plan for demolition and reconstruction is eligible to apply for incorporation in the urban renewal implementation plan, and other areas meeting the requirements can also proceed and apply for incorporation into the Urban Regeneration Unit in accordance with regulated procedures (Figure 5.11).

Since the adoption of the Urban Regeneration Unit in Shenzhen in 2009, in some areas with strategic locations and strong impact on regional urban development, urban regeneration has been challenged by insufficient market motivation and failure to achieve improvement goals. To encourage regeneration activities in those areas, the 2016 Provisional Measures introduced the Key Urban Renewal Unit to strengthen public intervention in a top-down approach. Compared with general Urban Renewal Units, in Key Urban Renewal Units, more difficult issues need to be tackled and less enthusiasm has been received from the market. Therefore, the project in the Key Urban Renewal Unit is organized by the government to guarantee smooth implementation for developing industries and significant infrastructure. Besides the government, developers with capacity, experience, and social responsibilities can also be selected to implement renewal practice (Table 5.7). In principle, the projects in the Key Urban Renewal Unit should be implemented as a whole, not in steps. In the case of phased implementation, public infrastructure, public services, resettlement housing, and policy housing projects should be prioritized.

Development of urban regeneration 85

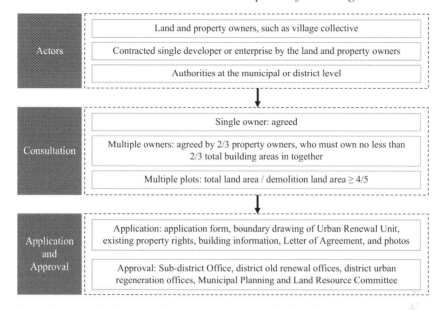

Figure 5.11 Application Procedure for Urban Renewal Units in Shenzhen.

Compiled from relevant sources: Planning and Land Resource Committee of Shenzhen (2018), Notice of Public Opinions Collection of the Planning and Land Resource Committee of Shenzhen on "Application Regulations on Urban Renewal Units for Demolition and Reconstruction in Shenzhen" (Opinion Collection Draft). Available at: http://www.szpl.gov.cn/xxgk/gggs/201808/t20180806_478165.html [Accessed October 22, 2018].

Table 5.7 Disposal of Historical Land in Urban Renewal Projects involving Demolition and Reconstruction in Shenzhen

Urban Renewal Projects involving Demolition and Reconstruction		Urban renewal land by successor agencies, %	Land banking by the government, %
General Urban Renewal Unit		*80*	*20*
Key Urban Renewal Unit	Percentage of legal land use≥60%	80	20
	60%>percentage of legal land use ≥50%	75	25
	50%>percentage of legal land use ≥40%	65	35
	Percentage of legal land use<40%	55	45

Sources: General Office of the People's Government of Shenzhen Prefecture (2016), Provisional Measures on Strengthening and Improving the Implementation of Urban Regeneration.

5.5.3 Shanghai: defining Urban Regeneration Unit through regional assessment

In Shanghai, an Urban Regeneration Unit is defined based on regional assessment. This is different to Guangzhou and Shenzhen, for the former's regeneration district is based on the Regeneration Database and the latter's on regulatory plans and applications. First, an area, particularly its public amenities, is assessed by the government to identify urban problems and the need for regeneration. Urban Regeneration Units are then identified within the assessed area. The size of an area for assessment basically follows the unit division of regulatory plans, while an Urban Regeneration Unit, as the basis for project implementation, can be as small as a neighborhood block. Moreover, unlike in Guangzhou or Shenzhen, where Urban Regeneration/Renewal Units or Districts have to be incorporated into an Annual Program for further implementation, in Shanghai the urban regeneration projects can be implemented immediately after the formulation of implementation plans.

5.6 Summary

In conclusion, the constitution of the institutional systems for urban regeneration in Guangzhou, Shenzhen, and Shanghai are distinctive, but share common features. First, a stable administrative system for urban regeneration, with the authorities at the municipal level for overall guidance and at the lower levels for implementation management, has been established in all three cities. Second, basic phases and administrative procedures for urban regeneration in all three cities have been developed, while the institutional arrangements for specific processes and target areas are being constantly improved. Third, the urban regeneration planning system has been well integrated into the conventional urban and rural planning system.

Notes

1 Urban Renewal Units in Shenzhen usually are regeneration areas for demolition and reconstruction.
2 Owing to the overall influence of national organizational reform, the Planning and Natural Resources Bureau was established in 2019 in Guangzhou according to the arrangements in the Institutional Reform Plan of Guangzhou, and the Committee of Planning and Land Resources and the Urban Regeneration Bureau were abolished. The responsibilities of the Urban Regeneration Bureau were divided between the Planning and Natural Resources Bureau and the Housing and Urban-Rural Construction Bureau.
3 Urban Regeneration Bureau of Guangzhou (2018), Notice of Guangzhou Urban Regeneration on Transfer of the Municipal Administrative Authorities to the District Level. Available at: http://www.gz.gov.cn/gzscsgxj/tzgg/201803/d1b03b6ac8e84f-cabad370940f979f22.shtml [Accessed October 12, 2018].
4 In 2016, with the objective of constructing a modern government and improving urban competence, decentralization was actively promoted in Shenzhen, with the devolution of administrative power and the promotion of responsibility transformation marking breakthroughs in this process.

5 On September 2, 2015, Luohu District issued the Implementation Opinions of Luohu District to Thoroughly Implement the "Decision of Shenzhen to Launch Reform Trials of Urban Regeneration in Luohu District", launching the institutional reform of planning and land resources administration.
6 Recommended Cases of the Urban Management Progress Award of China for 2012 (2011). The "1+3+N" Planning System of the "Three Olds" Regenerations of Guangzhou, *Information for Deciders*, 40:20–21; Lai, S., Wu, J. (2013), Speed and Benefit: Guangzhou "Sanjiu" Redevelopment Strategies for New Urbanization. *Planners*, 29(5):36–41.
7 The specific name of the planning might vary, for example the 13th Five-Year Plan of Urban Regeneration in Shenzhen is one such urban regeneration special plan.
8 Shanghai Municipal Government (2015), Implementation Details of Shanghai Urban Regeneration Land-Use Planning (Trials) (Draft for Opinion Collection).
9 With the constant change in renewal requirements, the Small-plot Renewal Units were later readopted in subsequent policies.
10 Regeneration Database ("drawings and information database")-related work includes defining urban regeneration plots on aerial maps, integrating information from the Land-Use Map and Land-Use Plan, establishing the "three olds" monitor database, etc.
11 In December, 2016, the Administration Measures on Data Collection and Investigation of Urban Regeneration of Guangzhou and the supplementary Investigation (Inspection) Guidance and Standards of Urban Regeneration Data in Guangzhou were officially published and distributed, strengthening the construction of the database.
12 Guangzhou Urban Regeneration Bureau (2017), Guangzhou Urban Regeneration Master Plan (2015–2020). Available at: http://www.gzuro.gov.cn/csgxjxxgk/7.2/201703/b340a8043e61416995b486579ff8a8de.shtml [Accessed October 28, 2018].

6 Spatial management and control of urban regeneration in the three cities

To achieve the overall objectives of urban construction and the integration of dispersed regeneration with orderly development, cities and districts need to clarify their management and control requirements, construction standards, and measures for restrictions and incentives to specific urban regeneration projects. Guangzhou, Shenzhen, and Shanghai, on the one hand impose comprehensive regulations on spatial management and control through the publication of supplementary policies, and on the other hand, strengthen spatial guidance on specific urban regeneration projects through regeneration planning and implementation planning, which involves functional requirements, development intensity, public elements, design guidance and fund-raising. Each of the three cities employs distinctive spatial management and control measures of urban regeneration, and many innovative tools have emerged from local practices.

6.1 Spatial management and control measures in the urban regeneration of Guangzhou

6.1.1 Function, intensity, and special regulations guidance in urban regeneration

6.1.1.1 Function guidance for regeneration

As proposed in the Guangzhou Urban Regeneration Master Plan (2015-2020), function guidance is required to connect land-use planning with urban-rural planning and urban environmental protection planning. The Urban Regeneration Master Plan has set the development direction of major functions (land uses) for all urban regions and sub-regions (Table 6.1). The plan also lays down that the functions of key regeneration regions shall be led and approved by the government; the function of land for municipal and public service amenities shall not be changed at discretion; urban regeneration for commercial purposes shall be complemented with necessary public services; and the scale and distribution of urban regeneration areas for residential purposes shall be reasonably determined.

6.1.1.2 Intensity guidance for regeneration

Development intensity is closely linked to urban morphology and increased revenue from urban regeneration. Guangzhou implements zoned control on the development intensity of urban regeneration, as shown in the Guangzhou Urban Regeneration Master Plan (2015-2020), which partitioned Guangzhou into four tiers of intensity zones based on the existing regulatory plans and rail transit grid plan (Table 6.2 and Figure 6.1). It is an important reference for the

Table 6.1 Function Guidance for Urban Regeneration in Guangzhou

Region	Sub-region	Function Guidance
Downtown	Old City	Modern service industries, including headquarters economies, commerce and offices, culture and innovation, and amenities and entertainment
	Northern Functionality Group	Residences, commercial services, and supplements
	Eastern Functional Group	Residences, commercial services, and supplements
	South-western Functional Group	Residences, commercial services, and supplements
	Southern Functional Group	Public services and supplements
Panyu	Fashion and Innovation Group	Service sector supplementing higher education
	Fashion and Shopping Group	High-end service sector, fashion, commerce, leisure, and headquarters economies
	High-End Services Group	Leisure, tourism, healthcare, high-end residences, and high-tech industries
	Fashion and Life Group	Commerce, residences, and comprehensive services
Nansha	Core Urban Area	Commerce, offices, and living services
	Northern Group	Industries including automobiles, equipment manufacturing, chemicals, logistics, and culture and innovations ("Internet+" and Industry 4.0 for the Qingsheng area of the free-trade zone)
	Western Group	Services for heavy equipment manufacturing, modern urban agriculture, culture, and tourism
	Southern Group	Production services
Eastern	Western Group	Residences, commercial services, and supplements
	Central Group	Industries and supplements
	Eastern Group	Public services and supplements
Huadu	Central Urban Area	Supplementary functions for airport economies
	Xinhua Area	Residences, commercial services, and supplements
	Western Area and the Huadu Automobile City	Research, education, trade, tourism, and residences
	Eastern Townships	Ecological corridors
	Other Areas	Ecological and supplementary services

(Continued)

90 *Spatial management and control of urban regeneration*

Table 6.1 (Continued)

Region	Sub-region	Function Guidance
Zengcheng	Core Area	Services
	Dongjiang Development Area	High-tech industries, high-end commerce, exhibitions, and logistics
	Science, Education, and Living New Area	Education, medicine, and healthcare
	Northern Ecological Area	Maintaining status quo and ecological regreening
Conghua	Central Core Urban Area	Complementing public services
	Northern Ecological Area	Leisure and healthy living, commerce, tourism, horseracing, ecological tourism, and tourism agriculture
	Southern Taiping Area	High-tech research, innovation industries, life and healthcare industries, and commercial services
	Western Aotou Area	Emerging strategic industries, advanced manufacturing, modern logistics, and modern urban agriculture

Compiled from relevant sources: Urban Regeneration Bureau of Guangzhou, Guangzhou Urban Regeneration Master Plan (2015-2020) [EB/OL] (2017-01) [2018-10-22] http://www.gzuro.gov.cn/gzsgxj/gxj/u/cms/www/201709/18090336bw0u.pdf.

Table 6.2 Urban Regeneration of Guangzhou: Development Intensity Classification

Intensity Level	Intensity Control
Intensity Level 1	Areas within 800 m of railway stations, where highly intensive development is encouraged if permitted by planning
Intensity Level 2	Areas except intensity level 1 areas, intensity level 3 areas, or ecological control areas. Appropriately intensive development is encouraged according to regional development conditions with planning permission
Intensity Level 3	Mostly policy-based regions, such as construction control areas. Development intensity must conform to regional regulations and planning requirements
Ecological Control Areas	Construction prohibition areas and construction restriction areas designated in Urban Master Plan, whose development intensity must conform to administrative requirements on ecology control lines

Sources: Urban Regeneration Bureau of Guangzhou, Guangzhou Urban Regeneration Master Plan (2015-2020) [EB/OL] (2017-01)[2018-10-22] http://www.gzuro.gov.cn/gzsgxj/gxj/u/cms/www/201709/18090336bw0u.pdf.

Spatial management and control of urban regeneration 91

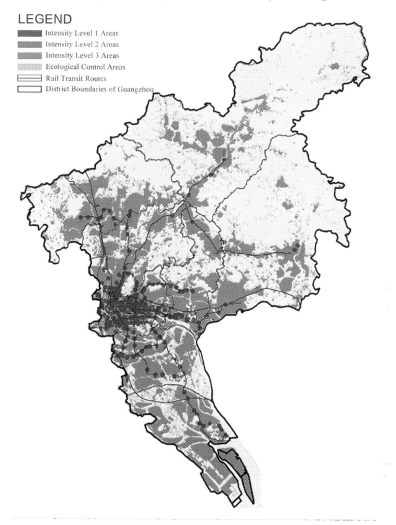

Figure 6.1 Urban Regeneration and Renovation of Guangzhou: Development Intensity Zones

Sources: Urban Regeneration Bureau of Guangzhou, Guangzhou Urban Regeneration Master Plan (2015-2020) [EB/OL]. (2017-01)[2018-10-22] http://www.gzuro.gov.cn/gzsgxj/gxj/u/cms/www/201709/18090336bw0u.pdf.

implementation of regeneration plans and projects. For areas with special regulations on urban character and landscape, development intensity control should follow the relevant special planning, and for a few specific urban villages, development intensity should be determined according to the situation on the ground.

6.1.1.3 Special regulations guidance

The Guangzhou Urban Regeneration Master Plan (2015-2020) proposed special regulations guidance on urban industrial upgrading, historical and cultural conservation, natural and ecological conservation, infrastructure construction, affordable housing construction, urban identity building, etc. For example, for supplementary amenities, it is necessary to complete urban infrastructure, improve urban living conditions, optimize community networks (opening dead-end roads, repairing damaged roads, etc.), and construct community pedestrian networks through urban "micro regenerations"; with reference to nature and ecology, connecting urban regeneration projects and old residential areas with natural resources (such as mountains and water bodies) and cultural resources for improving conservation of the ecology and environment is encouraged; with regard to affordable housing, 10% FAR of the regeneration projects targeting commercial residential buildings is required to be allocated for affordable housing, so as to solve the shortage of urban affordable housing.

6.1.2 Design guidelines for micro renovation of old residential areas

The improvement and renovation of old residential areas has always been a key focus of urban regeneration, while at the same time representing a continuous conundrum. In accordance with the requirements on old residential area renovation trials from the Ministry of Housing and Urban-Rural Development, the Guangzhou Urban Regeneration Bureau formulated the Design Guidelines on Micro Renovation of Old Residential Areas in Guangzhou (implemented on August 9, 2018), which provide refined administrative and planning guidance for old residential area regeneration by strengthening top-level policy design, safeguarding mechanisms, and technical support (Table 6.3). The Design Guidelines, which comply with the Guangzhou Three-Year Action Plan for Old Residential Area Micro Renovation (2018-2020), contain numerous design requirements and standards on old residential area micro renovation based on the integration of "water, roads, electricity, gas, fire control, waste, vehicles, and stations", to improve the standard and effects of old residential area regeneration across Guangzhou.

6.1.3 Establishment of "Urban regeneration special funds"

In order to coordinate the financial resources for urban regeneration at the municipal level, the Guangzhou Urban Regeneration Master Plan proposed "Urban Regeneration Special Funds" as a financing mechanism to compensate for the economic costs incurred in conservation of historic streets and ecologically sensitive areas (ecology control lines, ecology corridors, etc.) in special urban regeneration projects. The Guangzhou Urban Regeneration Bureau is responsible

Table 6.3 Classification of Element Guidelines for Micro Renovation of Old Residential Areas in Guangzhou

Module		Classification	Elements and Facilities
Basic Module	Buildings	1. Building Facilities	Renovation of building gates, intercom systems, wiring, fire control facilities, water supply facilities, drainage facilities, electrical appliances, corridor lighting, lighting protection, septic tanks, rainwater gutters, air-conditioning drainage pipes, mailboxes, household meters, pipeline gas, anti-theft wire meshes, and canopies
		2. Building Repairing	Corridor repairs, rooftop waterproofing, façade repairs, building outdoor structural components, accessible entrances and exits, and decorative façade
	Community Facilities	3. Service Facilities	Sanitation, wellness facilities, cultural facilities, services for the elderly, and public washing lines
	Road and Municipal Facilities	4. Community Roads	Community roads and pedestrian systems, facilities for the disabled, demolition of illegally constructed buildings, and passageway clearance
		5. Municipal Facilities	Wiring repairs, safety equipment, firefighting equipment, municipal lighting, drainage repairs, water and electricity supply
	Environment	6. Public Environment	Fence cleaning and repairs, signage, street furniture, and physical environment renovation
Enhancement Module	Buildings	7. Building Enhancement	Elevators, air-conditioning slot renovations, rooftop renovation and decoration, 3-dimensional greening, and energy-saving renovation
	Public Spaces	8. Community Public Space	Open activity spaces, alleyway activity spaces, pocket parks, residential area entrances, public benches, and landscape accessories
	Facility Enhancements	9. Public Facilities Enhancement	Rainwater and sewage disposal, parking facilities, non-motor vehicle facilities, information boards, public management facilities, express delivery facilities, and smart management

Sources: Urban Regeneration Bureau of Guangzhou. Design Guidelines on Micro Renovations of Old Residential Areas in Guangzhou [EB/OL] (2018-08-20) [2018-10-22] http://www.gzuro.gov.cn/csgxjxxgk/2.2/201808/d95be67019b04e8cafe59ba28e7aabac.shtml.

94 *Spatial management and control of urban regeneration*

for the overall management and supervision of the funds. The responsibilities include drafting an annual arrangement plan for the special funds, formulating budgets for urban maintenance and a construction fund for urban regeneration projects, clarifying the distribution of the urban regeneration special funds, and examining and approving the utilization of national policy funds for urban regeneration projects.

6.1.4 *"Transition period" favors for industrial land transformation*

To promote the transformation and upgrading of urban industries, the Implementation Opinions on Improving Urban Regeneration Standards and Promoting Economical and Intensive Land Usage indicated support for high-standard transformations of old state-owned factories to new industries and business areas. To reduce the pressure on old factories in terms of both finance and legal permissions during industrial transformation, regeneration projects are offered a five-year transition period under the Implementation Opinions, during which they are allowed to introduce new industries, such as R&D (research and development), and cultural and creative industries, without changing the original land use or paying land price compensation or concession fees. After the transition period, the land-use procedure is confirmed and completed based on the new industries, with the approval of the municipal government. The Implementation Opinions also dictate that self-renewal projects in old factories on state-owned land allocate a minimum of 15% of the total land area to building urban infrastructure, public services, or other welfare facilities conforming to the regulatory plans, which will eventually be transferred to the government for utilization and management.

6.1.5 *Land banking and revenue distribution*

In order to coordinate regional development and avoid sporadic land development, Guangzhou's policies encourage property owners to transfer their land to the government for centralized land banking. The land appreciation revenue is shared equally (1:1) between the government and the property owners, and a bonus of 10% appreciation revenue is awarded to property owners if the land transfer for depositing was timely (Table 6.4).

6.1.6 *Land premium payment in comprehensive renewal of old factories*

In Guangzhou, there are two typical types of comprehensive renewal of old factories (industrial lands), depending on the land premium payment approach:[1]

(1) *Self-renewal of old factories.* There are a variety of regeneration directions for old factories (industrial lands), including industrial to industrial, industrial to commercial, industrial to new industries, etc., and the government stipulates the land premium payment requirements for each industrial classification and regeneration direction (Table 6.5).

Table 6.4 Compensation Standards for Land Expropriation of Old Factories by the Government

Districts	3 Perimeter Districts (Huadu, Conghua, Zengcheng)	8 Central Districts (Districts other than Huadu, Conghua, and Zengcheng)
Compensation standards for land regeneration from industrial to residential	60% benefits to property owners, for a planned gross floor area ratio under 2.0 (50% + 10% rewards)	50% benefits to property owners, for a planned gross floor area ratio under 2.0 (40% + 10% rewards)
Compensation standards for land regeneration from industrial to commercial	60% benefits to property owners, for a planned gross floor area ratio under 2.5 (50% + 10% rewards)	50% benefits to property owners, for a planned gross floor area ratio under 2.5 (40% + 10% rewards)
Compensation standards for land regeneration in other scenarios	One-time compensation, calculated as 40% of the market appraisal price with a gross floor area ratio of 2.0	

Sources: Urban Regeneration Bureau of Guangzhou, Brief Introduction to Guangzhou Major Urban Regeneration ("Three Olds") Policies (2018); Recommendation Conference on Guangdong Province "Three Olds" Regeneration Projects, 2018-06-28, Guangzhou.

Table 6.5 Land Premium Payment for Self-Renewal

Regeneration Direction	Land Price
Industrial to industrial	Entitled to exemption from land premium payment
Industrial to commercial	Land premium according to market appraisal price based on new land use
Industrial to new industries	Entitled to a 5-year transition period
Scientific to scientific, educational to educational, medical to medical, sport to sport	Land premium calculated as a specified proportion of the market appraisal price of offices in the corresponding lot
Others	Land premium calculated as 40% of the market appraisal price

Sources: Urban Regeneration Bureau of Guangzhou. Brief Introduction to Guangzhou Major Urban Regeneration ("Three Olds") Policies (2018); Recommendation Conference on Guangdong Province "Three Olds" Regeneration Projects, 2018-06-28, Guangzhou.

(2) *Combination of self-renewal with land expropriation of old factories.* The government, following relevant regulations, retakes certain land and compensates the property owners accordingly, while the property owners are allowed to regenerate the remaining land (not for commercial housing) spontaneously or transfer it on to others by negotiation. Integral planning and regeneration can apply if all the land belongs to one corporation or involves multiple old factory regenerations on state-owned land (with a total area not less than 120,000 m^2).

6.2 Spatial management and control measures in the urban regeneration of Shenzhen

6.2.1 Regeneration intensity guidance

Like Guangzhou, Shenzhen employs zoned control to comprehensively manage urban regeneration development intensity. The Shenzhen development intensity guidance zone map takes account of traffic conditions, road layout, land scale, and plot land-use types (Tables 6.6–6.10) to roughly calculate floor area baseline and upper limit ratios, ensuring the orderly administration of the development intensity of urban regeneration projects throughout the city.

In Shenzhen, the floor area of a plot consists of three parts, the baseline floor area, the transferred floor area, and the rewarded floor area[2]: ① the baseline floor area of a plot is the part based on the baseline floor area ratio designated by the intensity zoning, modified according to microscopic factors (such as adjacent roads, metro stations, land size, etc.); ② the transferred floor area of a plot is the part that is transferred from other plots whose development is constrained by specific conditions, including public interest restrictions such as historic or cultural conservation, green public spaces protection, etc.; and ③ the rewarded floor area is the part rewarded for achieving certain public welfare objectives, and it should be less than 30% of the baseline floor area.

Table 6.6 Basic Regulations on Intensity Zoning of Urban Construction Land

Intensity Zoning	Intensity Level 1 Zones	Intensity Level 2 Zones	Intensity Level 3 Zones	Intensity Level 4 Zones	Intensity Level 5 Zones
Development and Construction Characteristics	High-intensity development	Mid-to-high-intensity development	Middle-intensity development	Mid-to-low-intensity development	Low-intensity development

Sources: Planning and Land Resources Committee of Shenzhen, Notice on the Publicity of the Partial Revision Draft (Chapter 4, Intensity Zoning and Floor Area Ratio) of the Shenzhen Urban Planning Standards and Principles by the Planning and Land Resources Committee [EB/OL] (2017-11-29) [2018-10-22] http://www.szpl.gov.cn/xxgk/gggs/201711/t20171128_458484.html.

Table 6.7 Floor Area Ratio Guidance for Residential Land

Intensity Zoning	Intensity Level 1, 2, 3 Zones	Intensity Level 4 Zones	Intensity Level 5 Zones
Baseline Floor Area Ratio	3.2	2.5	1.5
Upper Limit of Floor Area Ratio	6.0	4.0	2.5

Sources: Planning and Land Resources Committee of Shenzhen, Notice on the Publicity of the Partial Revision Draft (Chapter 4, Intensity Zoning and Floor Area Ratio) of the Shenzhen Urban Planning Standards and Principles by the Planning and Land Resources Committee [EB/OL] (2017-11-29) [2018-10-22] http://www.szpl.gov.cn/xxgk/gggs/201711/t20171128_458484.html.

Table 6.8 Floor Area Ratio Guidance for Commercial and Services Land

Intensity Zoning	Intensity Level 1 Zones	Intensity Level 2 Zones	Intensity Level 3 Zones	Intensity Level 4 Zones	Intensity Level 5 Zones
Baseline Floor Area Ratio	5.4	4.5	4.0	2.5	2.0

Sources: Planning and Land Resources Committee of Shenzhen, Notice on the Publicity of the Partial Revision Draft (Chapter 4, Intensity Zoning and Floor Area Ratio) of the Shenzhen Urban Planning Standards and Principles by the Planning and Land Resources Committee [EB/OL] (2017-11-29) [2018-10-22] http://www.szpl.gov.cn/xxgk/gggs/201711/t20171128_458484.html.

Table 6.9 Floor Area Ratio Guidance for Industrial Land

Intensity Zoning	Intensity Level 1, 2, 3 Zones	Intensity Level 4 Zones	Intensity Level 5 Zones
Baseline Floor Area Ratio for New Industries	4.0	2.5	2.0
Baseline Floor Area Ratio for Common Industrial Land	3.5	2.0	1.5

Sources: Planning and Land Resources Committee of Shenzhen, Notice on the Publicity of the Partial Revision Draft (Chapter 4, Intensity Zoning and Floor Area Ratio) of the Shenzhen Urban Planning Standards and Principles by the Planning and Land Resources Committee [EB/OL] (2017-11-29) [2018-10-22] http://www.szpl.gov.cn/xxgk/gggs/201711/t20171128_458484.html.

Table 6.10 Floor Area Ratio Guidance for Logistics and Storage Land

Intensity Zoning	Intensity Level 1, 2, 3 Zones	Intensity Level 4 Zones	Intensity Level 5 Zones
Baseline Floor Area Ratio for Logistics Land	4.0	2.5	2.0
Baseline Floor Area Ratio for Warehousing and Storage Land	3.5	2.0	1.5

Source: Planning and Land Resources Committee of Shenzhen, Notice on the Publicity of the Partial Revision Draft (Chapter 4, Intensity Zoning and Floor Area Ratio) of the Shenzhen Urban Planning Standards and Principles by the Planning and Land Resources Committee [EB/OL] (2017-11-29) [2018-10-22] http://www.szpl.gov.cn/xxgk/gggs/201711/t20171128_458484.html.

Floor area limits can be lifted, to the overall advantage of the city, on the condition that the service capacity of various facilities, including public services, traffic facilities, and municipal facilities, is satisfied. The extent to which limits are lifted can be calculated in accordance with the regulations for various modification factors (Tables 6.11–6.12).

98 Spatial management and control of urban regeneration

Table 6.11 Floor Area Adjusted for Road Adjacency

Road Adjacency	Unilateral Road Adjacency	Bilateral Road Adjacency	Trilateral Road Adjacency	Peripheral Road Adjacency
Factor	0	+0.10	+0.20	+0.30

Sources: Planning and Land Resources Committee of Shenzhen, Notice on the Publicity of the Partial Revision Draft (Chapter 4 , Intensity Zoning and Floor Area Ratio) of the Shenzhen Urban Planning Standards and Principles by the Planning and Land Resources Committee [EB/OL] (2017-11-29) [2018-10-22] http://www.szpl.gov.cn/xxgk/gggs/201711/t20171128_458484.html.

Table 6.12 Floor Area Adjusted for Metro Stations

Metro Station Conditions	Distance to Station (m)	Type of Station	
		Multi-line Station	Single-line Station
Factor	0~200	+0.70	+0.50
	200~500	+0.50	+0.30

Sources: Planning and Land Resources Committee of Shenzhen, Notice on the Publicity of the Partial Revision Draft (Chapter 4, Intensity Zoning and Floor Area Ratio) of the Shenzhen Urban Planning Standards and Principles by the Planning and Land Resources Committee [EB/OL] (2017-11-29) [2018-10-22] http://www.szpl.gov.cn/xxgk/gggs/201711/t20171128_458484.html.

6.2.2 Regeneration method guidance

In order to address the structural problems of urban regeneration, such as market preferences for certain methods, locations, and functions, and the loss of industrial land, the Shenzhen 13th Five-Year Plan for Urban Regeneration provided location and method guidance for zoning of regeneration projects , classifying regeneration into demolition and reconstruction priority zones, comprehensive renovation priority zones, and parallel demolition and reconstruction and comprehensive renovation zones (Figure 6.2). The zoning applied citywide, restricting the spatial expansion of regeneration of the demolition and reconstruction type and hence avoiding problems such as the occupation of advantageous locations by profit-seeking regeneration, individual regeneration methods, and the market-led dominance of demolition and reconstruction.

Ensuring the economic vigor of the city requires Shenzhen to ensure the provision of industrial land and buildings, and to avoid the drastic decrease in industrial land during urban regeneration. Therefore, Shenzhen regulates the structure of its regeneration projects through planning, and prioritizes the increase of scale of industrial and related complementary buildings while reducing the scale of commercial and office buildings, so as to realize the overall objective of guaranteeing a supply of industrial building areas even when the industrial land scale is diminishing. Thus, under the Shenzhen Special Urban Regeneration Plan, industrial block control lines are designated within which the old industrial areas are strictly protected from regeneration that changes the land function from industrial to commercial or from industrial to residential. For regeneration projects

Spatial management and control of urban regeneration 99

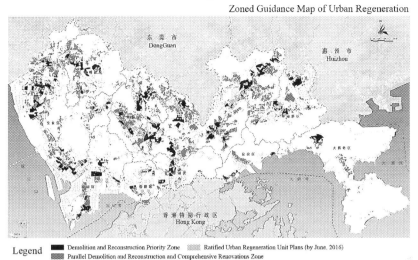

Figure 6.2 Zoned Guidance Map for Urban Regeneration in the Shenzhen 13th Five-Year Plan for Urban Regeneration.

Sources: Planning and Land Resources Committee of Shenzhen, Shenzhen 13th Five-Year Plan for Urban Regeneration[EB/OL] (2016-11-21) [2018-10-22] http://www.szpl.gov.cn/xxgk/ztzl/rdzt/csgx135/201611/t20161121_456427.html

located inside the industrial block control lines and intended for demolition and reconstruction, the land function after regeneration is in principle required to be industrial. A lower limit is set for industrial to industrial projects, which demand that "pure" industrial land should constitute no less than 50% of all regeneration areas in the next five years.

6.2.3 Construction guidance on policy-based housing and innovative industrial buildings

Shenzhen's urban regeneration policies imposed zone requirements on the construction of affordable housing, in order to improve people's living conditions and maintain peace and contentment. According to the Shenzhen Regulations on Complementary Construction of Affordable Housing in Urban Regeneration Projects, demolition and reconstruction projects involving housing after regeneration should complementarily construct a certain amount of affordable housing with reference to the ratio set for various zones: the ratios are 20%, 18%, and 15% for category I, II, and III zones respectively.[3] Increases or reductions of the ratio to satisfy the regulations apply during implementation to adjust for the situation on the ground. Demolition and reconstruction projects that contain commercial apartments and are located in category I, II, or III areas are required to transfer 20%, 18%, or 15% of the commercial apartments to the government as accommodation. This proportional provision of policy-based housing, along

Table 6.13 Complementary Construction Standards for Innovative Industries Buildings in Shenzhen High-tech Park

Subjects	Method of Development	Complementary Construction Ratio
High and new technology enterprises	Self-development	10%
Non-high-tech enterprises	Cooperative development with high-tech enterprises	12%
Non-high-tech enterprises	Self-development	25%

Sources: Planning and Land Resources Committee of Shenzhen, Regulations on the Complementary Construction of Innovative Industries Buildings in Shenzhen Urban Regeneration Projects [EB/OL]. (2016-10-18) [2018-10-22] http://www.sz.gov.cn/zfgb/2016/gb975/201610/t20161018_4994771.htm.

with market-led regeneration, not only increases the quantitative supply of policy-based housing, but also avoids certain location imbalances caused by the centralized development of affordable housing by the government in the past.

To promote the development of urban industries, the Shenzhen policies stipulate complementary construction requirements for innovative industrial buildings. In August 2016, the Planning and Land Resources Committee officially published the Regulations on the Complementary Construction of Innovative Industries Buildings in Shenzhen Urban Regeneration Projects, which required demolition and reconstruction regeneration projects that upgrade the building function into new industries to complementarily construct 12% of innovative industrial buildings. The regulations required that the complementarily constructed innovative industrial buildings should be centrally distributed and constructed by the project implementation actors in the process of regeneration. For regeneration projects located in the High and New Technology Industrial Park of the Shenzhen Special Economic Zone, independent requirements on complementary construction ratios were established in related policies (Table 6.13).

6.2.4 Public welfare land and public facilities

Complementing urban public services and improving the municipal infrastructure are among the important objectives of urban regeneration. There is an obvious shortage of public services and municipal infrastructure in Shenzhen, yet market-led urban regeneration is not motivated to improve old public goods or provide new public goods, and some regeneration projects even fail or evade the compulsory duty to complement public amenities. There is even a "fallacy of accumulation" that the planning scheme of a single regeneration project conforms to the specification requirements, but the sum of multiple projects may not. An example is the supply of educational facilities, where small-scale regeneration projects transforming old industrial areas into residential districts are unable to provide the land required for primary schools. The consequence of these

Spatial management and control of urban regeneration 101

accumulated breaches is that urban regeneration is unable to satisfy the ever-increasing demand for primary school places. Pertinent regulations are therefore published in Shenzhen in response to demands for public amenities and to protect the public interest. The policies require that a certain proportion of the land or space within the urban regeneration range has to be transferred freely to the government as "public welfare land" or "complementary public amenities" after the demolition and land sorting (Table 6.14). The area of the transferred public welfare land has to be greater than 3,000 m² and occupy no less than 15% of the total land area for demolition and reconstruction.

Table 6.14 Summary of Gratuitously Transferred Public Amenities

No.	Project Name	Size (m²) Building Area	Land Area	Land Price	Method of Transfer	Receiving Department
1	Community Police Stations	≥50	-	Free	Gratuitous	District Governments
2	Community Management Center	≥300	-	Free	Gratuitous	District Governments
3	Community Service Center	≥400	-	Free	Gratuitous	District Governments
4	Cultural Activities Center	8000~10000	-	Free	Gratuitous	District Governments
5	Cultural Activities Rooms	1000~2000	-	Free	Gratuitous	District Governments
6	Kindergarten	1600~5800	1800~6500	Free	Gratuitous	District Governments
7	Community Health Services Center	≥1000	-	Free	Gratuitous	District Governments
8	Community Elderly Daycare Center	≥750	-	Free	Gratuitous	District Governments
9	Small Waste Transfer Station	150~480	500~800	Free	Gratuitous	District Governments
10	Renewable Resources Recycling Station	60~100	-	Free	Gratuitous	District Governments
11	Public Toilets	60~120	90~170	Free	Gratuitous	District Governments
12	Accommodation for Sanitation Workers	7~20	20~30	Free	Gratuitous	District Governments

(Continued)

Table 6.14 (Continued)

No.	Project Name	Size (m²) Building Area	Land Area	Land Price	Method of Transfer	Receiving Department
13	Bus Stations and Depots	-	-	Free	Gratuitous	Municipal Transportation Committee or District Governments
14	Public vehicular rights of way	-	-	Free	Gratuitous	District Governments

Sources: Shenzhen Planning and Land Resources Committee, Provisional measures on strengthening and Improving the implementation of urban regeneration [EB/OL] (2017-01-05) [2018-10-22] http://www.szpl.gov.cn/xxgk/ztzl/rdzt/csgx_zxcs/201701/t20170105_456422.html.

The Shenzhen 13th Five-Year Plan for Urban Regeneration raised construction standards for the complementary public amenities in urban regeneration projects, and effectively increased public welfare projects. Services include public transport, public municipal facilities, medical and healthcare facilities, educational facilities, social welfare facilities, cultural and sporting facilities, green spaces, and public squares. For instance, the standard of public service amenities complementing the commercial apartments in Urban Renewal Units has been raised to meet the standards for housing in the Shenzhen regulations. After Urban Renewal Unit Plans have been approved, land for public amenities should be prioritized within the range of regeneration projects and included in the earliest phase of construction. Small-scale "industrial to residential" projects within a size range of 10,000-20,000 m² are strictly controlled, to relieve pressure on public services. In regions with weak capacity for support, renovation or construction of transport and municipal infrastructure are required to be prioritized.

6.2.5 Urban regeneration early warning and Key Urban Regeneration Units

Shenzhen has established a regeneration early warning system to strengthen the examination of regeneration projects based on big-data platforms; the urban regeneration early warning regions are delimited in what is called the "basic supporting ability evaluation map". The early warnings are identified based on the obvious disadvantages of urban regions, using basic information such as transport supply, municipal support, public amenity provision, and remaining development capacities. The early warnings provide important references for decision-making in the various urban regeneration approval procedures, such as choosing projects, designing preliminary conditions, determining the scales of renewal units, clarifying contributions, and completing public amenities.

The urban renewal of Shenzhen is mainly driven by the market. Problems in the implementation process include insufficient overall planning of the renewal areas and discrepancies between the renewal areas selected by the market and the key development areas prioritized by the government. The 2016 version of the Provisional Measures thus proposed regulations for Key Urban Regeneration Units, which are implemented top down with special policy supports. To solve the problem of the supply of affordable housing, some land use in Key Urban Regeneration Units may be changed from "industrial" to "affordable housing", if the original industrial land can be adapted for building affordable housing by revising the relevant land-use plan; meanwhile a proportion of commercial housing construction is also permitted by the government. This model partly solves the issue of industrial land redevelopment, while also motivating enterprises to participate in the construction and operation of affordable housing in collaboration with the government.

6.2.6 Land price charging and premium payment

Regulations on land price charging and premium payment are important policies for implementation of urban regeneration projects. Land price charging was regulated before 2016 by the Shenzhen Urban Regeneration Measures, and subsequently in the Notice of Provisional Measures for Strengthening and Improving the Implementation of Urban Regeneration, which includes details on the following.

6.2.6.1 Disposal of historically illegally used land[4]

For demolition and reconstruction projects, land to be disposed of can be transferred to the implementation body by negotiation for new development and construction, during which the land price will be charged at 110% of the baseline land price calculated according to the regenerated function and time limit of the land-use rights (10% is for the disposal of the historically illegally used land). For comprehensive renovation projects in old industrial areas, which increase the building area for production and business purposes, the land disposed of can be transferred to the successor agency by negotiation with a term of 30 years, and the building areas added can be registered in the name of the inheritor after the land price is paid, according to the 2016 Provisional Measures. In July 2018, the Disposal Measures of Historic Illegal Industrial and Public Amenity Buildings During the Urbanization of Rural Areas of Shenzhen (Draft for Comments) was published, Article 37 of which stipulates that historic illegal productive buildings, commercial buildings and office buildings can be registered as non-commercial properties once the relevant fine and the land premium have been paid.

6.2.6.2 Simplification of urban regeneration land price system[5]

In Shenzhen, the standard classifications of land prices are integrated, land price evaluation rules for urban regeneration projects are simplified, and a land price evaluation system based on the advertised baseline land prices is established. Provided the urban regeneration land price level remains relatively stable, the urban regeneration land price evaluation should be gradually integrated into the

104 Spatial management and control of urban regeneration

unified municipal land price evaluation system. Land prices in urban regeneration projects can be paid by installment and are interest free, with the first installment no less than 30% of the overall land price and the rest paid off within 1 year.

6.2.6.3 Land transfer by negotiation in old town and old village regeneration projects[6]

Under Article 62 of the Implementation Details, for old town and old village regeneration projects designated by the municipal government in the Opinions on the 70 Old Town and Old Village Regeneration Projects in Districts of Bao'an and Longgang (including projects like Xin'an Fanshen Industrial Area Regeneration), development and construction land defined in the Urban Renewal Unit Plans may be transferred to verified project implementers through negotiation after the payment of land prices.

6.3 Spatial management and control measures in the urban regeneration of Shanghai

6.3.1 Public elements list and life-cycle management

Shanghai implements life-cycle management of land for urban regeneration projects, imposing regulations on land use and construction requirements on regeneration in the form of a contract. The implementation of public elements defined by the Public Elements List in urban regeneration projects is ensured through contractual administration, with the required additional open spaces and public services defined in the land contracts. The Public Elements List for each Urban Regeneration Unit is determined in the regional assessment period to guide project implementation, including urban function, cultural character, ecology and environment, non-motorized traffic systems, complementary public service amenities, and public open spaces. There are two major aspects to the assessment: ①investigating the opinions of residents living in the range of regeneration units, which should reflect the problems that the residents most want to be resolved, clarify the issues that the regeneration implementation plans ought to focus on, and determine the degree of urgency for regeneration according to the lack of public amenities and public open spaces; and ②determining the control required over the public elements to be implemented in regeneration units, including the categories, sizes, forms, and distribution, with consideration of the construction criteria of the public elements and pertinent planning and land policies (Table 6.15).

6.3.2 Floor area ratio rewards and transfer

Shanghai implements incentive policies for urban regeneration projects facilitating public interest. In the implementation planning phase, projects capable of providing public amenities and public open spaces are eligible for additional building area, but generally not exceeding the upper limit set in the regulations

Table 6.15 Suggestions on Public Elements Lists

Content	Suggestions
Function	• Deciding whether current functions are aligned with the function development orientation, and proposing solutions and suggestions on improving the diversity and compositeness of functions
Public Amenities	• Determining the types, sizes, and spatial distribution of the community-level public amenities that should be added • Evaluating the improvement suggestions on neighborhood and block-level public amenities
Historic Character	• Compiling preservation requirements for historic and cultural character regions, cultural conservation units, outstanding historic buildings, and historic blocks • Proposing suggestions for improving urban cultural character and attractiveness
Ecology and Environment	• Determining whether environmental impact assessments are necessary, and deciding environmental problems pending solutions • Proposing suggestions on whether ecological construction is necessary
Slow Traffic System	• Proposing solutions to improve current non-motorized traffic systems, and creating guidelines for the construction of slow traffic pedestrian routes
Open Public Spaces	• Identifying problems, and proposing solutions with regard to the size, distribution, and pedestrian accessibility of current public spaces
Urban Infrastructure and Safety	• Identifying problems, and proposing solutions to improve the current infrastructure; resolving safety issues, including traffic service standards, road systems, public transport, municipal facilities, disaster prevention and refuge facilities, and accessibility design

Sources: Plan Formulation and Examination Center of Shanghai Municipality (2015), *Standards on Regulatory Planning Evaluation Reports and Urban Regeneration Area Assessment Reports*

(Table 6.16). The land award is reduced in proportion to the amount exceeding the upper limit (Table 6.17). Projects simultaneously providing public amenities and public open spaces are entitled to enjoy a combination of building area rewards. Inside a regeneration unit, the building areas can be transferred and compensated via floor area ratio transfer. For instance, in terms of regeneration projects conforming to requirements for preservation of their historic character,

Table 6.16 Upper Limits of Extra Floor Area for Commercial and Office Buildings

Scenarios	Providing Public Open Spaces (Area of land, m²)			Providing Public Facilities (Building Area, m²)	
	Independent land, the land property right is transferred to the government	Independent land, the land property right is not transferred to the government	Independent land, open for 24 hours a day, the property right is not transferred to the government (such as stilt building, public corridors, etc.)	Property right is transferred to the government	Property right is not transferred to the government
Multiplier	2.0	1.0	0.8	1.0	0.5

Notes: ① the above multipliers apply to areas within the outer ring road; those outside the outer ring road are awarded an extra multiplier of 0.8; and ② those providing underground public amenities are awarded an extra multiplier of 0.8. Sources: Municipal Government of Shanghai, Detailed Regulations on Urban Regeneration Implementation [EB/OL] (2015-05-27) [2018-10-22] http://www.shanghai.gov.cn/nw2/nw2314/nw2319/nw12344/u26aw42750.html

Table 6.17 Multiplier Discounting Factor when Exceeding the Requirements of Pertinent Regulations

	Part Exceeding Pertinent Regulations	Multiplier Discounting Factor
Public Open Spaces	Part ≤ 50%	0.8
	Part ≥ 50%	0
Public Facilities	Part ≤ 30%	0.5
	Part ≥ 30%	0

Sources: Municipal Government of Shanghai. Detailed Regulations on Urban Regeneration on Implementation [EB/OL] (2015-05-27) [2018-10-22] http://www.shanghai.gov.cn/nw2/nw2314/nw2319/nw12344/u26aw42750.html

newly identified historic buildings or structures can be exempt from the calculation of floor areas.

In summary, in order to protect the public interest and achieve public objectives, and to ensure the effectiveness of urban regenerations, various spatial management and control measures have been employed by Guangzhou, Shenzhen, and Shanghai. These measures have solved specific regeneration problems and difficulties faced by the cities, and broken the ice on some regeneration bottlenecks, providing learning and reference points for other cities and regions in China that have not yet embarked on similar work.

Notes

1 Urban Regeneration Bureau of Guangzhou, Brief Introduction to Major Urban Regeneration (Three Olds) Policies of Guangzhou (2018). Conference on Guangdong Province "Three Olds" Regeneration Projects, 2018-06-28, Guangzhou.
2 Planning and Land Resources Committee of Shenzhen, Notice on the Publicity of the Partial Revision Draft (Chapter IV, Intensity Zoning and Floor Area Ratio) of the Urban Planning Standards and Principles of Shenzhen by the Planning and Land Resources Committee [EB/OL] (2017-11-29) [2018-10-22] http://www.szpl.gov.cn/xxgk/gggs/201711/t20171128_458484.html
3 As stipulated in the Provisional Measures to Strengthen and Improve the Implementation of Urban Regeneration, the baseline complementary construction ratios of talent housing and affordable housing in categories I, II, and III zones are increased from 12%, 10%, and 8%, as stipulated in the Regulations on Complementary Construction of Affordable Housing in Shenzhen Urban Regeneration Projects, to 20%, 18%, and 15%.
4 Article 11, Point 4, 2016 version of Provisional Measures to Strengthen and Improve Implementation of Urban Regeneration.
5 Ibid., Article 15.
6 Ibid., Article 13.

7 Urban regeneration implementation paths in the three cities

Relatively clear implementation requirements for regeneration projects have been defined by the urban regeneration institutions in Guangzhou, Shenzhen, and Shanghai. Like Hong Kong and Taipei, all three cities used regional assessment or project application methods to determine their urban regeneration projects. Annual urban regeneration implementation plans are formulated and the projects proceed in an orderly fashion under procedural and substantive regulations.

7.1 Urban regeneration implementation paths in Guangzhou

7.1.1 Overall process based on urban regeneration annual plans

Urban regeneration annual planning is an effective method for the implementation of urban regeneration in Guangzhou. In 2016, Guangzhou formulated and implemented its first urban regeneration project and annual funding plan, which included deciding on the project name, administrative regions, regeneration range, subjects, and funding source and arrangement. The plan also provided the basis for the management of the year's urban regeneration activities. Through the formulation of annual plans, the urban regeneration of Guangzhou in 2016 was able to be carried out effectively to promote overall progression.

7.1.2 Practical exploration of different regeneration models

As a result of the transitions in urban regeneration policies, the urban regeneration of Guangzhou has undergone three different implementation phases since 2009. In 2009-2012, after the "three olds" renewal policies had been established, regeneration practices were mostly market-led single projects, and the subjects were predominantly urban villages and old factories being developed for real estate. In 2012-2015, the government took precedence over the market in leading urban regeneration, promoting comprehensive renewal and contiguous regeneration areas instead of single projects. The regeneration projects from this period were mostly old factories with an area of roughly 2-4 km^2, such as the regeneration of Financial City, Guanggang New City, Guangzhi Region, and Datansha Island. Since 2015, the establishment of the Urban Regeneration Bureau has enabled problems encountered in the earlier phases to be better addressed, for example, limited regeneration targets, short-term effectiveness, homogeneous methods, and comparatively single subjects and effects. In this phase Guangzhou innovated its regeneration methods, explored the micro-regeneration model, and emphasized multi-subject participation.

Urban regeneration implementation 109

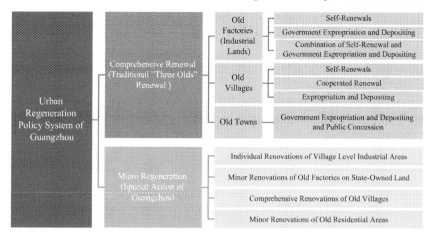

Figure 7.1 Major Models of Urban Regeneration in Guangzhou

Source: Luo, 2018. Practical Explorations of the Urban Regeneration of Guangzhou, in Conference of Interpretation on "Three Olds" Renewals Policies of Guangdong Province and Practices of Related Cities, July 20, 2018.

The comprehensive renewal and micro-regeneration currently practiced in Guangzhou reflect different implementation and operational paths for different scales, different intensities, and different subjects of urban regeneration (Figure 7.1). Through several phases of exploration, the urban regeneration of Guangzhou has shifted from urban growth to urban maturation, which focuses not only on land transfer revenues, but also on the functions and responsibilities borne by the land, as well as the long-term development of the city. The limits of action and the interaction and coordination between the government and the market need to be clearly defined in urban regeneration, in order to better exploit the enthusiasm of the market within appropriate limits (Table 7.1).

7.1.2.1 Comprehensive renewal

Comprehensive renewal in Guangzhou is implemented on the principle of government-led social participation. It is based on the macroscopic demands of urban and regional development, and emphasizes the optimization of urban structures and fulfillment of urban strategies. According to the 2017 Project and Financial Plan of Urban Regeneration of Guangzhou, there are main five types of comprehensive renewal project: old town renewal, old village renewal, self-renewal of old factories, village-level industrial area renewal, and land preparation. Multiple operational and implementation models have been explored in Guangzhou, as exemplified by the comprehensive renewal of urban villages. For example, after village-wide renewal following the "resettlement before demolitions, and rolling development" model, the Hengsha urban village, located in the commercial area of the Huangpu District, realized local development complemented by some degree of educational and medical infrastructure, which also allowed the original

110 Urban regeneration implementation

Table 7.1 Complementary Interaction between the Government and the Market in the Urban Regeneration of Guangzhou

Subject	Government	Market
Governance Framework	Pertinent legislation and policy regulations	Under government regulations, pursuit of economic benefits
Responsibilities	Formulation of rules, procedures and planning, and supervision of implementation	Investment, implementation, and operation
Principal Regeneration Subjects	Key regeneration regions	Sporadic and inefficient plots
Regeneration Models	Consecutive coordination and integration, comprehensive renovations	Individual projects and single plots
Regeneration Objectives	Comprehensive optimization of urban spatial structures and function configurations	Multiple win–win: Development profit, industrial upgrading, innovation nurturing, and market Activation

Sources: Building Alliance, The "Micro Regeneration" Model of Urban Regeneration of Guangzhou [EB/OL] (2017-11-27) [2018-10-22] https://www.sohu.com/a/207071699_188910.

property owners to exchange their living areas for shops to solve the income problems of the residents. Another example is the influential case of Liede Village. Liede Village used to be one of the poorest urban villages in the Tianhe District of Guangzhou, but its economic development was realized through the village-wide renewal guided by the government, which was implemented via the "selling land to raise money, one replenishment for one demolition" model. In this procedure, an enterprise collectively owned by the villagers was established, the market players were introduced, and the "nail household" problem was resolved through legal procedures. Thus, development of the village's collective economy, redevelopment of the village area, and improvement of the living environment have in general been achieved.

7.1.2.2 Micro-regeneration

Unlike comprehensive renewal, micro-regeneration features smaller-scale projects aimed at improving details of the living environment and achieving rapid implementation. Micro-regeneration applies to the regeneration of old towns, old villages, or old industrial lands, supported by supplementary policies including the Implementation Plans of the Micro Renovation of Old Residential Areas of Guangzhou, the Working Guidance of the Comprehensive Renovations of Urban Villages of Guangzhou and the Implementation Plan and Technical Guidance of the Remediation of "Three Wires" in the Minor Renovations of Old Residential Areas in Guangzhou (Trial). The micro-regeneration of Guangzhou follows the principle of "government induction and social dominance", and emphasizes stimulating urban vitality, improving the living environment, and protecting urban cultural heritage, with diverse implementation paths available for different projects. In 2016, 38 micro-regeneration projects were planned in Guangzhou. The number increased to 97 in 2017 and 828 in 2018, implementing a transition from "dot" projects to "dot-line-plane" interactive projects.[1] The environmental quality of numerous old residential areas in Guangzhou has been substantially improved through minor renovations, and at the end of 2017, Guangzhou was selected by the Ministry of Housing and Urban-Rural Development as one of the 15 trial cities in China, and the only first-tier city, for old residential area renovation. This program is epitomized by the "construction management committee" instituted in the Liwan District,[2] where community representatives established a committee and organized minor renovations of their environment through "resident self-governance". This made implementation easier and reduced the cost of minor renovations, while encouraging residents to begin self-governance and remediating the deficiencies of the asset management of old urban areas. Another example is the "resident consultancy committee" established in the Yangzhong Community of Yuexiu District. The committee, composed of residents' representatives, community enthusiasts, building group directors and community party members, participated in the publicity and opinion survey processes and promoted the "three wires" (electricity, communications, and cable television) and "three pipes" (water supply, gas, and drainage) improvements in the renovations of old residential areas. Yangzhong Community also established a quasi-asset management model for the community and formulated the Working Standards of Minor Renovations of the Yangzhong Community, Zhuguang Street of Yuexiu District, Guangzhou. Minor renovation practices that explored distinctive regeneration implementation paths rich in local characteristics include: the arcade-house renovations of No.225 Beijing Road by "arcade-house activation and implantation of cultural and innovation industries"; the *shifangzi* reading space renovation plan (renovating a reading space for children from poor families) featuring "caring for vulnerable groups, and operation by crowdfunding"; and the transformation of the Guangzhou Textile Machinery Factory into the T.I.T. International Fashion Center through "government platform building and enterprise-commercial cooperation".

7.1.3 Typical urban regeneration cases in Guangzhou

7.1.3.1 Liede Village renewal: comprehensive renewal of urban village guided by the government

Liede Village is located in the golden region of the planned Pearl River New City, the central business district of Guangzhou, and is the first comprehensive renewal project of an urban village in Guangzhou. Due to its importance for constructing a positive urban image for the Asian Games held in Guangzhou, the renewal of Liede Village has brought tremendous morphology changes through demolition and reconstruction since work began in 2007. The region was transformed from a multi-floor rural village to a modern urban functional area full of high-rise buildings. The comprehensive influence of the renewal of Liede Village is reflected in multiple aspects, including the organizational mechanism, renewal methods, fund-raising, and working concept. Although the renewal model of Liede Village was criticized for the "growth machine" formed by the government, the village collective and the market, as well as for the pursuit of economic benefit through high-intensity development, its implementation path served as an important reference for later urban village renewals in Guangzhou.

The organizational mechanism for the Liede Village renewal was "municipal/district government-led + village as implementor + introduction of market funds through land auctions", with trilateral coordination and division of work between city–district–village (Table 7.2). The government incentivized the village collective and the villagers by looking after the integral interests of the community. The corporation established by the village, Liede Economic Development Limited Corporation, was responsible for demolition, resettlement, applications for approval, project bidding, and delivery of resettlement compensation, which markedly reduced dissent from the villagers. To comply with the fund-raising requirements of Guangzhou at that time of "no direct investment from the government[3] and the village collective, and no direct involvement of real-estate developers", the renewal of Liede Village was implemented with a tripartite land-use model which divided the land into three parts: one for villager resettlement, one for commercial development, and one reserved for village collective economy development. The auction of the commercial part of the land realized land transfer fees[4] from the developers for Liede Village, revitalizing the village's land assets. The combination of the preparations for the Asian Games and the multilateral profit concession in the regeneration process resulted in a win–win scenario

Table 7.2 City-District-Village Collective Organizational Structure

Subject	Responsibilities
Municipal Government	Guiding urban village renewal, determining overall requirements, and providing policy support
District Government	Coordinating, organizing and guiding the formulation of urban village renewal plan; coordinating and solving the various problems encountered in the urban village renewal
Village Collective	Implementing the urban village renewal; responsible for land investigation and propriety confirmation, and organizing activities including land expropriation, demolition, compensation, and resettlement; and implementing the urban village renewal in accordance with fundamental construction procedures and requirements

Compiled from relevant sources: Wu, Z., Zhou, S. (2005), Solutions to the Renovation of Urban Village: Balancing the Interests among the Municipal Management, Urban Development, and Inhabitants – a Case Study of Wenchong Community in Guangzhou. *Urban Studies*, 2:48–53; Wu, Z., Fu, X. (2008), References for the Urban Regeneration in China from the Renewal Mode of Urban-Village of Liede, Guangzhou. Annual Urban Planning Conference of China, Dalian.

for the government, the village collective, the villagers, and the real-estate developers alike, guaranteeing the smooth progression of the renewal. Villagers were also compensated in respect of illegal constructions, and the final floor area ratio after renewal reached 5.0, much higher than the standard proposed earlier, which was below 4.0. The measures adopted by Liede Village to improve environmental quality and landscape were: land auction acquisitions were entirely devoted to urban village renewal; the government waived the taxes on renewal project on the principles of "demolish one, exempt one"; the construction of municipal roads and river renovation funded by the government were implemented concurrently with the renewal of Liede Village; and the renewal project was incorporated into the city's key projects and "green channel".

7.1.3.2 Enning Road regeneration: a historic street going from mass demolition to micro-regeneration

The first micro-regeneration project, which epitomizes the micro-regeneration of historic and cultural streets and neighborhoods in Guangzhou, is the renovation of Enning Road old town. Enning Road is located at the heart of the Xiguan old town, and is the longest and the most complete arcade building street, dubbed the "most beautiful old street of Guangzhou". The Enning Road old town regeneration project originally planned for complete demolition and the reconstruction of skyscrapers, but between 2006 to 2013, following widespread exposure in the media and opposition from residents, the direction of regeneration was diverted from the original redevelopment aim to preserve valuable buildings and spatial patterns. Tension culminated in the "Enning Road incident", in which the public questioned the opaqueness of the Enning Road renewal planning, claiming it was a violation of the public's right to know. The planned floor area ratio of the region was lowered to 1.2 from the previously determined 2.6–2.8, effectively increasing public participation in the urban regeneration of Guangzhou.

The Enning Road renewal plan began in February 2006, when the Liwan District government proposed using the redevelopment of consecutive decrepit buildings on Enning Road as a trial for old town regeneration, extending the renewal range to the neighborhood north of Enning Road, west of Baohua Road and south of Duobao Road. In May 2007, the extent of the proposed demolition was disclosed for the first time by the Liwan government, triggering media coverage of Enning Road. In 2008, the Guangzhou Planning Bureau reviewed and passed the Plan of Historic Building Conservation and Utilization in the Enning Road Decrepit Building Regeneration Region, which further explicated the demolition targets. Residents wrote to the National People's Congress accusing the demolition of violating the Property Law. The struggles of the residents and the media coverage of the Enning Road renewal project attracted more attention, and non-governmental student organizations began to investigate, organizing various activities to attract even more attention for the future of Enning Road. The government established an expert consultancy group for the project, and eventually settled on the conservation of the historic and traditional appearance of the area as the basic objective of the renovation, instead of the previous regeneration mindset that had prioritized economic gain. The function of Enning Road was thus reconsidered, changing from the previously planned residential neighborhood to a boutique cultural community combined with commercial functions. In 2011, the Enning Road Old Town Regeneration Plan and the Revised Guidelines for the Regulatory Plan of the Enning Road Old Town Renovation Plots were approved, permitting residents to initiate "spontaneous regeneration". As the project progressed, the residents, media, non-governmental organizations, and experts all became involved, collectively forming an interest group that greatly influenced the direction of the project and protected residents' rights. It not only promoted public participation and caused more citizens to recognize the value of history and culture, but also prompted the alteration of the official planning ideology.

The renovation and revitalization of the Yongqing area, as a miniature of the old town renovation at Enning Road, explored the "government leadership, enterprise implementation, public participation" model, and served as a trial of micro-regeneration theories. In 2015, led by the Urban Regeneration Bureau of Yuexiu District, the renovation of the Yongqing area of Enning Road was initiated and implemented by the Guangzhou/ Vanke cooperation. Major and minor renovation measures included:[5] ① repairs and improvements to primary renovation methods; ② comprehensive renovation was set as the objective and the continuation of historic links was emphasized, with 60 buildings evaluated and proposed for "restoration", "façade renovation", "restructuring", "demolition and reconstruction", or "construction anew"; ③ social participation was emphasized, and the functions of the area enriched – in addition to the long-let apartments, joint offices, and infant education devised by Vanke, other ideas were also conceived according to local realities and social resources, including designer-brand stores, old town workshops, Xiguan experience hostels, and cultural exchange activities. According to the *Evaluation Research on the Implementation of the Micro Regeneration of Yongqing Area of Enning Road in Guangzhou*, published by the Urban Regeneration Expertise Committee of the Urban Sciences Society in 2017, the Yongqing area was opened in October 2016 after renovation, encompassing the four major functions of shared offices, education camps, long-let apartments, and complementary commerce, with a total investment of 65 million RMB and a building area of 7,000 m². Forty-nine rooms were reutilized and 12 original households were preserved. The renovation created obvious environmental and economic improvements, while the main regret was that there was not much public participation, with some renovations restricting the rights of original residents. In October 2018, president Xi Jinping visited the Yongqing area during his inspection of Guangzhou, and celebrated the regeneration practice with its emphasis on the preservation of history and culture, highlighting local characteristics and the use of the "embroidering" approach to micro-regeneration, while also stating that the inheritance of urban civilization and the continuation of historical roots are vital, that tradition and modernity should develop in synchrony and that cities should be implanted with memories.

7.1.3.3 Tangxia Village: from old factory in urban village to long-let apartments

There has been a gradual rise in the prevalence of long-let apartments in China in recent years, providing youngsters with quality rented spaces and unified community services through renovation of existing buildings. In the renovation of six factories in the Tangxia Village of Guangzhou, Vanke transformed the original factory buildings into the largest set of long-let apartments in Guangzhou, with approximately 600 sets of rooms and an occupancy rate of 95%,[6] a change from the customary urban village practice of demolition and reconstruction. The design of the apartments employed the strategy of "combining old with new", i.e., introducing functional transformation and adding a few new elements to form a new building that has a mixture of old and new components. The street frontage part of the southernmost building was leased as shops; the ground floors of the main buildings were transformed into public spaces to serve as advice centers, coffee shops, fitness studios, audio-visual facilities and conference services for young people; the living spaces are box-shaped with concrete frames, measuring 5.1×2.5×4.5m; and the ground floors of the residential buildings contain communal areas, equipped with compact kitchen, bathroom, storage and laundry airing facilities. Well-known Chinese real-estate enterprises, including Vanke,[7] Longfor, Country Garden, Cifi, and Kangqiao, have recently conducted innovative explorations in Guangzhou and Shenzhen, transforming urban villages or old housing into long-term leasing apartments, altering the previous model of demolition and reconstruction in urban village renovations, following the policy direction of promoting the development of the lettings market, and attracting widespread social attention. However, these market-reliant renovations have inevitably led to a rise in rents, and low-income groups unable to keep up with the rents were forced to leave. This implicit "gentrification" also sparked new social concerns and reflections.

7.1.3.4 Institutions and open activities: design competition and community planner system for minor renovations

To attract planners, architects, artists, and citizens to participate, and to accelerate the minor renovations of old residential areas of Guangzhou, a design and planning competition for old residential area minor renovations was held in 2017. Five old residential areas were chosen and designs invited from the public. 33 designs were submitted, which received roughly 2,200 residential votes and over 220,000 online votes, diversifying the implementation paths of old residential area regeneration. As a result of this experience, Guangzhou later organized a second old residential area renovation planning and design competition.

In 2018, Guangzhou began to promote the community planner institution. Community planners, as a pivot between the government and residents, serve the more than 160 sub-districts and towns of Guangzhou. As of April 15, 2018, more than 180 planners and enthusiastic residents had applied to become community planners. The first micro-regeneration project in Guangzhou with the introduction of community planner is the minor renovation of Zhusigang Neighborhood, Nonglin Street. After becoming a community planner, Ye Min, architect and director of Guangzhou Fei Arthouse, invited the modern artist Song Dong to work together on a public space design to change the thick wall between the wet market and Fei Arthouse into a transparent new wall made of leftover wooden window panes from demolished houses.[8] After the completion of renovation, activities routinely held at the site of this "borderless wall" site included film shows, drama performances, and calligraphers writing couplets for residents in the Spring Festival, making it an attractive tourist destination.

7.2 Urban regeneration implementation path in Shenzhen

7.2.1 Overall process based on Urban Renewal Unit Annual Plans

The Urban Renewal Unit Annual Plans are effective tools for the implementation of urban regeneration in Shenzhen, determining the chronology and requirements of the implementation of renewal unit projects. Shenzhen requires areas for demolition and reconstruction to be delimited as Urban Renewal Units which should be included in the Urban Renewal Unit Annual Plans for implementation. The published content of the Urban Renewal Unit Annual Plan comprises mainly sub-district and unit names, declaration subjects and the land area planned for demolition and reconstruction. For each Unit included in the Annual Plan, a supplementary graph facilitates management. Since the "district empowerment, power concession" reform of 2017, the formulation of Urban Renewal Unit Annual Plans has become the responsibility of the districts (Table 7.3).

7.2.2 Periodic adjustment and optimization of urban regeneration policies

Shenzhen periodically adjusts and optimizes its urban regeneration policies with the publication of Provisional Measures for Strengthening and Improving the Implementation of Urban Regenerations, which on one hand maintains the stability of the core policy, the Shenzhen Urban Regeneration Measures, and on the other hand enables timely corrections or supplements to the regeneration regulations, adjusted to take account of changes and demands of the market and society. As of 2016, a total of three versions of the Provisional Measures had been issued by the municipal government, summarizing experiences and improvements to the urban regeneration practices of recent years (Table 7.4), and acting as important policy indemnities for deepening the implementation of the "district empowering, power concession" administrative reform and ensuring the improved quality of urban regeneration.

Following the cycle of national socio-economic five-year plans, Shenzhen has been actively publishing reports on the implementation status of urban regeneration in Shenzhen, and periodically summarizes the basic status, innovative practices, practical effects, and current problems of urban regeneration practice. For

Table 7.3 Urban Renewal Unit Annual Plan of Longgang District in 2018 (Third Batch)

Sub-district	Unit Name	Subject of Declaration	Planned Area of Demolition and Reconstruction	Notes
Bantian	Urban Renewal Unit of Fuhao Villa Old Residential Area	Office of Bantian Sub-district, Longgang District, Shenzhen	19228.6 m^2	① Planned direction of renewal commercial and residential; ② No less than 6,730 m^2 of public-interest land should be implemented within the planned range of demolition and reconstruction
Henggang	Xianhe Village Renewal Unit in Silian Community	Shenzhen Henggang Silian Joint Corporation Limited	122259.1 m^2	① Planned direction of renewal commercial and residential ② No less than 42,791 m^2 of public-interest land should be implemented within the planned range of demolition and reconstruction
Baolong	Urban Renewal Unit of Longdong Shitang Region	Shenzhen Longdong Joint Corporation Limited	64003.2 m^2	① Planned direction of renewal commercial and residential ② No less than 22,401 m^2 of public-interest land should be implemented within the planned range of demolition and reconstruction

Sources: Urban Regeneration Bureau of Longgang District, Shenzhen, Notice on Third Batch Plan of the 2018 Longgang District Urban Renewal Unit Plan [EB/OL]. (2018-04-18) [2018-10-22] http://www.lg.gov.cn/bmzz/csgxj/xxgk/qt/tzgg/201804/t20180418_12094268.htm.

example, in April 2018, Shenzhen published the Report on the Status of Urban Regeneration in Shenzhen, which sets out the keys to deepening urban regeneration: ① promoting contiguous area development (abolition of small-plot Urban Renewal Units, promoting contiguous industrial area renewal, and facilitating the implementation of key regeneration units); ② intensifying comprehensive renovations; ③ strictly adhering to the public bidding method of selecting cooperating enterprises for urban village renewal projects; ④ establishing enforcement institutions through legislation to solve demolition and resettlement problems; and ⑤ further regulating urban regeneration affairs.

Table 7.4 Comparison Between the 2012, 2014, and 2016 Versions of the Provisional Measures in Shenzhen

Policy	Background	Main Contents
2012 Version of Provisional Measures	Fulfillment of the 12th five-year urban regeneration objectives	① Accelerate the disposal of historic illegal land for urban regeneration ② Complete urban regeneration land price policies ③ Strengthen urban regeneration implementation management
2014 Version of Provisional Measures	Further strengthens and improves the implementation of urban regeneration	① Accelerate the disposal of historic illegal land for urban regeneration; ② Complete urban regeneration land price policies; ③ Encourage the upgrading and renovation of old industrial areas; ④ Trial small-plot urban renewal; ⑤ Strengthen urban regeneration implementation management
2016 Version of Provisional Measures	Fulfillment of the 13th five-year urban regeneration objectives	① Innovate implementation institutions, and trial the development of key regeneration units; ② Simplify urban regeneration land price policies; ③ Improve the construction intensity of complementary public amenities; ④ Extend measures for the construction of affordable housing through multiple channels

Compiled from relevant sources: Provisional Measures for Strengthening and Improving the Implementation of Urban Regeneration (Shenzhen Government Office [2012] No. 45), Provisional Measures for Strengthening and Improving the Implementation of Urban Regeneration (Shenzhen Government Office [2014] No. 8), Provisional Measures for Strengthening and Improving the Implementation of Urban Regeneration (Shenzhen Government Office [2016] No. 38).

7.2.3 Practical exploration of different regeneration models

Shenzhen flexibly employs different models of urban regeneration to realize effective project advancement and ensure multilateral success in various regions (Table 7.5). Examples include: 1) upgrading urban villages and old factory buildings through "demolition and reconstruction" to complete regional functions, improving quality of living environment, and increasing urban infrastructure supply; 2) performing structural adjustments to old villages and old industrial areas through change of use to satisfy the functional demands of urban development; and 3) improving and reusing old towns, old factories and ancient buildings through "comprehensive renovation" to activate unutilized resources.

Table 7.5 Typical Examples of Different Urban Regenerations in Shenzhen

District	Project	Type of Regeneration	Characteristics	Before Regeneration	After Regeneration
Futian District	Gangxia Heyuan Region	Urban Village	The only urban village in central area of Futian; completing the functional and spatial structure of the central area	① Disorderly and dense buildings; ② Poor living conditions; ③ Insufficient complementary infrastructure; ④ Hindering the development of central urban regions	① Consummating the functional and spatial structures of the central area, with the construction of CBD complementary area and comprehensive development regions; ② Introduction of educational and medical infrastructure; ③ Improving living conditions
	Seg Hitachi	Old Industrial Area (Industrial to Industrial)	Upgrade existing high energy consumption, high pollution industries to headquarter industries	① Original industry in decline, factory production halted, with industrial upgrading pressure; ② High pollution, high energy consumption industries	① Constructing a headquarters base for listed manufacturing companies, and establishing headquarters economies (innovative industries housing, commercial services amenities, and high-grade commercial apartments); ② Improving the surrounding traffic environment
Luohu District	Caiwuwei Village	Urban Village	Five-way win in urban regeneration, with the establishment of core financial district	① Located in the central financial district of Caiwuwei, hindering regional development; ② Poor living conditions	① Five-way win for enterprises, the public, the collective, villagers, and the government ② Realization of regional development and increase in residential incomes
	Kingway Brewery Factory	Old Industrial Area	Combination of industrial upgrading and preservation of industrial remains	Brewery acquired, and the factory left for renovation	① Largest gold-and jewelry-themed urban complex in Shenzhen; ② Preservation of remains of old industrial area, and establishment of industrial heritage district

(Continued)

Table 7.5 (Continued)

District	Project	Type of Regeneration	Characteristics	Before Regeneration	After Regeneration
Longgang District	Days AnYun valley	Old Industrial Area, Urban Village	Construction of special economic zone integration, demonstration project for industrial upgrading, fulfillment of innovative industry housing (70,000 m²)	① Industrial area for low-end manufacturing, comprising farm housing and old factories ② Mostly traditional labor-intensive industries, including metalwork and plastics	① "New bird for old cage", with industrial upgrading completed and smart industrial zone established ② Completed infrastructure, large quantities of public amenity land transferred
	Xipu New Residence	Old Village	Activation and Exploitation of Antique Buildings (Comprehensive Renovation)	① Hakka enclosed houses; ② Buildings in urgent need of protection and repair	① Property rights of land and houses in Xipu New Residence remained unchanged after regeneration; ② Served as the branch venue for Shenzhen biannual exhibitions
Nanshan District	Dachong Village	Urban Village	The largest-scale urban village renewal project in current Shenzhen	① Dense buildings; ② Poor living conditions; ③ Fragile infrastructure; ④ Surrounded by high-tech park, with a fortunate location but hindering regional development	① Development of commercial and services sectors to support the high-tech park ② Improved living conditions; ③ Improved infrastructure (affordable housing, educational and medical facilities); ④ Regional development; ⑤ Residents resettled, with preserved ancestral halls, temples, and old banyans, combining cultural heritage preservation with urban construction

Dapeng New District	Honghua Dyeing Factory	Old Industrial Area	Activation of abandoned industrial area, transformation into cultural innovation and international art and tourism district (comprehensive renovation)	19 long-abandoned factory buildings and dormitories of Honghua Dyeing Factory	Elevation of the original industrial area into cultural innovation and international art tourism destination through comprehensive renovation
	Jiaochangwei	Old Village	Composite urban regeneration, effective guidance on spontaneously formed homestay tourism industry	① Shortage of living facilities; ② Hidden perils of water supply and drainage, and fire protection	① Followed the ideas of "preservation first", and "preservation along with regeneration"; ② Followed the "natural growth, government induction, non-government organization, and market operation" models; ③ Comprehensive renovation of water and electricity services, traffic, environment, and views in the region

Sources: Compiled from relevant sources by the author.

7.2.4 Typical cases of urban regeneration in Shenzhen

7.2.4.1 Urban Renewal Unit Planning of Yangmei New Village: demolition and reconstruction[9]

The Urban Regeneration Unit of Yangmei New Village is classified as the "demolition and reconstruction" type of regeneration from village to residential. It was listed in the second batch of Urban Regeneration Unit plans in 2014 and the fourth batch in 2018. In October 2014, the project initiator, Shenzhen Hongtai Industries Limited, instructed Shenzhen Urban Planning and Design Research Institute to formulate a plan for the regeneration unit, but the outcome was rejected after submission to the Urban Regeneration Bureau in April 2016. The main reasons were first, that a feasibility report from the traffic department was required, since the area was involved in railway and subway planning, and second, that the plan was in conflict with the approved statutory plan with which it was required to comply. The planner submitted a revised plan to the Urban Regeneration Bureau, after acquiring official responses from the metro and railway departments and strengthening the connection with the statutory plans. Throughout the project planning process, comprehensive calculations of the "land" and "buildings" development areas, and the spatial layout of buildings are key to project planning. Meanwhile the two thematic research areas, function plan and urban design, were conducted in parallel.

The existing land use of the Urban Renewal Unit is mostly urban villages (R4), with some residential land (R2) and commercial land (C1). The planning first determined the area of land available for construction and the area of public-interest land required to be freely transferred to the government under the urban regeneration land disposal policies (Table 7.6). After calculation and verification,

Table 7.6 Calculation of Land Available for Redevelopment in Yangmei New Village

No.	Item			Area (m^2)
1	Land area for demolition			36,197.0
	of which…	Land with clear ownership		22,604.4
		Land without expropriation or transferring records		13,952.5
		of which …	About 20% would be included in government land deposit	2,790.5
			About 80% could be transferred to the receiver for urban renewal	11,162.0
2	Land with complete legal documents			33,766.4
	of which …	No less than 15% for land devotion		5,065.0
		85% for redevelopment and construction		28,701.4
3	Sporadic land			3,000.0
4	Land for redevelopment and construction			31,701.4

Source: Shenzhen Urban Planning and Design Research Institute Corporation Limited (2016), Urban Renewal Unit Plan of Yangmei New Village, Yantian District.

Urban regeneration implementation 123

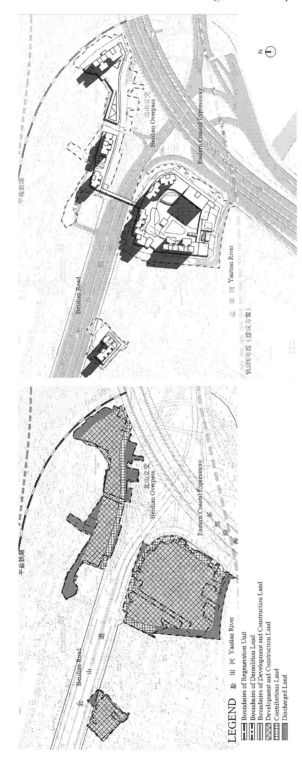

Figure 7.2 Land Range (left) and Construction Plan (right) of Yangmei New Village Urban Renewal Unit Plan, Yantian District
Source: Shenzhen Urban Planning and Design Research Institute Corporation Limited (2016), Urban Renewal Unit Plan of Yangmei New Village, Yantian District.

the total area of the renewal unit was determined as 50,000 m², of which 36,000 m² was designated for demolition and 32,000 m² for construction, with a transfer rate of public land of 21.7%.

According to local calculation, the baseline building area was 136,000 m², with a baseline floor area ratio of 4.25. Taking the affordable housing, public amenity and public open space areas into account, as well as the rule that the rewarded area should not exceed 30% of the baseline building area, the rewarded development area was calculated to be approximately 40,000 m². The development floor area ratio (FAR) of the regeneration unit should be 5.51, yet the final development area is set at 220,000 m² with a floor area ratio of 6.87, because it would be hard to attain an economic balance with a development FAR of 5.51 in view of the large volume of buildings. The progression of the planning saw endless conflicts in which the interests of the government, developers and planners had to be balanced, on the subjects of planning preconditions, breaching or bridging of the statutory plan, and definition of the final development volume and floor area ratio of the buildings (Figure 7.2).

7.2.4.2 *"Mountain City" iD Town: from abandoned factories to international art community*

In 2003, Honghua Dyeing closed down, and the factories were left abandoned. In 2013, Shenzhen selected eight old industrial areas as first trials for comprehensive renovations, including the Honghua Dyeing factories, with a planned area of 7.9 hectares. The project revitalized the old industrial area while preserving historic traits through comprehensive environmental improvements and renovation, and the completion of complementary public amenities. The renovated Mountain City iD Town contains two major functional modules, the innovative offices area and the self-operated complementary area. Industrial upgrading and environmental improvement of the inventory land were achieved through a combination of innovative cultural industry and tourism, by integrating innovative design, international art communication, workshops, education and training, fashion publishing, and tourism. The planning and design followed the principle of "urban regeneration and industrial upgrading on the condition of little to no demolition", and the original factory buildings of Honghua Dyeing were retained, with new functions introduced through spatial renovation. Examples include the Manjinghua Art Gallery, which used to be the Honghua Dyeing packaging workshop, and the iD Town Youth Hostel, developed using the internal space and external façades of the original staff dormitory.

7.2.4.3 *Futian Shuiwei LM Youth Community: reusing "handshake buildings" in urban village as affordable housing for talent community*

The LM Youth Community in Shuiwei, Futian is the first affordable housing for talent in an urban village. Since the reform and opening up, many urban villages surrounded by modern urban spaces have been formed in Shenzhen.[10] Despite the hygiene, safety, and social issues, these urban villages have provided cheap living spaces for low-income earners and entrepreneurs. Currently, the rapidly soaring cost of living and accommodation has caused a large amount of industrial talent to be drained from Shenzhen, leading the city to establish an affordable housing system for talent as a counter measure. However, with limited land resources and the difficulty of renewing old areas, it is hard to provide enough affordable housing in the central area. Thus, the exploitation of urban villages and refurbishment of "handshake buildings" into affordable housing communities for talent became a new direction for exploration.

The LM Youth Community was upgraded and renovated following the public–private partnership model:[11] the Housing and Urban-Rural Development Bureau of Futian led the effort, and Shum Yip Group as the implementer of the project rented the village buildings from Shuiwei Limited, established by the village collective, and then formulated the renovation plan for the buildings based on the requirements of youth talent. The buildings were leased to the Futian government as affordable housing after renovations were completed. The total renovation land area was around 8,000 m^2.29 village buildings yielded 504 apartments for talent, with 18 unit types varying from 15 m^2 to 55 m^2,[12] amounting to a total building area of 15,472 m^2. The project not only synchronously upgraded the internal and external environments of the buildings and preserved the original texture of the urban village, but also innovatively added elevators and corridors to forge a modern living community suitable for young talent. The apartments also have various open spaces designed to cater to the living preferences of different types of young people, including community kitchens, community cafeterias, reading rooms, drawing rooms, gyms and patio courtyards, as well as full exploitation of the "fifth façade", the roof, where relaxation areas and functional spaces are set up, including rooftop gardens, laundry rooms, vegetable gardens, and leisure gardens.

7.2.4.4 "Small and Smart Design" urban micro-regeneration competition

Borrowing experience of organizing urban design competitions from Hong Kong, Guangzhou, and Shanghai, the Shenzhen Urban Design Promotion Center organized a succession of urban design competitions called "Small and Smart Design" in Nantoucheng Community of Nanshan District, Lixin Community of Luohu District, Xinxiu Community of Luohu District, and Longling Community of Longgang District,[13] seeking to attract planners and designers to participate in community construction. The competitions have already been held four times; in addition to design, entrants had to communicate with different parties in the community, balancing demands and establishing trust. They even experienced obstacles such as plans aborted due to objections from villagers, "sneaky" construction, and the demolition of completed constructions for various reasons. However, after numerous attempts and explorations, the bottom-up direction of the project operation gradually became clear. The "Small and Smart Design" competitions further matured the organization by selecting communities with relatively good systems of autonomy for residents or community empowerment

126 *Urban regeneration implementation*

agencies, focusing on projects with clear dialog subjects, and providing "acupuncture" research and design solutions. The influence of the competition is also reaching wider audiences.

7.3 Urban regeneration implementation paths in Shanghai

7.3.1 *Regional assessment, implementation planning, and regeneration trials*

The combination of regional assessment and implementation planning is the main method of urban regeneration management and control in Shanghai, based on which regeneration projects are determined and the directions and emphases of projects are highlighted. Before the implementation of urban regeneration projects, thorough and systematic assessment of the regeneration regions are required to delimit Urban Regeneration Units and determine lists of public elements. Then, based on the regional assessment results, the Urban Regeneration Unit Plan and implementation plan are formulated. Urban regeneration trials of multiple types are the most straightforward implementation path for urban regeneration in Shanghai. For example, in 2016, Shanghai proposed the "12+X" action plans respectively for shared communities, innovation parks, charming cityscapes, and entertainment networks (Table 7.7, Figure 7.3), which intentionally explored urban regeneration practices by identifying the setting of different objectives and various types of regeneration project.

Table 7.7 Four Action Plans of Shanghai Urban Regeneration (12+X, 2016-2017)

Regeneration Dimension	District	Project Name	Themes of Action
Shared Communities Plan	Putuo	Caoyang New Village	LOHAS Community, Happy Caoyang
		Wanli Community	Charming Community, Happy Wanli
	Pudong	Minor Renovations of Tangqiao Community	Space Creation with Ideas, Community Enlightenment with Culture
	Changning	Regeneration of Tianshan Community, Changning District	-
	Minhang	Renovation of Shanghai Theater Academy	-

Table 7.7 (Continued)

Regeneration Dimension	District	Project Name	Themes of Action
Innovation Parks Plan	Pudong	Regeneration of Scientific and Innovation Communities in Zhangjiang Science City	Vigorous Zhangjiang, City of Science of Innovation
	Jing'an	Pan-Shanghai University Filming Industry Community Construction	Coordination of Four Districts, Synergy and Symbiosis
	Minhang	Creation of Innovative and Enterprising Atmosphere in Zizhu High-Tech District	Innovative and Enterprising Zizhu, Vigorous Town
Charming Cityscape Plan	Huangpu	No. 197 Neighborhood in the Bund Community	Revisiting Histories of the Bund, and Reproduction of Neighborhood Appearances
	Xuhui	Renovation Hengfu Appearances District	-
	Yangpu	No.228 Neighborhood, Changbai Community	Continuation of Historic Context, and Preservation of Shanghai Nostalgia
	Jing'an	Renovation of Ankangyuan	-
	Changning	Renovation of Shanghai Biological Products Research Institute	-
	Hongkou	Project of Plot No. 1, Duolun Road, Hongkou District	-
Entertainment Networks Plan	Pudong, Huangpu	Slow-Traffic Leisure System on Banks of Huangpu River	Riverside Promenade, Tour of Huangpu Promenade on Riverside, Happy Shanghai
	Jing'an, Changning	Suzhou River Banks Leisure System	Three Axes and Three Districts, Elevation of Energy Levels
	Xuhui	Shanghai Gymnasium Open Fitness and Leisure Spaces	Top Events at Shanghai Gymnasium, Community of Leisure and Networks

Sources: Urban and Land Resources Bureau of Shanghai. 12 Key Projects of the Four Action Plans of Urban Regeneration Initiated in Shanghai [EB/OL] (2016-05-25) [2018-10-22] http://sh.newhouse.fang.com/2016-05-25/21271004.htm

128 *Urban regeneration implementation*

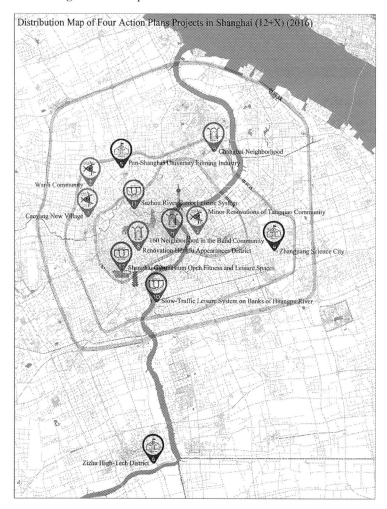

Figure 7.3 Distribution Map of Four Action Plans Projects in Shanghai (12+X, 2016)

Sources: Urban and Land Resources Bureau of Shanghai. 12 Key Projects of the Four Action Plans of Urban Regeneration Initiated in Shanghai [EB/OL] (2016-05-25) [2018-10-22]. http://sh.newhouse. fang.com/2016-05-25/21271004.htm

7.3.2 *Minor community renovations through multiple channels*

7.3.2.1 *"Walking in Shanghai" plan for community space minor renovations*

"Multiparty participation, joint contribution and shared benefits" is the working principle proposed in the Shanghai Urban Regeneration Implementation Measures. In 2016, the Planning and Land Resources Bureau launched the "Walking in Shanghai" plan for community space minor renovation, realizing the "mutual

Urban regeneration implementation 129

construction, co-governance, and sharing" of community management through stimulating public participation. The community space minor renovations plan selects 11 trial projects each year[14] from volunteer designers and public-interest activities, with proper bonuses and rewards for the designers. The renovation subjects cover all aspects of the communities. For example, the subjects of the 11 projects selected in 2016 are green spaces, public squares, activity spaces, and

Table 7.8 Walking in Shanghai - Community Space Minor Renovation Plan (2016, 2017)

2016		2017	
District	Project	District	Project
Changning	Daxi Villa, Huayang Sub-district	Huangpu	Aimin Alley, East Nanjing Road
	Jinguyuan, Huayang Sub-district		No. 500 Tianjin Road Neighborhood, East Nanjing Road Sub-district
	Hongxu Residential Area, Xianxia Sub-district	Xuhui	Ground Floor Space of West Asia Hotel, Xujiahui Sub-district
	Shuixia Residential Area, Xianxia Sub-district		Guilinyuan Public Space, Hongmei Road Sub-district
Pudong	Entrance Square of the Jinpu Residential Area, Tangqiao Sub-district	Hongkou	Central Green spaces in Dongti Residential Area, Quyang Road Sub-district
Qingpu	External Spaces of the Activity Room, Hangyun New Village, Fuxing Community, Yingpu Sub-district		Entrance to the Marriage Registration Center of the Hongkou Civil Affairs Bureau, Quyang Road Sub-district
Jing'an	Shangong New Village, Daning Sub-district	Yangpu	Zhengtong Road, Wujiaochang Sub-district
	Ninghe Residential Area, Daning Sub-district		Concentrated Green Spaces in No.491 Xiangyin Road, Wujiaochang Sub-district
	Yikangyuan, Pengpu New Village	Putuo	Entrance Square of Dahua Yujinghuating, Wanli Sub-district
Xuhui	Camellia Garden, Kangjian Sub-district		Central Green Spaces in No.4 Neighborhood, Wanlicheng, Wanli Sub-district
Putuo	Shiquan Sub-district	Changning	Green Spaces at the Corners of Pingtang Road and Jinzhong Road Intersection, Beixinjing Sub-district

Compiled from relevant sources: "Walking in Shanghai 2016 – Community Space Minor Renovation Plan" Initiated in Shanghai [EB/OL]. (2016-05-08) [2018-10-22] http://www.shanghai.gov.cn/nw2/nw2314/nw2315/nw4411/u21aw1128103.html.

130 *Urban regeneration implementation*

waste rooms, and the subjects of the 11 projects selected in 2017 are neighborhoods for the preservation of traditional scenes, public activity squares, public artworks, streets, entrance squares, and internal community spaces (Table 7.8). The plan established a platform for community residents, professionals, and students (planners, architects, artists, and college students) to participate in urban micro-regeneration and to include various social parties in the exploration of new paths of minor community renovation.

7.3.2.2 Community planner institution

The community planner institution aims at: improving construction standards of public space through cooperation between communities and professional planners; and organizing residents to participate in planning and design, forming a community design model with close-knit bottom-up and top-down approaches. In January 2018, the community planner institution was created in Yangpu District, Shanghai, and 12 experts from the departments of planning, architecture, and landscape of Tongji University were appointed as community planners for Yangpu District. In April 2018, Putuo District recruited 11 community planners. In June 2018, Hongkou District government issued the Implementation Measures of the Community Planner Institution of Hongkou District (Trial), which regulated the responsibilities, selection, training, evaluation, and trial arrangements of community planners, providing policy support for the community planner institution. After initiating the "colorful communities" project, Pudong District also appointed 36 experts as community planning mentors in January 2018, and appointed an additional 72 community planners in April 2018, forming the technical guidance model of "36 + 72" for the district, or "1 + 2" for each sub-district and town, ensuring the delivery of one-to-one instruction on the "colorful communities" construction during the whole process.

7.3.3 Typical cases of urban regeneration in Shanghai

7.3.3.1 No.228 Neighborhood, Yangpu District: preservation and exploitation of historical buildings and neighborhoods

Twelve "20,000 households (workers' new village)" buildings in No.228 Neighborhood, Changbai Community, Yangpu District were constructed in the 1950s, and are the only intact and contiguous neighborhoods of such type remaining in Shanghai. Planning in the past followed the traditional redevelopment model of demolishing and reconstructing residential and commercial buildings here, but the transition of urban regeneration ideas and growing understanding in recent years have provided a renaissance for No.228 Neighborhood. In May 2016, the project was chosen to demonstrate the "12 + X" urban regeneration program, and was listed among the "charming cityscapes" of the four action plans. In accordance with the relevant policies, the project combined regional assessment and implementation plans, exploring combined development by realizing the mutual construction and benefit of regional development through the relocation of development volumes.

Basic information about the neighborhood was collected through on-site investigation, public interviews and surveys, and the direction of regeneration was clarified taking regional development appeals and existing problems into account:[15] ① sub-community-level public services within a 300 m and 500 m radius of the regeneration area were investigated and evaluated, which established that public toilets, public car parks and public-interest facilities most closely related to residential living needed to be replenished; ② in reference to public spaces, the results of the assessment proposed an "addition to quality, subtraction from volume" adjustment method, mitigating the problem of narrow spaces in old communities through relocation of development volume (FAR transfer), reduction of development intensity, and addition of public spaces; ③the assessment required the 12 "20,000 households" buildings to be preserved, and "20,000 households" exhibition halls and experience hotels were included in the planning. On top of this, partial adjustments to the regulatory plan were made, in terms of the optimization list and the public element list of the Urban Regeneration Unit (Table 7.9).[16] The planning department of the government also organized "memories of time, stories of the past, entrustment of outlooks, and conversations of the future" dialog activity in the publicity phase of the planning draft to promote and deepen citizens' recognition of the project.

The original planned volume of development was rendered infeasible by the need to preserve historic buildings, and the relevant departments of the district decided, after deliberation, to relocate the development volumes (transfer FAR) for balance. The surplus development volume was transferred to the five development plots in the riverside region to enhance the location's liveliness and functionality. In December 2016, the Shanghai municipal government officially ratified the adjustments to the No.228 Neighborhood regulatory plan. The pre-concession evaluation of the project has since been completed and the project is currently in the detailed building schemes phase.

7.3.3.2 West Bund: founding state-owned development group to conduct riverside regeneration

The West Bund is situated on the bank of the Huangpu River, in the east of Xuhui District, with a shoreline of 11.4 km, an area of 9.4 km^2 and a total development volume of 9.5 million m^2. The Xuhui riverside area, within which the West Bund is located, used to be one of the cradles of modern Chinese national industries, with a conglomeration of numerous important national enterprises, including Longhua Airport, Nanpu Railway Station, Beipiao Coal Docks and Shanghai Cement Factory, serving as Shanghai's main transport, logistics, and processing hub, and encapsulating a century of national industrial history.[17]

Benchmarking La Rive Gauche in Paris and London's South Bank, the West Bund follows the "planning lead, culture precursor, ecology priority, and scientific innovation dominance" development strategy against the background of brownfield renaissance and the opportunity of Shanghai Expo, making the overall transition from a productive shoreline to a living shoreline. The construction and management of the regeneration of the West Bund underwent several

132 *Urban regeneration implementation*

Table 7.9 Urban Regeneration Unit Public Elements List

Content	Category		Constraining Requirements	Urgency
Function	–		Rectify lack of complementary community facilities; establish composite functions such as characteristic commerce, innovation and offices, and cultural exhibitions; and increase public amenities and public open spaces	Urgent
Public Amenities	Community Level	Cultural Facilities	-	-
		Sports Facilities	Insufficient. Suggested to append this category of facilities to the community-level inventory land for public amenities; and when feasible, open sporting facilities in schools to the public as community-level sporting facilities	Average
		Retirement Facilities	-	-
		Administrative Facilities	Insufficient. Suggested to append this category of facilities to the community-level inventory land for public amenities	Average
		Commercial Facilities	Insufficient. Suggested to set up community-level complementary facilities within No. 228 Neighborhood, including a supermarket no less than 2,000 m^2	Urgent
	Neighborhood Level	Cultural Activities Station	Insufficient. Suggested to set up in combination with community-level cultural facilities or neighborhood centers	Average
		Swimming Pool	Insufficient. Append to community-level inventory land for public amenities in the vicinity	Average
		Childcare facilities	Insufficient. Append to community-level inventory land for public services in the vicinity	Average
	Block Level	Children's Playground	Insufficient. Append.	Average
		Indoor Fitness Equipment	Insufficient. Append.	Average

Historical Appearances	"20,000 Households" Buildings	Preservation, repair and change of use	-
Ecology and Environment	-	Improving overall environmental quality in the neighborhood	-
Traffic Calming System	-	Establishing open blocks; optimizing the cross-section forms of surrounding roads, including Changbai Road and Antu Road	-
Public Open Spaces	-	Preservation of central "20,000 households" garden and southwestern open space formed after the demolition of multi-story residential buildings, and establishment of an open community activity center for the region	Urgent
Urban Infrastructure and Urban Security	-	Preservation of the existing transformer substation; creating public car parks with at least 50 spaces, public toilets, and an east–west pedestrian corridor to increase connectivity and accessibility, the specific positions and forms to be decided by urban design plans	Urgent

Sources: Zhou S. From Old Town Renovation to Urban Regeneration - Case Study on 228 Neighborhood, Yangpu District (2017). 2017 Annual Conference of Urban Planning of China. Dongguan.

distinct phases. First, the urban regeneration was initiated using the opportunity of Shanghai Expo, with construction starting in 2007 and ending in 2010 with the Expo. Second, in 2010, Shanghai began a "comprehensive development plan for Huangpu riverbanks", and the riverside area of Xuhui became one of the six key functional areas in Shanghai's 12th Five-Year Plan. Third, in 2012, the Xuhui government decided to found the Shanghai West Bund Development (Corporation) Limited (short name "West Bund Group") to implement the first-phase project in depth and to construct the second-phase project. The West Bund Group, consisting of nine first-level subsidiaries and 17 second-level subsidiaries, including Shanghai Xuhui Land Development Limited, Shanghai Guangqi Cultural Industry Investment and Development Limited, Shanghai Xuhui Riverside Development, Construction, and Investment Limited, and the West Bund Media Port Construction Limited, became an important state-owned enterprise responsible for the development and construction of the riverside area of Xuhui.

The West Bund Group gradually introduced various resources to construct cultural facilities through planning and land policies. The art and culture function of the West Bund was also progressively installed with the introduction of galleries, art organizations, and art resources, such as the Long Museum and the West Bund Bonded Warehouse of Arts. Meanwhile, the organization of activities such as music festivals, biannual exhibitions and art expos increased the social influence of the West Bund. Cultural elements both strengthened the West Bund brand and promoted the industrial development of its three regions (Table 7.10), the West Bund Media Port, the West Bund Intelligence Valley, and the West Bund Financial City.

Table 7.10 Industrial Layout of the West Bund, Shanghai

Region	Scale	Settled Enterprises	Industries
West Bund Media Port	Land Area: 190,000m^2 Building Area: 1,000,000 m^2	Shanghai Dream Center, Tencent, Hunan Television, Yoozoo, Guosheng Corporation, Volkswagen, and Nuobu	Filming services, digital media, and cultural exhibition
West Bund Intelligence Valley	Land Area: 638,000m^2 Building Area: 1,120,000m^2	Xiaomi, SenseTime, Terminus, United Imaging, Speech, Netposa, and EM Data	Artificial Intelligence, aviation services, healthcare, information technology services, etc. Innovative finance
West Bund Financial City	Land Area: 890,000m^2 Building Area: 1,700,000 m^2	Shanghai Cultural Industry Innovation and Entrepreneurship Fund of Funds, China Media Capital, Oriental Pearl Cultural Investment Fund	

Compiled from relevant sources: Shanghai West Bund Group. Key Projects [EB/OL] [2018-10-22] http://www.westbund.com/cn/index/KEY-PROJECTS/All-Projects/show_list.html

The urban regeneration of the West Bund is the product of systematic urban planning. In 2003, Shanghai formulated the Structural Planning of the Southward Extension of Huangpu River, designating the structural division of the functional regions in the riverside area of Xuhui. In 2008 regulatory plans were drawn up for the relevant regions, determining core contents such as the spatial structure, functions and development scales of riverside Xuhui, and gradually forming the legal basis for land development and redevelopment (Figure 7.4). More detailed planning forms and results followed: international plans were invited, and special complementary plans and relevant node designs provided important technical support for the development of the West Bund. Examples are the 2012 Urban Design and Overall Construction of the West Bund Media Port of Xuhui, and the special plans covering transportation, municipal services, infrastructure, and intelligent facilities formulated based on the Three-Year Action Plan of the Construction of Public Spaces on the Huangpu Riverbanks (2015–2017).

7.3.3.3 Beautiful Homeland Communities in Pengpu Town: public participation based on community self-governance

To explore improvements in the community environment and living conditions through community self-governance and co-governance, the original Zhabei District (later merged with Jing'an District) began the Beautiful Homeland Construction in July 2015. The Beautiful Homeland Planning of Pengpu Town proposed the community P+P (planning + participation) model, which combined dynamic planning with self-governance and co-governance. During the Beautiful Homeland construction process, planners conducted in-depth investigations in the community, listened to residents' problems and demands using communication platforms such as "three conferences and one representative"[18] and "1+5+X"[19] established by the neighborhood committees. The planners exchanged opinions with neighboring committees, proprietor committees, asset management companies and residents, inviting residents to participate in both self-government and co-government through planning. The main contents of community planning include the four aspects of safety maintenance, transportation organization, environmental improvement, and building renovation, while the five project phases are planning, investigation and plan formulation, public decision, construction and management, and maintenance. In the planning phase, planners help the government to conduct willingness surveys; in the investigation and plan formulation phase, planners listen to residents' opinions, inviting opinions and feedback on the plan under the community self-governance model, and establishing a platform for communication between planners, government, proprietors and the constructor; in the public decision phase, all residents vote on the plan, with a 2/3 majority required to pass; in the construction phase, planners are responsible for coordination and proprietors are responsible for supervision; in the management and maintenance phase, the finished environmental facilities would be transferred to the neighborhood committees, asset managers, and proprietors to be managed and maintained. The Beautiful Homeland plan not only renovated and improved

136 *Urban regeneration implementation*

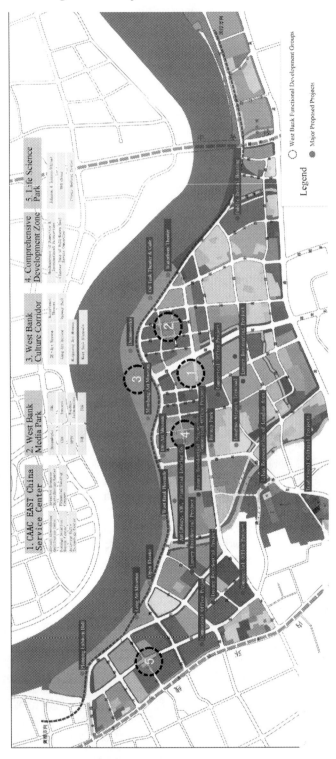

Figure 7.4 Map of Land Use Plan in Xuhui West Bund.
Sources: Aedas (2012). Urban Design and Overall Construction of the West Bund Media Port of Xuhui.

the community environment, but also realized the long-term development of the community in terms of building social relationships and implementing self-governance mechanisms.

7.3.3.4 Chuangzhi Agriculture Garden and Herb Garden: minor community garden experiments

Community gardens are horticultural venues for residents, created by mutual construction and sharing. Without changing their existing spatial properties, community gardens improve public participation and encourage the establishment of communities.[20] Since 2014, faculties and students from the landscape department of Tongji University, having conducted minor renovations and operations in various green spaces in Shanghai, have improved the spatial qualities of open spaces in intensely developed areas in Shanghai, and realized public participation and community cohesion through the construction of gardens by the people. As of the second half of 2018, the Tongji team has conducted regeneration practices in around 40 community gardens and mapped out relatively mature methods for participation in horticulture construction and micro-space renovation. The team employed differential regeneration strategies according to the individual characteristics, users, and participation subjects for green spaces in different land uses,[21] including residential areas, streets and campuses, and formed diverse renovation models – "neighborhood committee-led, resident participation" and "complete residential self-organization" – by making good use of government policies and renovation funding upside and addressing user concerns downside. The construction of community gardens emphasizes their use for all time by people of various ages, habits, and vocations, and takes into consideration the life-cycle operation and maintenance in planning events and activities. The once little cared for public spaces are transformed into catalysts of community vigor, as these minor regenerations have a profound influence on the behaviors and actions of residents, with prime examples such as the Chuangzhi Agriculture Garden and the Herb Garden in Yangpu District. The spatial design of the Chuangzhi Agriculture Garden emphasizes three functions: daily services, community interaction, and nature education. The garden is divided into a facility services area, public activities area, permaculture vegetable garden, one-meter vegetable garden, and interactive horticulture area, with space to hold more than 20 categories of activities in the compact area, such as public-interest lectures and street markets. Its daily operation emphasizes its social organization function, making it a platform for residents to communicate with the government, different enterprises, and universities. The first phase of the Herb Garden project, which occupies only 200 m², is funded by the sub-district, led by the neighborhood committee, designed by the landscape department of Tongji University, supported by the public-interest organization of Clover Nature School, and constructed and managed by residents' participation, construction, and sharing,[22] which tightened social relationships in the vicinity.

7.3.3.5 Urban design competition

Since 2016, Shanghai has invited urban designs of designated areas through design competitions that channel the wisdom of society into projects closely related to people's everyday lives. The idea is an innovative way to attract media attention, garner urban publicity, encourage public participation, and promote urban regeneration. The competitions are organized by the Planning and Land Resources Bureau of Shanghai and the district governments, and are hosted by higher education or professional organizations such as the Shanghai Urban Planning and Design Research Institute, and the School of Architecture and Urban Planning of Tongji University. The competitors are divided into two groups: professionals and the general public. The former is open to students, academics, and professionals in the architecture, urban-rural planning, and landscape fields, while the latter group is open to any members of the public interested in the urban construction of Shanghai. Three competitions have been held so far, with location and topic both actively exploring new methods and ideas for urban regeneration, such as the Hengfu appearances area and Suzhou riverbanks area in 2016, the Panyu Road region in Changning District in 2017, and the "four southern plots" region of Jiading District, and the vicinity of the 80,000-ton silo in Minsheng Dock, Pudong District in 2018. Each year the urban design competitions have attracted a vast number of entries from industrial, education, and research institutes and the public worldwide, and this low-cost, high-yield consultation approach has become a useful addition to Shanghai's urban regeneration practice. For example, the urban design Binjiang Attractions: Event-driven Waterfront Public Green Space Revitalization, submitted in 2017 by the Harvard University team, proposed the establishment of smart spatial event auxiliary tools in the riverside area of Baoshan District, and spatial regeneration to strengthen interactions between people and the environment.

Alongside the process of urban regeneration implementation in Guangzhou, Shenzhen, and Shanghai discussed in this chapter, constant attention from other markets and industries – as well as mutual promotion of interests – are also beneficial to communication and learning, For example, in 2014, the first domestic urban regeneration society was established in Shenzhen by 18 well-known real-estate developers supporting urban regeneration, and in 2017 Shenzhen Real-Estate Society established the Urban Regeneration Expertise Committee which has continued to serve the real-estate industry through cooperation of professionals from various sides. In 2017, the Guangzhou Urban Regeneration Bureau founded the Guangzhou Urban Regeneration Society, which initially consisted of 16 businesses including the Pearl River Enterprises Group, the Guangzhou Urban Regeneration Planning and Design Research Institute, and the Guangzhou Metro Group; it now numbers 113 members from the real-estate, valuation, agency, design, research, finance, and law industries.

Notes

1 Ou J (2018). The Idea of Co-governance in "Minor Renovations" of the Urban Regeneration of Guangzhou. *Intelligent City*, 11: 86–87.
2 Liwan District issued the Three-Year Action Plan for Liwan District Old Community Minor Renovations (2016–2018), which established a "community construction management committee" institution.
3 There were two reasons why the precedent of government investment in renewal should not be established at that time: the substantial local fiscal expenditure for the Asian Games, which limited the financial capabilities of the local government, and the 138 "urban villages" in Guangzhou, the renewal of all of which would cost as much as 250 billion RMB, unaffordable for the government.
4 A total of 93,928 m^2 of land has been auctioned, raising over 4.6 billion RMB .
5 Zhu Z, Song G (2017). "Micro-Renovation" Becomes Reality: Reviewing the Renovation of Yongqing District of Enning Road. *Architecture Technique*, 11: 66–75.
6 PBA Architects, Tumushi Architects. Tangxia Vanke Port-Apartment in Guangzhou [EB/OL] (2017-03-28) [2018-10-22] https://www.gooood.cn/tangxia-vanke-port-apartment-guangzhou-china-by-tumushi-architects-pba-architects.htm
7 The Vanke brand long-let apartments are called Port-Apartment, signifying the establishment of a harbor and shared community for young people working in the cities. Vanke also promoted the "ten thousand villages' revival" urban village renovation plan (the Wancun plan), and established the Shenzhen Wancun Development Limited Corporation. Vanke implements follows the "comprehensive renovation + professional operation" model to upgrade use and renovate environmental facilities, improving quality of life while preserving the original neighborhood character and appearance and low cost of living model.
8 When Wet Market Becomes Arthouse, Grocery Shopping is an Art. *Nanfang Metropolis Daily*, June 6, 2018.
9 The contents of this section are sourced from the Yangmei New Village Urban Renewal Unit Plan, Yantian District formulated by the Shenzhen Urban Planning and Design Research Institute in 2016, which is an unratified procedural planning file, thus devoid of legal status in terms of data and decisions.
10 In the past, regeneration of urban villages meant complete demolition and reconstruction, as well as mass relocations. After the renewal, almost all urban villages became high-rise commercial and residential districts.
11 http://shenzhen.news.163.com/17/1219/12/D613UF4A04178D6R.html.
12 http://shenzhen.news.163.com/17/1219/12/D613UF4A04178D6R.html, http://www.szgzw.gov.cn/szgq/qydt/201811/t20181130_14764563.htm.
13 https://mp.weixin.qq.com/s/iiBHkYhomdGzhLXqjIZnxg.
14 The "Walking in Shanghai" minor renovations plan is promoted by the Planning and Land Resources Bureau, yet the projects are not designated by the Planning and Land Resources Bureau, but declared by districts, sub-districts, or even residents. Thus, the awareness, abilities, and motivation of low-level officials and the public greatly influence the implementation of the projects.
15 Zhou S. From Old Town Renovation to Urban Regeneration – Case Study on 228 Neighborhood, Yangpu District (2017). 2017 Annual Conference of Urban Planning of China. Dongguan.
16 Ibid.
17 http://www.westbund.com/cn/.
18 The institutions that neighborhood committees are responsible for establishing for decision hearings, conflict resolution conferences, governance revision conferences, and public affairs representatives.

19 The "1" refers to residential area Party branches; the "5" to community police, neighborhood committee chairs, proprietors' committee chairs, heads of asset management firms, and heads of mass groups or relevant social organizations; and the "X" to incumbent Party members and heads of the residential area.
20 Liu Y, Yin K, Ge J (2018). Community Participation, Co-Sharing, Approaching Perfection – A Case Study of Shanghai Community Garden Space Micro-Regenerations. *Journal of Human Settlements in West China*, 33(04): 8–12.
21 On the basis of not involving property right alteration, change of development volume, or change of use, the team cultivate the original green space meticulously based on public participation.
22 Liu Y, Yin K, Ge J (2018). Community Participation, Co-Sharing, Approaching Perfection – A Case Study of Shanghai Community Garden Space Micro-Regenerations. *Journal of Human Settlements in West China*, 33(04): 8–12.

8 Urban regeneration fulfillment and experiences in the three cities

With the systematic development of policies and laws, the sporadic and scattered exploration of urban regeneration practice in Guangzhou, Shenzhen, and Shanghai has entered a new phase characterized by a more stable standardized framework for administration and management. The following sections review and reflect on the activities of a decade of intensive urban regeneration experience in the three cities, taking the goals and measures into account, and seeking to contribute to the improvement of institutional construction in China.

8.1 Objectives and fulfillment of urban regeneration in Guangzhou, Shenzhen, and Shanghai

8.1.1 Guangzhou

Through the implementation of several large projects, including Green Hills and Clear Waters, the Blue Sky Project, and the Guangzhou Asian Games, the private sector has been highly motivated to take part in the "three olds" renewal movement in Guangzhou, leading to a series of "three olds" projects, which have improved the urban environment and urban image dramatically. The redevelopment project for the Asian Games has had a significant impact in changing urban regeneration policies in Guangzhou. However, to enhance the urban image in support of the mega event of the Asian Games, the planned urban renewal projects must at all costs be completed before the opening of the Games, which will result in some inappropriate measures and high costs. The financial pressure of the large investment of the Asian Games forced the local government to pursue more land benefit through redistribution of land value surplus in the urban renewal process after the Games. Meanwhile, the fragmentation problems of urban regeneration projects were to be solved by strengthening control over profit-seeking redevelopment projects by the private sector. Since 2012, urban regeneration practice in Guangzhou has featured more government intervention and promoted contiguous area regeneration, such as the Financial City, Tongdewei, Guanggang New City, Civil Financial Street, and Wanbo City projects. Subsequently, the "three olds" renewal practice in Guangzhou slowed down due to reduced motivation for market participation,[1] together with more attention being paid to improvement of urban infrastructure, preservation and inheritance of historic culture, protection of public interest, and the promotion of sustainable urban development.

8.1.1.1 "Three olds" regeneration before the establishment of the Urban Regeneration Bureau in 2015

Until December 2014, the 310 "three olds" projects approved in Guangzhou (Table 8.1) included 22 old towns, 37 old villages and 251 old factories (industrial lands). The regeneration of old factories is the most popular type and has greater benefits, due to the relatively simple property rights and considerable land transformation incomes. In terms of total land area, there were 50.8 hectares of old towns, 577.7 hectares of old villages and 294.8 hectares of old factories, with old villages occupying the largest area. When it comes to land area of the completed projects, there were 61.5 hectares of old towns, 100 hectares of old factories, and 108.5 hectares of old villages. There have been fewer renewal projects in the old towns due to more complicated property rights and higher regeneration costs compared with the other two types.

8.1.1.2 Progress of urban regeneration after the establishment of Guangzhou Urban Regeneration Bureau in 2015

The new agenda for urban regeneration that was developed in 2015 in Guangzhou focuses on policy development, clarification of responsibilities, and improvement of institutions. This development includes the issue of "1+3" documents, formulation of "three olds" regeneration plans, revision of the Guangzhou Three Olds Regeneration Plan (2010–2020), and the launch of the 2015 Guangzhou Annual Urban Regeneration Program/Plan (First Batch). A further 23 complementary

Table 8.1 "Three Olds" Regeneration Projects Before the Establishment of Urban Regeneration Bureau (projects till December 2014)

Type	Approved Number	Total Area (hectares)	In Preparation Number	Total Area (hectares)	Under Construction Number	Total Area (hectares)	Completed Number	Total Area (hectares)
Old Towns	22	148.0	9	35.6	9	50.8	4	61.5
Old Villages	37	1718.8	18	1041.1	16	577.7	3	100.0
Old Factories/ Industrial Lands	251	1294.8	173	891.5	59	294.8	19	108.5
In Total	310	3161.6	200	1968.3	84	923.3	26	270.0

Sources: Urban Regeneration Bureau of Guangzhou. "Three Olds" Regeneration Projects Approved in Guangzhou [EB/OL]. (2015-04-16) [2018-10-22] http://www.gzuro.gov.cn/csgxjxxgk/7.2/201504/8c8c840fbc814da68d47f57611dbb024.shtml.

measures and technical guidance have been drafted, including Management Regulations on the Application of Implementation Plans of Urban Regeneration Projects and the Guidance on Cost Accounting of Old Village Regeneration in Guangzhou. The 2015 Guangzhou Annual Urban Regeneration Program (First Batch) included urban regeneration districts, urban village renewal projects, old factories renewal projects and community renovation projects. Among the 44 urban regeneration districts listed in the Annual Program, 13 were under implementation with a total area of 101 km², 11 were at the organization and planning stage, with a total area of 18 km², and 20 were under preparation, with a total area of 17 km².[2] In 2016, the first Annual Program of Urban Regeneration and Funding was issued in Guangzhou. Among the 58 listed regeneration projects in a total area of 24.54 km², 26 were under planning, 19 were approved, eight were being implemented, and three were completed. Around 96% of projects have been implemented to a certain extent, with a total fund allocation of 261 million RMB, which constitutes 99% of all planned public funds in Guangzhou (Urban Regeneration Bureau of Guangzhou, 2017). Meanwhile, trials of micro-regeneration have been carried out in 48 old residential districts with a total area of 10.5 km².[3] Further, in the 2017 Annual Urban Regeneration and Funding Program,[4] 111 regeneration projects were planned, including around 100 micro-regeneration projects, demonstrating rapid growth. Focusing on projects that facilitate strategic urban development and optimize urban function, the location of urban regeneration projects was concentrated in the old urban districts of Yuexiu, Haizhu, and Liwan, where 45% of total funds were allocated. In 2017, 464 million RMB of funding was allocated to 122 planned urban regeneration projects with a total area of 16.46 km², of which 90 were old residential area regeneration projects funded with 202 million RMB (Urban Regeneration Bureau of Guangzhou, 2018). In 2018, urban regeneration tasks emphasized active promotion of the regeneration of old residential districts and urban villages, increasing land pooling or banking, and upgrading industrial buildings on state-owned land. The 2018 Annual Urban Regeneration Program (First Batch)[5] consisted of 223 projects, with a total area of 42.95 km², of which 26 were comprehensive renewal projects, 174 were micro-regeneration projects, and 23 were land pooling or expropriation (land banking) projects (see Table 8.2).

From "three olds" regeneration movement to "comprehensive urban regeneration", from "campaigns" to "norms", urban regeneration practice is becoming more and more significant in Guangzhou. Various groups of actors have undertaken urban regeneration projects: in urban villages, it is usually village collectives or developers; in old residential and commercial areas, land is always expropriated by the government and transferred onwards through a public bidding process for renewal, which also applies to old industrial areas to be redeveloped as residential areas; and factory owners are eligible to undertake renewal projects for old factories to be redeveloped as non-residential areas.[7] As reported in the 2018 "Three Olds" Regeneration Projects Promotion Conference by the Urban Regeneration Bureau, the following objectives had been achieved by June 2018.[8]

144 *Urban regeneration fulfillment and experiences*

Table 8.2 Urban Regeneration Annual Program/Plan of Guangzhou (2015–2018, till the first batch in 2018)[6]

Year	Projects in Planning (area in km²) Number	Area	Projects under Implementation (area in km²) Total Number	Area	Comprehensive Renewal Number	Area	Micro-Regeneration Number	Area	Land Pooling or Expropriation (land banking) Number	Area
2015 (planned)	11	18	13	101	–	–	–	–	–	–
2016 (planned)	6	4.6589	52	19.8842	12	2.4346	38	17.3547	2	0.0931
2016 (finished)	–	–	58	24.54	–	–	–	–	–	–
2017 (planned)	22	65.4059	111	14.1629	12	0.8593	97	13.0312	2	0.2364
2017 (finished)	32	75.05	122	16.46	21	–	101	–	–	–
2018 1st batch (planned)	1	6.191	223	42.9527	26	17.8869	174	23.1181	23	1.9477
2nd batch	1	123	658	38.5111	3	0.0647	654	38.4278	1	0.0186

Notes: Data for 2015 (planned) are sourced from pertinent works of the Guangzhou Urban Regeneration Bureau; data for 2016, 2017, and 2018 (planned) are sourced from the annual urban regeneration plans; data for 2016, 2017 (finished) are sourced from annual work summaries. In the 2017 implementation plan, the Research and Development Base of Navigation Technologies Headquarters of China Railroad Construction Corporation project was listed as "combination of self-renewal of old factories and government expropriation and depositing", and was counted as a government land expropriation plan in this table.

(1) *Facilitating industrial restructuring and upgrading, and boosting economic growth.* Altogether 293 old factory renewal projects with a total land area of 15 km^2 were approved, and five technology incubators were built. After renovation of 46 buildings in old industrial parks, 62 enterprises and publicly traded corporations were hosted, achieving an annual economic output of 133 billion RMB, an annual tax income of 16 billion RMB yuan, and the creation of 120,000 jobs.

(2) *Improving living conditions and safeguarding urban security.* 121 km of "three wires and lines" have been rectified, 933 fire protection facilities have been repaired, 11 km of drainage pipes have been repaired and replaced, 50 standardized waste stations were established, 9,151 m^2 of illegal buildings (theft-protection nets) have been demolished, 16,558 m^2 of green space have been added, and 901 m^2 of historical buildings have been renovated.

(3) *Revitalizing inefficiently used land, and promoting the economical and intensive use of land.* The annual urban regeneration area was 26.38 km^2, which has been exceeded with 34.53 km^2 completed in practice. Thus, a completion rate of 130.9% has been achieved. In old villages, with the demolition of 1,030,000 m^2 illegal buildings, the green space rate increased from 5% to 30% and the building density decreased from above 60% to under 30%.

(4) *Promoting coordinated development between cities and villages, new and old urban districts.* In the regeneration of old towns and old villages, resettlement was organized before demolition and public services have been improved during the process, so as to solve the problems of untidy and low-profit land use in rural areas. Coordinated development integrating cities and villages, new and old urban districts has been promoted, and villagers and farmers' incomes have increased. Altogether, 438 public services amenity sites have been developed, with a total area of 2,070,000 m^2. Further, 1,140,000 m^2 of relocation housing has been constructed, as well as 134 schools (including kindergartens) and 166 nursing homes.

(5) *Inheriting Lingnan[9] heritage and branding urban culture.* Funded with 600 million RMB, 207 sites of historic monuments, industrial heritage, and historic buildings were preserved and renovated, with a total area of 140,000 m^2.

8.1.2 Shenzhen

Through urban regenerations, 991 km^2 of land in built-up areas has been reused, comprising 1.6% of construction land in Shenzhen. A fixed-asset investment of 358.5 billion RMB has been completed, comprising 14% of all contemporary fixed-asset investment in Shenzhen.[10] Besides the improvement of public amenities, land has been used more economically and efficiently and urban functions have been optimized. During the 12th Five-Year period, urban renewal activities have shown positive effects such as boosting economic growth, enhancing land-use efficiency, improving urban functions, balancing spatial structure, and solving historic problems (Zou, 2017). As stated in Reports on the Status of Urban Regeneration in Shenzhen by the Municipal Planning and Land Resources

Committee (Shenzhen Planning and Land Resources [2018] No. 292), the following have been achieved.

(1) *Demolition and reconstruction projects.* By the end of 2017, 644 projects had been listed under the regeneration type of demolition and reconstruction in Shenzhen, with a total area of 50.15 km^2 to be demolished (Table 8.3). In the 404 approved Urban Regeneration Unit Plans, a total area of around 31.32 km^2 was to be demolished, and a total area of 113 million m^2 was approved for new construction, including 4.2 million m^2 of policy-based housing, 810,000 m2 of innovative industrial space and 2.62 million m^2 of space for public amenities (Zhang and Liu, 2017). By the end of 2016, approximately 3.25 million m^2 of policy-based housing had been constructed, over-fulfilling the original plan (Table 8.4), and various types of public services had been developed, including 102 primary and secondary schools, 210 kindergartens, three hospitals, 189 community healthcare centers and 130 bus termini (Shenzhen Special Zone Daily, 2017). By the end of 2017, a total area of 16.27 km^2 of land had been released, 5 km^2 of which was transferred to the government, and a total of 116.8 billion RMB of land fees had been collected.

Table 8.3 Approved Areas in Urban Regeneration Unit Plans involving Demolition and Reconstruction in Shenzhen (to the end of 2017)

Item		Total Area	Area Transferred to the Government	
			Area	For Projects
Land Area Approved in the Plans		31.32 km^2	9.92 km^2	118 primary and secondary schools, 3 hospitals, and 5 nurseries
Floor Area Approved in the Plans		113 million m^2	7.66 million m^2	–
Specific Floor Area	Residences	56.28 million m^2	4.20 million m^2	Talent housing and affordable housing
	Industrial buildings	18.44 million m^2	810 thousand m^2	Innovative industrial space
	Commercial buildings	26,650,000 m^2	30,000m^2	Talent apartments
	Public Amenities	2,620,000 m^2	2.62 million m^2	239 kindergartens, 216 community healthcare centers, 161 bus termini, etc.

Note: According to the service standards in the Standards and Principles of Urban Planning in Shenzhen, 239 kindergartens could provide convenient infant education services to approximately 1.6 million people after completion, and 216 community healthcare centers could provide convenient nearby healthcare services to approximately 3.3 million people.Sources: Planning and Land Resources Committee of Shenzhen (2018). Reports on the Status of Urban Regeneration of Shenzhen by the Municipal Planning and Land Resources Committee.

Table 8.4 Annual Program/Plan of Urban Renewal Units in Shenzhen (2010–2017)

Year	1st Batch	2nd Batch	3rd Batch	4th Batch	5th Batch	6th Batch	Total
2010	89	22	–	–	–	–	111
2011	18	13	11	11	4	–	57
2012	5	13	15	13	18	–	64
2013	18	13	–	–	–	–	31
2014	18	11	7	20	–	–	56
2015	10	22	31	12	–	–	60
2016	20	12	11	19	10	19	91
2017	14	3	2	–	–	–	19

Sources: Compiled from the urban regeneration annual plans published on the website of Shenzhen Planning and Land Resources Committee, http://www.szpl.gov.cn/.

(2) *Comprehensive renovation projects.*[11] In 2009, a round of comprehensive renovation of urban villages was completed at a cost of 240 million RMB, including 333 urban villages, transforming dirty, untidy and poor urban villages, eliminating potential fire hazards, and improving living conditions. Further, to progress the comprehensive renovation trial of old industrial areas, a series of preferential policies were issued in 2014 to allow building extensions, change of use, and land-use term extensions. Meanwhile, nine old industrial areas were selected as trial projects, including Luohu Art and Exhibition Center and Dapeng Honghua Dyeing Factory. In the years 2016 and 2017, 790,000m² and 1.16 million m² of floor area were comprehensively renovated in old industrial areas, coupled with the improvement of public amenities and extension of industrial space.

With the streamlining of administration and delegation of authority in Shenzhen in October 2016, the district governments were able to publish their respective urban regeneration measures and plans. In the 13th Five-Year Plan of Urban Regeneration in Shenzhen released in November 2016, the required size of Urban Renewal Units (demolition and reconstruction) during the period was specified as between 30 and 35 km². Urban regeneration tasks were allocated to each district (Table 8.5), including the required scale of the area to be renewed and the affordable housing and public service requirements, such as education, health, cultural and sports facilities. Disposal Opinions on the Several Problems on Regulating Urban Regeneration Practice (One), issued in April 2017 by Shenzhen Planning and Land Resources Committee, dealt with Urban Regeneration Units with long-term implementation difficulties; as a result 70 projects were required to be withdrawn from the regeneration plan by the end of June 2017.

In general, after nearly a decade of urban regeneration practice, redevelopment of built-up areas has become an important task for the new round of urban

Table 8.5 Distribution of Urban Renewal Unit Areas in Various Districts during the 13th Five-Year Period in Shenzhen

District	Total Urban Renewal Unit Areas (in hectares)	Percentage %
Futian	140–200	4.0
Luohu	35–480	9.6
Nanshan	210–300	6.0
Yantian	110–160	3.2
Bao'an	740–1060	21.2
Longgang	170–1560	33.6
Guangming	185–300	5.2
Pingshan	185–300	5.2
Longhua	370–520	10.4
Dapeng	55–120	1.6
Total	3500–5000	100

Sources: Shenzhen Planning and Land Resources Committee, 13th Five-Year Plan of Urban Regeneration in Shenzhen [EB/OL]. (2016-11-21) [2018-10-22] http://www.szpl.gov.cn/xxgk/ztzl/rdzt/csgx135/201611/t20161121_456427.html.

development of Shenzhen. The following two aspects of urban regeneration practice have had particularly positive effects in the urban development of Shenzhen.[12]

(1) *Facilitating the integration of the special economic zone and boosting economic growth.* With increased investment in urban regeneration projects, the percentage of urban regeneration project investments in total fixed-asset investments increased from 8% prior to 2016 to 16.7% in 2016. Up to the end of 2016, the percentage of commodity housing produced through urban regeneration increased annually, reaching roughly 50% in 2016, i.e., half of all commodity housing was generated on brownfield sites instead of new land. Altogether, 92 industrial upgrading projects with demolition and reconstruction were approved, which would provide approximately 1 million m² of industrial space after regeneration (Table 8.6).

Table 8.6 Land Supply through Urban Regeneration and the Development of New Land in Shenzhen (2010–2015, in hectares)

Type	2010	2011	2012	2013	2014	2015
Land Supply through Urban Regeneration	96	105	205	183	209	266
Land Supply through the Development of New Land	512	270	154	162	152	150

Source: Edited by authors.

(2) *Ongoing enhancement of land-use efficiency, upgrading of urban function, and improvement of public services.* Urban regeneration has shown comprehensive effects in the urban development of Shenzhen, including solving historical land-use problems, strengthening economical and intensive land use, optimizing urban function and promoting industrial upgrading. The affordable housing and innovative industrial space required to be constructed in Urban Renewal Units in accordance with the principle of prioritizing public interest was over-fulfilled almost every year in 2010–2017 (Table 8.6). Furthermore, substantial achievements were made in regard to contributing land to the government. Within Urban Regeneration Units, a certain amount of land is designated as "public interest/welfare land" and should be transferred free of charge to the government to develop projects in accordance with the public interest, such as urban infrastructure and public amenities (Xu, 2017).

8.1.3 Shanghai

After the publication of the Shanghai Urban Regeneration Implementation Measures, Shanghai progressed its urban regeneration trials by launching 17 urban regeneration projects in 10 central districts of the city (Table 8.7), which covered various land types: ① regeneration of old residential areas, such as the "20,000 households" in Yangpu District and the Caoyang New Village; ② regeneration of historic preservation areas, such as the area along North Sichuan Road; ③ regeneration of commercial areas, such as Lujiazui and areas along Century Avenue; ④ development of industrial parks, such as the pan-Tongji University area; and ⑤ the upgrading of traffic hubs, such as the urban complex along New Gonghe Road, and the regeneration of Sleepless Town area. The regeneration strategies are mostly either regional regeneration or plots regeneration, and their objectives emphasize exploration of quality improvement and policy and pathway innovations, such as coordination mechanisms, working methods, innovating community governance, public participation, and urban regeneration fund construction.

To coordinate the existing urban regeneration trial projects, Shanghai has been actively integrating urban regeneration into planning and land management, based on the work of 2015. In 2016, the previous regeneration projects were upgraded into the three-year Four Regeneration Action Plans, flexibly managed via the "12+X" method.

From the perspective of the methods and subjects, the urban villages and old residential areas in Shanghai were mainly renewed through the "shanty-town renewal" [13] approach under government leadership; old commercial districts were renovated by proprietors or market players; and old industrial areas were either publicly conceded by the government after expropriation and depositing, or spontaneously renovated by the original proprietor.[14] The Shanghai Urban Regeneration Implementation Measures have narrower applicability than those of Guangzhou and Shenzhen, as some regions designated by the municipal government, such as old area renewal, industrial land transformation, and urban village renewals, were not covered in the measures. Shanghai is endeavoring to motivate

Table 8.7 Shanghai Urban Regeneration Trial Projects (September 2015)

Type of Regeneration	Trial Project	District	Innovative Mechanisms
Regional Regeneration (6 projects)	Pan-Tongji University Strategy	Yangpu	Exploration of coordination mechanisms between educational institutions, communities, and enterprises; chief planner institution
	Regeneration of Areas along North Sichuan Road	Hongkou	Working methods of area overall regeneration; community governance
	Research on Lujiazui and Areas along Century Avenue	Pudong	Working methods of area overall regeneration; public participation
	Regeneration of Xujiahui Commercial Area	Xuhui	Working methods of area overall regeneration
	Regeneration of West Nanjing Road Area	Jing'an	Community governance; establishment of urban regeneration funds
	Regeneration of the Sleepless City Area	Jing'an	Working methods of area overall regeneration; public participation

Plots Regeneration (13 projects)	"20,000 Households" Buildings Renovations in Yangpu	Yangpu	Binding mechanisms for floor area ratio redistribution between different areas
	Renovation of Caoyang New Village	Putuo	Community governance
	Zhonghuan Bailian Project of Changzheng Community	Putuo	Activating regional commercial vigor
	Renovation along Handan Road in Dabaishu	Hongkou	Exploring policy mechanisms for scientific and innovative center construction
	Shanghai Theater Academy Renovations	Minhang	Coordination between educational institutions and communities
	Renovation of the Xinmin Hotel	Minhang	Exploring the formulation of urban regeneration implementation plans
	Chuanqi Square in Zhangjiang	Pudong	Community governance
	Urban Complex along New Gonghe Road	Baoshan	Exploring urban regeneration multilateral cooperation working mechanisms (government, investors, proprietors, and tenants)
	No. 6 Department Store in Xujiahui	Xuhui	Increasing public open spaces, and rewarding building height
	Ganghui Henglong Square	Xuhui	Increasing public open spaces, and rewarding building height
	Coordinating Mechanism of the Featured District	Xuhui	Preservation mechanisms for historic streets; binding mechanisms for building area transfer
	Changjiang Computer Factory, and Aviation Terminals	Jing'an	Community governance
	No.123, 124, 132 Neighborhoods of Huaihai Community	Huangpu	Compensation mechanism for public spaces, green spaces, and development intensities

Sources: Kuang (2017). Research on the Difficulties and Countermeasures for Urban Renewal in Shanghai. *Scientific Development*, 3:32–39.

proprietors and market powers to participate in urban regeneration through government selection and trial projects. Some trials progressed very smoothly, while others had more issues requiring case-by-case discussion, limiting scope for applying past experience. One such example is the regeneration of the northwest Zhangjiang area, which was intended to be transformed from an industrial area to a comprehensive urban district, yet was limited to some small-scale public space renovations and public facility improvements due to property-right constraints (Ge, Guan and Nie, 2017).

8.2 Reflections on the experience of the institutional construction of urban regeneration in the three cities

8.2.1 Achievements in Guangzhou

The urban regeneration of Guangzhou progressed from the trials and explorations of the "three olds" regenerations to policy adjustments and comprehensive urban regeneration, with every stage of the institutional construction accompanied by some fundamental changes in policy direction. In the process, the urban regeneration institutions of Guangzhou were gradually stabilized and completed, with the following major achievements.

8.2.1.1 Innovating administrative organizations

The establishment of the Guangzhou Urban Regeneration Bureau, a specialized independent organization exclusively in charge of urban regeneration, had a special significance in China and signified the deepening and refinement of the division of responsibilities in urban construction management. The establishment of the independent Bureau was an innovative experiment to address urban construction issues in the "inventory" era, unlike Shenzhen and Shanghai, where the urban regeneration authorities were established under the planning and land resources departments. Constrained by the structure in the conventional review and approval of urban construction projects, this institutional innovation faced the challenges of establishing good connections with existing mechanisms and institutions and adapting to national organizational reforms. The Urban Regeneration Bureau, which inherited the personnel- and institution-specific working experiences of the "three olds" office, was gradually transformed to create an administrative team with relatively diverse experiences, high levels of expertise, and familiarity with local practices. The Urban Regeneration Bureau is charged with the responsibilities of policy making and project supervision and operation - from the formulation of policies and legislation, the arrangement of funds and preparation of land, to project implementation, supervision, and management, a comprehensive procedure that is conducive to reinforcing the coordinated administration and the advantages of a specialized authority.

8.2.1.2 Balance of interest under government leadership

Guangzhou promotes profit sharing to stimulate the driving force of urban regeneration, especially at the initial stages of the "three olds" regenerations, when the government, market players, and the original village collectives shared the profits and created a win-win situation (Lai and Wu, 2013). On the other hand, Guangzhou also strengthened control of the distribution of regeneration profits by continuously tightening government administration, preventing inadequate contributions to the city and the loss of public-interest income in urban regeneration as a result of profit seeking by the market. The government gradually held onto the key elements, balancing multilateral interests in the long-term development of urban regeneration institutions, including profits, functions, and volumes, refining these elements into requirements such as gratuitous transfer area, public interest contribution ratio, land premium payment standards, and demolition compensation standards, to realize regeneration profit management under government leadership, according to the different environments and regeneration requirements and objectives of different time periods. From equal distribution between government, developers, and villagers in the early stages of the Liede Village project, to the "depositing of all land that could be deposited" by the government in the later stages, the dominance of the government in balancing interests can be seen clearly.[15]

8.2.1.3 Interconnecting policy and planning systems

Guangzhou published a series of urban regeneration policies and associated documents, gradually establishing an urban regeneration institution system centered on "1+3", and forming the "1+3+N" urban regeneration planning system that corresponded with regeneration policies and conventional statutory plans. The policies and plans are interconnected and progress interactively, which is helpful for clarifying instructions from various administrative levels and the key points of the various regeneration plans, and also conducive to guaranteeing that regeneration activities correspond to the expected objectives through multiple levels of plans and projects to realize the fused development of urban regeneration and traditional urban and rural planning. The overall urban regeneration plan adheres to the Guangzhou Urban Regeneration Measures, and mid-to-long-term macroscopic guidance is also established, based on the urban master plan. The old town conservation and regeneration plan, old factory renovation special plan, and urban village renovation guidance, in association with regulatory plans, provide classified guidance on the implementation of regional regeneration, while the regeneration plans formulated for specific projects and plots function together with the binding plot plans.

8.2.1.4 Special institutional arrangements addressing the "three olds"

The urban regeneration institutional system of Guangzhou was developed from the former "three olds" regeneration system. While the concept of urban regeneration is now widening, the original "three olds" types of land use - old towns, old villages, and old factories/industrial lands - remain the core subjects of urban regeneration in the management of regeneration activities. After undergoing years of exploration and adjustment, the current urban regeneration management system for addressing the "three olds" has gradually established sub-systems with clearer and more complete objectives, targets, methods, and pathways. The three special institutional arrangements have also become more sophisticated and synchronized, including coordination between the management of old factories and old villages, to address the dilemma of the high percentages of collectively owned industrial land in Guangzhou. In long-term practice of "three olds" regenerations, Guangzhou has also thoroughly investigated critical information such as the distribution, size, and property rights of the "three olds" land within the city, which is beneficial for in-depth exploitation of regeneration potential, policy adjustment, and the supply of specialized institutions.

8.2.1.5 Parallel implementation of micro-regeneration and comprehensive renewal

Guangzhou has been exploring the "minor regeneration" model since 2016, and has differentiated it from "comprehensive renewal" institutionally by establishing a quick and easy implementation pathway for minor renovation and repair projects with simple property-right transfers. Minor renovations focus on the activation and utilization of spaces, and emphasize improvements of living conditions and cultural and historic inheritance, on the basis of preserving and maintaining built-up areas, such as the "minor" regeneration activities in historic and cultural neighborhoods, old residential areas, urban villages with poor living conditions, and old state-owned factories. The Guangzhou Urban Regeneration Measures stipulated the inclusion of minor renovation projects conforming to regulatory planning in annual urban regeneration plans, and more detailed regulations were further stipulated in respect of implementation measures for old towns and old villages. On the policy level, Guangzhou prioritizes urban regeneration funds for minor renovation projects, and encourages the active participation of relevant proprietors. In 2018, the Implementation Plans and Technical Guidance of "Three Wires and Lines" Renovations in the Minor Renovations of Old Residential Areas in Guangzhou (Trial) was issued, effectively accelerating minor renovations in residential areas. Among the 428 projects listed in the Annual Urban Regeneration Plan of Guangzhou (2nd Batch), published in May 2018, 422 were minor renovation projects. Recently, Guangzhou issued the Design Guidelines for Minor Renovations of Old Residential Areas of Guangzhou, indicating continued acceleration and expansion of minor renovations in the future, and the intention of establishing minor renovations as the main route towards achieving demand-oriented urban regeneration.

8.2.1.6 Innovating investment and financing mechanisms

Supported by the government, Guangzhou has innovated investment and financing mechanisms for urban regeneration through state-owned banks, state-owned enterprises, and social and market capital, abolishing the model where government was the sole source of funding.[16] In 2017, large municipal state-owned enterprises, including the Guangzhou Yuexiu Corporation and Guangzhou Metro, collectively initiated and established an urban regeneration fund of 200 billion RMB, with multiple privately owned real-estate funds also targeting the regeneration market and actively seeking cooperation. In the PPP financing model, market capital is responsible for funding but does not participate in operations, such as the regeneration of Yongqingfang by Vanke; meanwhile, Guangzhou is also exploring the BOT model, where enterprises are directly involved. To expand the range of finance available to regeneration players, the trust model, where government credit and project land is mortgaged, is also one of the choices. By innovating investment and financing models, market-based financing channels have relieved the government of fiscal pressures by introducing external capital, while at the same time imposing economic sustainability requirements for urban regeneration projects. Thus, in future the government will still need to seek a balance between external capital profit and public-interest protection.

8.2.1.7 Comprehensive electronic data platform based on drawings and information database

The drawings and information database (regeneration database) started in the "three olds" regeneration period of Guangzhou, and gradually developed to become a fundamental data platform for the dynamic management of urban regeneration. Guangzhou strictly followed the drawings and information database regulations, and inclusion in the database has become a prerequisite for the implementation of urban regeneration, helping administrative departments with coordination, statistics, and analysis of all potential regeneration projects within the city limits. The Guangzhou database is currently expanding its categories to include collection of demographic, economic, industrial, and historical information. In the future, the database is expected to further progress the smart management of urban regeneration in Guangzhou, and it will become a decision-making platform guiding the government in the formulation of urban regeneration planning and programs, as well as acting as a public participation platform in addition to its data integration function.

8.2.2 Challenges in Guangzhou

Along with the in-depth development of urban regeneration, the situation faced by Guangzhou is growing in complexity, creating the following four outstanding problems.

8.2.2.1 Sluggish overall project progress

Having retained power and assumed leadership over urban regeneration in 2012, the government found the urban regeneration of Guangzhou has advanced sluggishly, with market and proprietors less motivated to participate. As of 2016 and 2017, there was little change in the overall sluggish trend in the implementation of urban regeneration plans (Urban Regeneration Bureau of Guangzhou, 2018). For example, of the 58 projects, totaling 24.54 km^2, included in urban regeneration plans of 2016, only three were actually completed, and eight were under construction[17] (Urban Regeneration Bureau of Guangzhou, 2017). Urban regeneration land in the Guangzhou Regeneration Database amounted to 590 km^2, and as of June 2018, 1,070 urban regeneration projects had been approved by the city (including officially programmed), with a total renovation area of 102 km^2. However, as regards implementation progress, 144 projects had been completed, totaling 11.08 km^2, only 1.88% of the volume in the Regeneration Database; 1.14 million m^2 of relocation housing was approved, 110,000 m^2 of which were completed, a rate of only 10%; 10.61 million m^2 of villager relocation housing and reconstructed commercial housing were completed, and 31.47 million m^2 were under construction, both at relatively low levels (Luo, 2018).

8.2.2.2 Regeneration imbalance due to profit seeking

The urban regeneration of Guangzhou currently follows the principle of "government led, market operation", yet the market, driven by its pursuit of profit, always picks up on the function, location, and difficulties of the regeneration projects, causing imbalance in regeneration projects.[18] Some regions in urgent need of regeneration were therefore unable to be regenerated due to lack of potential profits. In terms of function, the market prefers plots with clear and simple property-right relationships, whose function could be transformed to residential; for locations, downtown districts such as Liwan and Yuexiu are more popular, while suburban districts like Huadu, Zengcheng, and Panyu receive insufficient regeneration interest; and when it comes to models, many real-estate enterprises prefer regeneration projects with large investment and quick returns to accelerate their cash flow, with no interest in long-term ownership and operations. To counteract these trends, the government issued policy measures such as restrictions on industrial-to-residential renovations, which, however, aggravates the inefficient driving force and progress of urban regeneration. The government often measures all projects "with the same ruler", further exacerbating the slowing down, with regeneration projects falling out of favor with market players, and accumulating to eventually become nagging problems. The government should therefore further strengthen and supply differential policies according to the individual characteristics of regeneration projects in order to break free from the "uniformity then death" situation, starting from economic analyses and profit distribution to balance, adjust, or reduce the profit gap between regeneration projects with different locations and functions.

8.2.2.3 Emphasis on indicators, and neglecting quality

In the urban regeneration of Guangzhou, projects under both government and market leadership had the problem of emphasizing indicators while neglecting quality to varying degrees, the main reason being the difficulty of quantifying quality and the uncertainty of long-term profitability. The government's goal is to advance annual regeneration plans, and the market players' goal is to maximize expected housing price and profits – both emphasize quantity rather than quality. Consequently, some regions over-emphasize the activation of built-up land, with careless site and location choices and heavy regeneration mission workloads, causing oversized planned areas and further numerous problems in the process of planning, implementation, property-right determination and profit distribution (Wang, 2018). The urban regeneration implementation plans, in their connection with regulatory planning, guarantee fulfillment of indicator requirements relatively well, while lacking profound reflection on improvement of the integral environmental quality and subsequent operations. Establishing a quality assessment system for urban regenerations, including user satisfaction and the economic output of successive land users, would represent a way out. For market implementers, on the one hand, the review of planning based on urban planning and urban design should be strengthened, and on the other hand, more inductive requirements could be included in land concession conditions to implement contracted management.

8.2.2.4 Lack of overall coordination between regeneration projects

Although overall urban regeneration planning on the macroscopic level provided mid-to-long-term guidelines on the advancement of urban regeneration, Guangzhou still lacks comprehensive urban regeneration coordination, with regeneration projects focusing more on individual efficacy than integral efficiency. The distribution of the three types of old spaces – towns, villages, and factories – was relatively sporadic and scattered, so that separate administration is more conducive to implementation, but this will also limit the efficacy of regeneration projects if there are no comprehensive coordination of urban function integration. This may lead to inconsistent regeneration and a mismatch between regeneration directions and demands in the vicinity (Urban Regeneration Bureau of Guangzhou, 2017). On the other hand, the annual urban regeneration plan only provides fundamental project information, and lacks the integrated management of projects at the same time period and in the same region. Furthermore, coordination between the regeneration project and the vicinity is also often lacking, with regulatory plans usually serving as the sole basis, neglecting regional-level environmental coordination and infrastructure replenishment or sharing. In the future, urban planning and design should focus on the regional impacts of regeneration projects in key regions; the regeneration objectives of scattered projects should be unified to form a joint propulsion force for regional development; and comprehensive impact evaluation, including social, economic, and environmental aspects, should be performed for projects in the same administrative division or urban function conglomeration, helping to realize regeneration coordination on different levels.

On November 2, 2018, the Implementation Details of Profoundly Propelling Urban Regenerations (Opinion Solicitation Draft) (with 33 articles), formulated by the Guangzhou Urban Regeneration Bureau, invited opinions from the public. The Implementation Details optimized and completed the current urban regeneration policies, proposing new measures for innovating a regional balance of old village renovations, optimizing cost accounting in old village renovations, lowering the land concession fee standards and elevating the old factory expropriation compensation standards to improve the appeal of urban regeneration and motivate society and the market to participate.[19] The measures in the Implementation Details cover six aspects: ① dynamic adjustment of the "three olds" regeneration databases; ② advancing the comprehensive renewal of old villages; ③ strengthening old factory renovation revenue supports on state-owned land; ④ promoting continuous and contiguous area regenerations; ⑤ strengthening support for urban regeneration projects; and ⑥ accelerating the completion of historic land-use procedures. The details, once officially implemented, could profoundly influence the conduct of urban regeneration activities in Guangzhou.

8.2.3 Achievements in Shenzhen

The systematic construction of urban regeneration institutions in Shenzhen started earlier than in Guangzhou and Shanghai, and the Shenzhen Urban Regeneration Measures was the first local government policy legislation concerning urban regeneration in China. In the process of its institutional construction, Shenzhen has strongly emphasized marketization, regulated operations, and adhered to the "government guided, market participation" principle, thus maintaining steady progress in institutional development and policy continuity, with the following major experiences.

8.2.3.1 Continued fulfillment of the policy system

Institutional innovation granting more local legislative power is a typical reform activity in Shenzhen, as Shenzhen, with the status of a special economic zone in China, enjoys more freedom in independent legislation than Guangzhou and Shanghai. Unlike the frequently changed policies in Guangzhou, the urban regeneration of Shenzhen consistently pushed for a market orientation in the construction of its institutions, while publishing a succession of legislation and policies to effectively manage and promote the various fields of urban regeneration. Currently, Shenzhen has an institutional system with two core documents forming the basis of its operations – the Regeneration Measures and Implementation Details. At the same time, Shenzhen also emphasizes regular revision and updating of policies, such as the biannual revision of the Provisional Measures on Strengthening and Improving the Implementation of Urban Regeneration in Shenzhen, to support timely adjustments in specific urban regeneration procedures and operations and continue to improve public service standards.

8.2.3.2 Strengthening systematic planning management and control

Shenzhen values the leadership effect of urban regeneration planning in spatial management and control, while the formulation of regeneration plans is integrated with the urban and rural planning system, mutually promoting the orderly conduct of urban regeneration activities through macroscopic urban regeneration special planning and microscopic urban regeneration unit planning. On the municipal level, Shenzhen formulates mid-to-long-term "urban regeneration five-year plans" (urban regeneration special plan) based on the district development requirements determined in the urban master plan, overall land-use plan, relevant special plan, and economic and social development plan, to "coordinate the objectives, structures, scales, and public service amenities supply of the regeneration projects at various stages, and put forward the necessary mandatory requirements" (Planning and Land Resources Committee of Shenzhen, 2018). On the district level, Shenzhen formulates district-level urban regeneration special plans based on the overall urban planning for the districts, and imposes requirements on "coordinated regional regeneration planning". On the microscopic level, urban regeneration "breaches the traditional practice where stand-alone plots serve as the main objects of regeneration, employs 'urban regeneration unit (region)' as the basic management unit to establish a urban regeneration unit planning institution" (Planning and Land Resources Committee of Shenzhen, 2018), and connects Urban Regeneration Unit Plans with statutory plans and detailed blueprints to serve as the basis of administrative permissions in development control.[20]

8.2.3.3 Diversification of renovation models

Shenzhen was an early explorer of the different models in urban regeneration, and the 2009 Urban Regeneration Measures set out the three regeneration models of comprehensive renovation, function alteration, and demolition and reconstruction. Comprehensive renovation does not involve changes in property rights, functions, and volume (development intensity), and only improves fire safety control, public services, spatial appearance, etc., thus rarely involving distribution of interest, and features simpler regeneration procedures. Function alterations involve changes in function and volume, and are relatively difficult to implement. Demolition and reconstruction usually involves substantial changes in terms of property rights and function, and is subject to complicated requirements for operational procedures and implementation. Shenzhen focuses on the core concerns of relevant stakeholders in the three categories of regeneration, based on actual demands and regeneration characteristics, and appropriately adds or reduces procedures for revision and management to realize differential institutional supply. Judging from the practices, "demolitions and reconstructions are the major urban regeneration model in Shenzhen, capable of effectively balancing interest between the government and the market; the model of comprehensive renovations was introduced later and therefore still under consummation and promotion - the comprehensive renovations of urban villages are led and organized by the government, and the comprehensive renovations of old industrial areas are mostly led by the government, with enterprise participation also encouraged; and function alterations are faced with an low-interest market due to low rate of investment return" (Planning and Land Resources Committee of Shenzhen, 2018).

8.2.3.4 Respecting rights and market demands

The urban regeneration of Shenzhen has a high marketization level, and the government, as "night watchman", only serves as an inductor and supervisor, completing the bottom-up urban regeneration route in project application, approval, and implementation. "Urban regeneration shall fully respect the legal rights and interests of stakeholders at the time of planning, and willingness solicitation is required for every project. Urban village renewal projects shall be approved by the shareholder council of the successor enterprises of the original village collectives, while other projects shall be approved by over two thirds of all proprietors" (Planning and Land Resources Committee of Shenzhen, 2018). Market players are able to participate in the whole urban regeneration process: in the project application phase, developers or capable private proprietors are responsible for preparing application materials, and provide a feasible plan around critical elements, including property rights and economic compensation; in the project establishment phase, professional planning and design organizations are tasked with plan formulation according to the relevant legislation and regulations; in the implementation phase, with the exception of public interests, such as affordable housing and public open spaces, power to negotiate economic benefits is delegated to the market to avoid administrative commands distorting the market. Therefore, despite the harsh negotiation procedures before and during the implementation of regeneration projects, there are rarely disputes over profit distribution in the post-implementation stage.

8.2.3.5 Public-interest priority and indemnity[21]

The urban regeneration of Shenzhen prioritizes public interest, which is indemnified by gratuitous land transfer and the complementary construction of public facilities and policy-based housing. At the end of 2016, Shenzhen proposed the development of "key regeneration units" under government leadership,[22] which were intended to improve the fulfillment level of some large public facilities[23] that are difficult to realize if dependent on market forces. For Urban Renewal Units, the actual rate of gratuitous land transfer in Shenzhen currently stands at about 30%, while the talent housing, affordable housing, and innovative industry buildings complementarily constructed according to the policies are to be transferred to the government after construction by the implementers at cost price (Planning and Land Resources Committee of Shenzhen, 2018). For the complementary public facilities, not only must urban regeneration fulfill the requirements

Urban regeneration fulfillment and experiences 161

of statutory plans, but the implementers must also construct a certain number of kindergartens, waste disposal stations, and community healthcare centers, which should be gratuitously transferred to the government after completion.

8.2.3.6 Coordinated advancement by municipality and districts

When it introduced the "district strengthening and power concession" reform, Shenzhen established a two-level coordination system between the municipality and the districts: the municipal urban regeneration departments formulate policies, legislation, and macroscopic plans, while district governments and urban regeneration departments formulate differential management details and district-level urban regeneration five-year plans, fulfill the requirements of the municipal departments, and lead the project establishment and implementation. Having regard to the various situations of the districts, including the differences in functions, development stages, and land supply, the strengthening of the regeneration management of districts has been beneficial for adapting urban regeneration to meet specific development demands and improve the efficiency of regeneration in the long term.

8.2.4 Challenges in Shenzhen

However, while market operations achieved positive results, the following problems exist in the urban regeneration of Shenzhen.

8.2.4.1 Homogeneity in regeneration models and function due to market profit seeking[24]

In recent years, the housing prices in Shenzhen have been continually rising, and market profit seeking has resulted in the concentration of urban regeneration projects in new residential area development through demolition and reconstruction. The market prefers projects with good locations and would not actively invest in urban regeneration projects with poor locations or high regeneration difficulties, as well as the upgrading of urban public facilities. According to pertinent statistics, 90% of all urban regeneration projects in Shenzhen are demolitions and reconstructions, and nearly 50% of these are residential areas after regeneration, nearly 15% are commercial areas and only 12% of the land is still used industrially after regeneration (Table 8.8) (Miao, Zou and Zhang, 2018). Commercial and residential land thus squeezed the space released by other land uses. In recent years, multiple incidents, epitomized by the outward migration of Huawei's research and development headquarters due to rising house prices,[25] have exacerbated social concern over the function and structure of land use in Shenzhen. Since the inherent foundation supporting the development of Shenzhen remains the prosperity of the real economy (industries), urban regeneration, as the major channel of land supply in Shenzhen, needs to hold the bottom line of land management on land use and quota control, and balance the relationship between short-term profit earning and long-term sustainable development.

Table 8.8 Land-Use Proportions after Regeneration of Approved Urban Renewal Units in Shenzhen

Land use	Percentage %
Residential land	48.3
Commercial and Services Facilities	13.7
Public Management and Services Facilities	6.4
Industrial land	12.6
New Industries	0.9
Warehousing	1.0
Green Spaces and Public Squares	6.5
Road Traffic Land	0.8
Public Amenities	1.1
Special Purposes	0.1
Other Land Uses	1.5
Others (Roads)	7.1

Sources: Miao, C., Zou, B., Zhang, Y. (2018). Market-Oriented Development under Government Regulation in Urban Renewal: The New Idea for the 13th Five-Year Plan of Urban Renewal in Shenzhen. *Urban Planning Forum*, 4: 81–87.

8.2.4.2 Lack of government coordination and fragmentation of regeneration

Regeneration activities led by the market focus more on single-project construction and lack coordination with the vicinity and the larger areas, therefore taking on a "fragmented" outlook (Zhao, 2013; Fan, Sheng and Zhao, 2015), causing an inability to supply continuous space for accommodating industries of scale and creating difficulties with completion of public service facilities in urban districts. The comprehensive strategic objectives and the integral upgrading of urban regeneration are also compromised. For "continuous and contiguous areas", renewals are lacking in Shenzhen, the scale of industrial land renewals is particularly undersized, restricting industrial concentration and contiguous spatial development. Too many small-scale urban renewals[26] have made some regions even more fragmented, with scattered demolitions and reconstructions, again presenting difficulties with completion of public amenities. Some market-led projects would "devour the meat, and spit out the bones", with limited capability to implement the large public facilities that are urgently needed in regional development. Therefore, Shenzhen tries to strengthen planning guidance and control in "regional coordination", and restricts the launch of small-scale renewal, to better realize orderly urban regeneration management with allocation of work based on "integral consideration, individual constructions".

8.2.4.3 Excessive growth in construction scale caused by renewal

Due to the lack of diverse interest adjustment mechanisms, the regeneration revenue of market players mostly comes from elevating floor area ratios and changes of use, causing a substantial rise in the scale of urban construction in the process of regeneration. As of 2017, more than 500 urban regeneration projects had been approved and established in Shenzhen, with an equivalent future development scale of 150 million m^2, which means the building area of Shenzhen will increase by 10% over the 1.02 billion m^2 of 2014 (Miu, Zou and Zhang, 2018), reflecting the fact that the urban regeneration of Shenzhen is still highly dependent on the stimulating effect of floor area ratio increments. Shenzhen needs to induce market players to pursue revenue generation by improving spatial quality in the future, for example by learning the Japanese "seed base" model,[27] optimizing the relocation of original proprietors to reduce the compensation costs, and reducing the proportion of volume-expansion profits in total revenues through tax discounts and subsidies to the developers.

8.2.4.4 Insufficient comprehensive renovations

Comprehensive renovations in Shenzhen have been limited, focusing mostly on brightening up façades, fire safety improvements, and demolition of illegal constructions rather than comprehensive governance improvements or completion of facilities. The upgrading and renovation of industrial areas have been congested due to the interlocking administrative procedures for illegal building disposals, fire prevention standards[28] and quality inspections, and have thus not been enthusiastically received by the market; and the renovations of urban villages are also mostly trivial, such as façade improvements and fire risk elimination (Planning and Land Resources Committee of Shenzhen, 2018). In principle, the main structures and functions of the old buildings remain unchanged in comprehensive renovations, with no additional facilities, yet the objectives of realizing public services and municipal facilities are difficult to accomplish under current regulations, and partial alterations to the buildings and functions are sometimes necessary. Therefore, emphasizing the "comprehensiveness" of comprehensive renovations, horizontally bridging the urban regeneration regulations, codes, and standards on fire prevention, evacuation, and lighting, and issuing supplementary policies and acts relevant to the characteristics of comprehensive renovations, are key to promoting the efficacy of comprehensive renovations and improving the intensity of their implementation.

8.2.4.5 Lack of restrictions and standards on regeneration compensations

The urban regeneration of Shenzhen is relatively marketized, and the relocation and compensation issues of renewal projects are subject to spontaneous negotiations between the participants, without pertinent financial or physical restrictions or standards. Although it is convenient for developers and proprietors to reach a consensus on compensation standards to avoid further disputes, proprietors often seek astronomical compensation prices in negotiations, and developers usually compromise to save time, thus greatly increasing both demolition costs and the property prices after regeneration. The disadvantages are that on the one hand, developers might be less motived to participate in regeneration due to cost uncertainties, on the other hand, the costs would eventually become a burden to the

164 *Urban regeneration fulfillment and experiences*

public in various forms, such as a rise in house prices or a breach of development intensity. Therefore, restrictive measures on compensations might be beneficial for controlling regeneration costs and reasonable distribution of revenues.

8.2.4.6 Insufficient governance capability in the power concession process

Although "district strengthening and power concession" is beneficial to the coordination between the municipality and the districts, and reinforces the power of district governments and district-level urban regeneration departments,[29] the work of the districts has consequently suffered from problems of contradictory policies, lack of unified standards in management procedures, relaxation of function and floor area ratio control to benefit districts, and insufficient human resources. From the beginning of the "district strengthening and power concession" movement, the districts started to formulate their own rules, and as of September 2017, the districts of Shenzhen had issued 21 policy documents related to urban regeneration. Some districts even formulated district-level regeneration plans beyond the statutory plans, and designated them as the reference documents for project reviews and approvals. The differences in management and plan formulation across districts increased the difficulty for market players to participate in regeneration projects citywide, of urban regeneration is invisibly increased, as the need to learn the policies and planning of all districts adds hidden costs and implementation difficulties. From the viewpoint of market players, even though "district strengthening and power concession" has simplified regeneration procedures, the improvement in efficiency was still insignificant due to the policy uncertainties and limited managerial skills at the district level, with the addition of occasional adjustments to approval procedures and covert extension of the time limits by district governments. The differential implementation of the policies by districts causes unfairness in project approval and even encourages approval of regulation violations for district interests, damaging the integrity of planning and land-use management.

On November 5, 2018, the Planning and Land Resources Committee of Shenzhen issued the Shenzhen Overall Urban Village (Old Village) Planning Draft Opinion Survey (2018–2025), which addressed the problem of homogeneous regeneration methods and insufficiently comprehensive renovations, in order to fulfill the government's "strategic arrangement on preserving urban villages" and to "orderly induct the districts to conduct urban village regeneration with mostly comprehensive renovations, supported by other auxiliary methods of facility replenishments, function alterations, and regional demolitions". Under this plan, 99 km^2 of urban villages are included in the comprehensive renovation zone, 56% of which, amounting to 55 km^2, is in the planning phase. Meanwhile, the designated percentages of comprehensive renovation areas must be no less than 75% in Futian, Luohu, and Nanshan, and no less than 54% in other districts. The publication of this overall planning draft marks the transition of Shenzhen urban village regeneration from predominately demolition and reconstruction comprehensive renovations, and establishes that land in the comprehensive renovation zone should not be included in urban renewal unit plans, land preparation plans, and shanty-town renewal plans for demolition and reconstruction.[30] The plan required that a "one-map" geospatial information database for the comprehensive renovation zone of urban villages should be established, and the unified leasing and renovations of urban village housing progressed and scaled up in an orderly manner, with those conforming to requirements entitled to be included in the affordable housing system. After the draft was issued, there was an incident in Sungang Village, where villagers under renovation protested with banners against comprehensive renovations and demanded urban renewal.[31] The fact that the villagers believed that there was insufficient communication in the renovation process, doubted the necessity and effectiveness of renovation, and were expecting better urban renewal benefits reflects the complexity of the situation, which also reflects the challenges of overall planning implementation.

8.2.5 Achievements in Shanghai

The urban regeneration of Shanghai has followed a path that combines institution construction and trial activities. The Urban Regeneration Implementation Measures have a narrower applicability than in Guangzhou and Shenzhen, which are mainly applicable to regeneration projects spontaneously applied by the proprietors and advocated by the government, without including other forms of regeneration. The following sections summarize the progress made in the urban regeneration of Shanghai in recent years.

8.2.5.1 Transformation of regeneration ideas, and establishment of the urban regeneration policy system

Before the publication of its Urban Regeneration Implementation Measures, Shanghai reflected the shortcomings of the mass demolitions and reconstructions in urban regeneration of the 1990s, and gradually transformed the pertinent ideas and implementation thinking on urban regeneration. Thus, while urban planning guidance was more important in urban regeneration, urban regeneration remained an important part of comprehensive spatial quality improvement. Multiple policy documents, represented by the 2009 Opinions on Further Advancing the Old Area Renovations, diverted the direction of regeneration and advocated parallel methods of "demolition, renovation, preservation, and repairing", so as to explore the regeneration model with joint government and market forces. After the publication of the Shanghai Urban Regeneration Implementation Measures, the Planning and Land Resources Bureau refined and completed the pertinent policies and regulations in order to establish a more complete urban regeneration institutional system, issuing supplementary documents including the Land Implementation Details of Urban Regeneration Planning in Shanghai (Trials), the Operational Regulations of Urban Regeneration Planning Management of Shanghai and the Result Standard of Regional Assessment Reports of Urban Regeneration of Shanghai, to safeguard the implementation of urban regeneration practices.

8.2.5.2 Participatory negotiation based on regional assessment and implementation planning

The urban regeneration of Shanghai has a relatively good public-interest indemnity mechanism, implemented through the "three steps" of regional assessment mechanism, public elements list, and regeneration unit planning. Regional assessments focus on urban function aspects, public services, historical features, ecology and environment, traffic-calming systems, and public spaces, imposing specific requirements in terms of "what is lacking" and "what should be added".[32] The evaluations place a high value on public opinion, and formulated a constant participation indemnity institution. In the "regional assessment – implementation planning"[33] procedure, the following have been achieved: public opinion has been widely sought on regional development objectives, development demands and livelihood appeals at the regional assessment stage, with public participation achieved through questionnaires, interviews, and online investigations; and in the implementation stage, efforts to establish a communications platform were made, and strong cooperation between proprietors and relevant government departments have been realized by intentional plans and regeneration unit construction plans, gradually improving the self-governance capability of citizen communities.

8.2.5.3 Thematic urban regeneration trials and micro-regeneration activities

Shanghai used the "trial regeneration" method, and the government-formulated trial projects are very thematic. Examples include the "Four Regeneration Action Plans" proposed and conducted in 2016, and the "shared community plan, innovative park plan, charming cityscape plan, and the entertainment network plan". Each action plan had a wide system of objectives, and all 12 trial projects have their own characteristic themes. These case-by-case trials and innovation experiments were beneficial additions to regeneration policies and urban regeneration practice in general. In recent years, Shanghai has actively advocated urban micro regenerations, and the districts have conducted numerous activities such as the "Walking Shanghai" community minor regeneration plan and community garden movements, realizing the activation of urban regions and widespread social influences and effects at relatively low cost, experiences worthy of referencing and promotion.

8.2.5.4 Public elements list and floor area ratio rewards and transfer

The public elements lists determined from regional assessments in the urban regeneration of Shanghai involve infrastructure, ecologic preservation, history and culture, and public spaces, reflecting the role of urban regeneration in the protection of public welfare, while the requirements of relevant elements would be further reflected in the formulation of Urban Regeneration Unit Plans, direct influencing the implementation of regeneration projects. To encourage the proprietors to provide more public facilities and public spaces, the urban regeneration of Shanghai lays down rewards for function alterations, height increase, volume increments, and land price payments, bundling floor area ratio transfers and development within a relatively flexible institutional arrangement.[34] Buildings and structures preserved and protected due to their characteristic appearance, and historical and cultural heritage in regeneration units, are entirely or partially exempt from floor area calculations. Meanwhile, to motivate a variety of players to participate in renovations, Shanghai also relaxed the existing policy requirements concerning property-holding proportions, and the division of revenue between the municipality and the districts (Zhuang, 2015b).

8.2.6 Challenges in Shanghai

A review of the trials and other regeneration practices suggests some problems in the institutional construction and implementation process of the urban regeneration of Shanghai, as follows.

8.2.6.1 Narrow applicability of urban regeneration institutions

The Shanghai Urban Regeneration Implementation Measures have the narrowest applicability among the three cities, applying only to "urban regeneration regions designated through municipal government-stipulated procedures in the built-up area of the city, while many regions of old area renovations, industrial land transformations, and urban village renovations confirmed by the municipal government shall be within the ambit of other pertinent regulations". This systematic separation causes general fragmentation and lack of coordination in the institutional arrangements of urban regeneration, harmful for learning and understanding of the pertinent policies, and thus limiting the convenient and rapid deployment of practical experience. Therefore, Shanghai should fully involve urban regeneration departments in the integral coordination and comprehensive management of various categories of regeneration, and gradually merge the regeneration categories beyond the scope of the Urban Regeneration Implementation Measures into one integrated policy system to form a more coordinated regeneration institutional framework to complete the systems and platforms of urban regeneration.

8.2.6.2 Lengthy urban regeneration timescale

The actual urban regeneration of Shanghai has involved long periods and trivial works, with years spent in assessment, project establishment, and plan formulation and adjustments, reducing the overall efficiency of and motivation for urban regeneration. The negotiation process is also time-consuming, and lacks efficient communication mechanisms between the government, organizers, implementers, and other stakeholders. The cost in time is often unacceptable for certain regeneration parties (Kuang, 2017); therefore, the difficulty of involving market forces and non-government capital has restricted the large-scale promotion of regeneration activities (Ge, Guan and Nie, 2017), and successful trial projects have so far been limited to practices organized by property owners or state-owned enterprises. In order to improve the efficacy of urban regeneration and better serve society, it is necessary to implement trans-departmental coordination and administrative simplification, integrating unnecessary regeneration procedures managed by various departments and issuing detailed regulations covering review and timescales for departments. For matters involving the handover and coordination of departments, the limits of responsibility and powers should be clear to avoid disputes.

8.2.6.3 Limited reward mechanisms insufficiently attractive to the market

The details of the implementation measures of Shanghai (Act 31) proposed "floor area rewards", yet the types of public elements eligible for floor area rewards are few and far between, implementation has proved difficult in trials, and the profits are not so attractive to the regeneration parties (Kuang, 2017). Therefore, even though Shanghai's urban regeneration policies pay a great deal of attention to urban quality, public interest, and social justice, enabling floor areas to be granted as rewards for renewing public facilities and providing open spaces, floor area adjustments are in reality extremely cautious, and the magnitude of the adjustments strictly restricted and monitored by the government.[35] As a result of the difficulty of implementation and the low profitability, these rewarding policies failed to fully motivate the market as intended.

8.2.6.4 Incomplete institutional system

The current institutional system for urban regeneration in Shanghai still has scope for refinement in terms of policy complements, technical standards, and operational guidance. It has been some time since Shanghai promoted trials of urban regeneration, and the imperative is to transform the experiences in the trials into legislation, policies, and institutional indemnity. For example, due to the lack of codes specially designed for urban regeneration projects, urban regeneration often encounters difficulties in implementation because many buildings and spaces after regeneration fail to meet fire safety, amenity, and green space standards which were originally designed for new builds. Regeneration projects in historic areas are particularly susceptible, as they are more restricted by multiple objective conditions.

8.3 Summary

A summary of the above analyses shows that practices and projects for institutional implementation of urban regeneration have made progress in Guangzhou, Shenzhen, and Shanghai, particularly demolition and reconstruction projects or complete renewals, whose benefits are substantial, and micro-regeneration projects actively advocated and invested in by the government. The implementation of projects has not only realized efficient and intensive use of land and improved living conditions and urban functions, but has to varying degrees also promoted the shaping of social relationships, as well as historical and cultural preservation. However, in general, the actual implementation status of projects in the three cities continues to lag behind regeneration plan concepts, and every so often the implementation processes encounter various unexpected obstacles and resistance, causing schedules to overrun or even projects to be halted. Summarizing the gains and losses in the construction process of these projects through examination and feedback can significantly optimize the further achievement of urban regeneration institutions in the three cities. Although the three cities have encountered similar problems in the development of regeneration institutions, the systems in Guangzhou, Shenzhen and Shanghai embody different ideas and operational models, and possess different implementation difficulties and future directions for reform as a result of the differences in the internal demands and external environments of the three cities. Guangzhou and Shenzhen have to find more ways to improve their regeneration practices, such as renovation and remediation, while Shanghai needs to contemplate how to further motivate the market and proprietors to participate in regeneration, in order to extend urban regeneration practices beyond mere trials.

Notes

1 However, according to the government summary, some believe the "three olds" regenerations did not stop, but rather had different volumes and models, actually covering a larger area and scale of renovations.
2 http://gz.bendibao.com/news/201578/content192358.shtml.
3 https://711810.kuaizhan.com/44/21/p444341163863e6.
4 2017 Urban Regeneration Projects and Funding Plan (official plan, regional plan), http://www.gzuro.gov.cn/csgxjxxgk/7.2/201702/e35c6e7fe9314201a1f5c551cc4c5752.shtml.
5 2018 Annual Urban Regeneration Plan of Guangzhou, http://www.gzuro.gov.cn/csgxjxxgk/7.2/201802/9f74d734dea048c8a04e2ffb81487308.shtml.
6 In 2017, the government expropriation and deposition project was implemented in combination with self-renewal of old factories, with a total area of 4.14 hectares. The project was the Research and Development Base of Navigation Technologies Headquarters of China Railroad Construction Corporation.
7 Planning and Land Resources Committee of Shenzhen (2018). Reports on the Status of Urban Regeneration of Shenzhen by the Municipal Planning and Land Resources Committee.
8 Urban Regeneration Bureau of Guangzhou (2018). Brief Introduction to Major Policies of the Urban Regeneration ("Three Olds" Regenerations) of Guangzhou. 2018 "Three Olds" Regeneration Projects Recommendations Conference of Guangdong, Guangzhou, June 28th.
9 Lingnan is a general name for five mountains in southern China – Yuecheng, Dupang, Mengzhu, Qitian and Dayyu – which range mainly from the east of Guangxi to the east of Guangdong and the borders of Hunan and Jiangxi provinces. Historically, the Guangdong area (including Hainan, Hong Kong, and Macau), Guangxi, parts of eastern Yunnan province and southwestern Fujian Province were roughly included in Lingnan.
10 Planning and Land Resources Committee of Shenzhen (2018). Reports on the Status of Urban Regeneration of Shenzhen by the Municipal Planning and Land Resources Committee.
11 Ibid.

12 Zou B (2017) Practices, Effects, and Challenges of the Inventory Development Pattern: The Assessments and Extended Thoughts of Urban Renewal Implementation of Shenzhen. *City Planning Review*, 41(1):89–94.
13 A special urban regeneration policy and movement launched by the state in China, promoting regeneration through demolition and reconstruction by introducing the participation of developers.
14 Planning and Land Resources Committee of Shenzhen. Reports on the Status of Urban Regeneration of Shenzhen by the Municipal Planning and Land Resources Committee (Shenzhen Planning and Land [2018] No. 292), printed and distributed on April 24, 2018. The report pointed out that the old commercial area renovations and industrial-to-residential renovations in Guangzhou, and the urban village renovations in Shanghai had stronger government leadership, while old residential area renovations and comprehensive renovations were dominated by the government in all three cities, and market participation is allowed in other types of regenerations.
15 Reasonable control and adjustments of critical indicators are beneficial for balancing the appeal of multilateral interests and motivating participation in urban regeneration. It is also possibly profit motivation tool for other market players in special circumstances, when the government had limited fiscal capabilities.
16 Comprehensive renewal usually relies on the introduction of market funds, such as the comprehensive renewal project of , Pazhou Village urban village in Haizhu District, which introduced state-owned enterprises for project operation and redevelopment. In minor renovation, investment from multiple sides is also encouraged, including government investment, residents' funding, proprietary funding, and market-funding models.
17 19 were approved, and 26 had plans formulated.
18 Many urban regeneration projects in Guangzhou are real-estate development through demolition and reconstruction, targets usually being old factories and old villages.
19 Urban Regeneration Bureau of Guangzhou (2018). Explanation of the Main Contents of the Implementation Details of Profoundly Propelling Urban Regenerations (Opinion Solicitation Draft) by the Urban Regeneration Bureau of Guangzhou. Available at: https://wenku.baidu.com/view/b8b10b7852d380eb63946d40.html [Accessed October 22, 2018].
20 The Urban Regeneration Unit Plans, according to the controlling requirements of higher-level statutory plans, connect with special plans, including traffic and municipal plans, and determine indicators such as the range of development land use, function of land use, and floor area ratio based on the prefectural technical regulations, and would serve as the basis of administrative permission after government revision and approval.
21 Planning and Land Resources Committee of Shenzhen. Reports on the Status of Urban Regeneration of Shenzhen by the Municipal Planning and Land Resources Committee (Shenzhen Planning and Land [2018] No. 292), printed and distributed on April 24, 2018.
22 Key regeneration units further strengthen government leadership, and the application, project establishment, and planning formulation of the key regeneration units should be organized by the government. In the key regeneration units, the demolition area shall be no less than 150,000 m^2 if within the special economic zone, and not less than 300,000 m^2 if outside the special economic zone. Shenzhen requires around 10 key regeneration units to be trialed in the 13th Five-Year period.
23 Such as sewage treatment plants over 50,000 m^2, boarding schools over 40,000 m^2, and comprehensive hospitals over 40,000m^2.
24 Miao, C., Zou, B., Zhang, Y. (2018). Market-Oriented Development under the Government Regulation in Urban Renewal: The New Idea for the 13th Five-Year Plan of Urban Renewal in Shenzhen. *Urban Planning Forum*, 4: 81–87.
25 https://www.chinatimes.com/cn/newspapers/20181016000096-260309.

26 The average size of a renewal project is 80,000m². To address the regeneration demands of scattered plots in the special economic zone, Shenzhen issued small plot renewal policies in 2014, allowing the scale of demolition areas to be under 10,000 m² but not less than 3,000 m². As of the first half of 2018, 37 small plot projects had been listed in urban renewal unit plans, accounting for 6% of all projects and showing relatively fragmented distribution.
27 For details refer to Chapter 2, Section 2.3.2 "Urban renewal model innovation".
28 Since fire safety standards for urban regeneration projects are the same as for new buildings in China, it is always difficult to achieve renovation of old buildings under the current system of administrative permissions.
29 The authority for approval, originally undertaken by the municipality, was delegated to the districts, with the exception of the approval of toponyms, surveying, advance real-estate sales, real-estate registrations, and document management.
30 Except for urban infrastructure, public services designated by statutory plans, as well as land for urban public-interest projects, land for clearance, and land legally bound to be demolished. See Planning and Land Resources Committee (2018). Shenzhen Overall Urban Village (Old Village) Planning (2018–2025) (Draft Opinion Survey). Available at: http://www.szpl.gov.cn/xxgk/gggs/201811/t20181105_479731.html. [Accessed 19 Nov. 2018].
31 https://mp.weixin.qq.com/s/qMfh2HnTHQ-vhNSJJP99-A; http://www.sohu.com/a/273987984_440566.
32 http://www.huangpuqu.sh.cn/xw/001009/20180102/03930d6e-a469-4e4d-b243-1b07290be116.html.
33 Ge Y, Guan Y, Nie M (2017). The Evolution Character and Innovation Research of Urban Regeneration Policy in Shanghai. *Shanghai Urban Planning Review*, 10:23–28.
34 Floor area ratio transfer and reward ensured that the urban regeneration of Shanghai prioritized the value of "public interests", yet in actual implementation, they appeared unattractive to the market, with insufficient levels of reward.
35 Differences in the following four aspects are reflected in the setting of adjustments levels: better to provide public open spaces than public facilities, better to offer property rights than not, better to configure in conformity with planning requirements than outside, and better in downtown areas than suburbs. Ge Y, Guan Y, Nie M (2017). The Evolution Character and Innovation Research of Urban Regeneration Policy in Shanghai. *Shanghai Urban Planning Review*, 10:23–28.

9 Critical elements and future development of institutional innovations in urban regeneration in China

The examination of urban regeneration institutions in Guangzhou, Shenzhen, and Shanghai indicates that despite urban regeneration being a comprehensive topic involving multiple factors, the influences and constraints of three particular elements are the most fundamental and vital in the process: property rights, function (land use and building functions) and volume (development intensity). It can be said that numerous breakthroughs and controversies in institutional innovations of urban regeneration are focused around these, and each novel institutional reform, whether large or small, inevitably touches upon the three critical elements, reflecting the redistribution of rights and interests among different stakeholders behind the scenes (Figure 9.1).

9.1 Property right, function, and volume in urban regeneration

9.1.1 Property right

The first problem to be dealt with in the implementation of urban regeneration projects is the disposal of existing urban development and the property rights settlement relating to existing buildings, structures, and landscapes

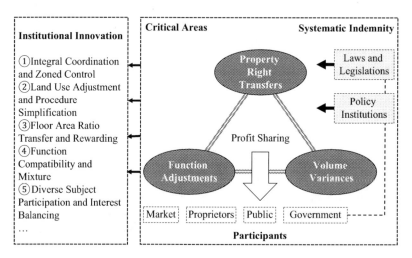

Figure 9.1 Three Critical Areas of Urban Regeneration Institution Innovations.
Source: Drawn by authors.

within built-up areas. The property right concerned in urban regenerations is usually the ownership of properties, i.e., the right of the owner to legally possess, expend, profit from, and dispose of the properties. In reality, urban regeneration activities encounter situations of complicated property ownership and property rights due to property transfers, equity transfers, historical changes, and policy reformations over the years, which substantially constrain or even dictate the possibility of demolition, renovation, or rectification in the regeneration process.

The complexity of the subjects of urban regeneration in China is reflected in the differentiation between "land properties" and "building properties", and in the differences between "uniform property rights" and "composite property rights", in the differing statuses of "public properties", "private properties" and "ambiguous properties", and in the different property-right time-limit regulations of 40, 50, or 70 years. With the exception of spontaneous regenerations by property owners and similar cases, other implementers involved in urban regeneration projects can only acquire the right of disposal of existing property after managing to conclude property-right sharing, concession, or compensation contracts with the relevant property owners. Property rights have therefore emerged as one of the primary factors dictating the possibility of advancing urban regeneration practices in China: for old residential areas and old villages, the difficulty is often the acquisition of the unanimous consent of the numerous individual property owners with conflicting demands; for most commercial and office areas, the property-right ownership is clear and uniform, the difficulty being the bargaining scope on property-right transfers; and for industrial areas, the property-right problem centers on whether the industrial land property rights are divisible, whether the time limit is eligible for adjustment,[1] and whether the land can be contractually conceded.

9.1.2 Function

The alteration of the "function" of existing constructions by urban regeneration results in direct changes such as appreciation in the redevelopment. After the land use, or the legally planned or regulated land-use properties, are changed, regeneration subjects can usually acquire economic gains, and reasonable distribution of these profits might involve a land premium payment to the government, or land repricing through "bidding, auctions, or listing", or a profit distribution agreement being reached among the stakeholders. Two typical examples of land-use transformation achieved by urban regeneration are industrial to residential and residential to commercial. Some proprietors with regeneration capacity or willingness may choose not to regenerate or upgrade their land, out of concerns that they might not be able to secure the re-acquisition of land-use rights in the bidding, auction and listing procedure if land use is altered,[2] preferring to ensure economic benefits by simply leasing the property or buildings. The urban regenerations in Guangzhou and Shenzhen have solved these problems through land institution reforms, allowing spontaneous and self-renovations and land transfer by negotiation (agreed transfer).

174 *Critical elements and future development*

According to conventional urban planning construction and management procedures, a prerequisite for land-use alteration is a legal process of revision of regulatory plans of the land, which incurs substantial costs and presents implementation dilemmas with specific renovations of existing buildings that were flexibly reused for other purposes without demolition and reconstruction, such as conservation regeneration of industrial buildings. Innovation and cultural industry on industrial land obviously does not fit the original intended usage, yet adjustments to the regulatory plan will involve entanglement of property right and interest definitions and require land relisting on the basis of usage alterations. The direction of land-use alteration is also difficult to define due to the characteristics of innovation and cultural industries and the uncertainties of predicting development demands. These complexities in adjusting regulatory plans have rendered domestically and internationally recognized cultural and innovation districts, like Beijing 798 - its "informal" regenerations that do not conform to planning and management requirements, which have aggravated unstable phenomena such as disagreements between landlords and constantly changing tenants. Therefore, innovation and reform in regeneration institutions, such as improving "land-use compatibility", promoting "flexible land use", making some land uses freely interchangeable, and providing industrial "transition period" discounts could promote urban function adjustment and upgrade through regeneration, strengthen the legal management authority, and reduce unnecessary administrative intervention and regulation, all the while avoiding frequent adjustments to regulatory plans.

9.1.3 Volume

Floor area ratio is one of the most sensitive elements in urban regeneration. It is an index of land development volume, an important indicator for balancing cost and benefits and an important factor for deciding development appreciation in the urban regeneration process. Many urban regeneration projects appear to be founded on inventory and decremental planning, yet in essence are still "incremental" over decremental – generating more revenue by improving floor area ratio to balance the cost and increase attractiveness of the development – and therefore propel the implementation of plans. Therefore, volume changes remain the pillar of numerous urban regenerations and the center of conflicts of interest in urban regeneration projects involving real-estate developers.

Urban regeneration where implementation is solely dependent on volume support is unwise and unsustainable in the long term. If regeneration revenues cannot be ensured through quality improvements and if constructing ever taller buildings with greater floor areas is the sole method of attracting regeneration development, urban construction may eventually become out of control in terms of its intensity and density. Therefore, certain cities have employed active measures in the innovation of urban regeneration institutions: setting the upper limit of floor area ratio; and proposing that a prerequisite for getting floor area ratios raised is public contributions to the city, such as increasing public spaces, constructing public facilities, and providing public affordable housing, etc.

9.2 Property-right regulations in urban regeneration institutional innovation

A review of urban regeneration institution construction practices in Guangzhou, Shenzhen, and Shanghai shows that the key measures of property-right institution innovations are focused on resolving historical problems, multi-subject implementations, contracted land concessions, pursuing and motivating spontaneous regeneration of the original proprietors, boundary adjustments in property-right plots, and property-right time limits on regeneration projects.

9.2.1 Organization of historical property rights of buildings and land

Thorough investigations of the property-right situations of the land, buildings, and structures within the range of the regeneration, and the effects of relevant historical problems, are prerequisites for urban regeneration projects. In Shenzhen, though the nationalization of all land was nominally achieved in 2004, the original rural collectives still occupy more than 300 km^2 of construction land, encompassing hundreds of millions of square meters of illegal construction, and continuing the simple and extensive leasing economic model, which creates the management dilemma of "government inability to take, community inability to use, and market inability to act" (Geng, 2015). The Implementation Details of Urban Regeneration Measures in Shenzhen stipulate that prior to the formulation of Urban Renewal Unit plans, supervising departments should set out the properties, belongings, functions, and area of land within the range of the renewal units, and inspect and compile property and building area information. Informal land use, buildings, structures, and attachments whose property rights have not yet been registered and are not illegal uses or buildings, accordingly have to be disposed of and have their registration procedures completed before they can be regarded as legitimate subjects for regeneration with clear property rights. Urban regeneration, therefore, has become an important method of solving the historic problems created by the rapid urbanization of Shenzhen. The Guangzhou Urban Regeneration Measures stipulated that land conforming to the regulations can be included in urban regeneration projects only after inclusion in the provincial "three olds" regeneration database, that land with relevant property rights problems should have the registration procedures for historically left-over land completed, and should undergo land-use disposal in conformity with the regulations. In its promotion of "three olds" renewals, Guangdong Province has employed multiple measures to handle the historical property-right problems of buildings and land through land policy reformations called "turning legal", "turning properties", and "turning land category".[3]"Turning legal" refers to transforming part of the previously illegal regulation-violating land use

176 Critical elements and future development

to legal. To support the "three olds" renewals, the Ministry of Land Resources specifically allocated certain land-use quotas to the disposal of regulation-violating land from the past, and local governments also introduced varying severities of penalties for regulation violations. "Turning properties" refers to turning collectively owned land in urban planning areas into state-owned land, which mainly undergoes land premium payment and property transformation procedures. "Turning land category" refers to allowing manufacturing or mining enterprises to turn land or public interest land into operational land such as commercial, or commercial and residential land, which, if the original land-use adjustment procedures are followed, should be returned to the government and redeveloped through the "bidding, auctions, and listing" procedures.

9.2.2 Multi-subject implementation of regeneration projects

All three cities encourage multilateral participation in urban regeneration projects and Shenzhen has even established procedural channels for "multi-subject application" for urban regeneration, with implementors such as real-estate developers or original proprietors waiting to be determined. The Guangzhou Urban Regeneration Measures state that "the implementing subject of urban regeneration can be municipal government departments, district government (or its departments), single land proprietor, or unions of multiple land proprietors, comprehensively employing the various renovation models of government expropriation, negotiated purchase with the proprietors, and spontaneous regeneration by the proprietors". According to the renovation measures for old villages, old factories, and old towns issued in 2015, comprehensive renewal of old villages may be implemented in one of the three models of land expropriation and deposition, self-renewal, or collaborated renewals: the renovation models for old factories include government expropriation and deposition, spontaneous renovation and combined government expropriation and spontaneous renovation, while comprehensive renewals and micro renovations are both available for old town regenerations. The Implementation Details of the Urban Regeneration Measures of Shenzhen stipulated that the applicants for renewal units should be determined in the following ways: self-renewal by property owners; single-market applicant delegated by property owners; and application by relevant municipal or district government departments. When Urban Renewal Units are applied for, if the buildings are shared by multiple property owners, the consent of over 2/3 of the owners is required to start urban regeneration. To reduce disputes, avoid negotiation unpleasantness, and maintain social justice, the Provisional Measures on Strengthening and Improving the Implementation of Urban Regenerations issued in Shenzhen in 2017 explicitly stipulated that urban renewal agreements by property owners in the scattered residential areas should be 100% (Wen, 2017), which reduced community disputes at the expense of increasing implementation difficulties of demolishing old residential districts, while also lowering market enthusiasm for participation.

9.2.3 Agreed land transfer in regeneration areas

Effective progress in urban regeneration is inseparable from land policy support. Guangzhou and Shenzhen are more progressive on the reform of land institutions in urban regeneration, with the most influential measure allowing land to be regenerated for land transfer by negotiation if it conforms to certain conditions and procedures, breaching the restriction that the renewal implementors in market operations could only acquire land development rights in the "highest-bidder-gets-it" form of bidding, auctions and listing. The Implementation Details of Urban Regeneration Measures of Shenzhen sets out implementation methods for demolition and reconstruction urban regeneration projects, including: self-implementation by property owners; independent implementation by market implementors; collaborative implementation (collaboration between property owners and the market); and government-organized implementation, which includes agreed land transfer mechanisms providing indemnity for both individual and collaborative implementation. The agreed land transfer gives the original property owners the opportunity to select market collaborators by negotiation.

9.2.4 Spontaneous regeneration by the original proprietors

Spontaneous regeneration activities initiated by the original proprietors are important components and project categories in the urban regeneration practices of the three cities. The property-right problems involved in these spontaneous regenerations are relatively simple, the difficulties residing in proprietors reaching a consensus over the regeneration direction and construction requirements when multiple proprietors are involved. Spontaneous regenerations initiated by the original proprietors are the major type covered by the Shanghai Urban Regeneration Implementation Measures. The Shanghai Urban Regeneration Planning Land Implementation Details of (Trials) (2015) stated that "the implementor of regeneration projects could be undertaken by the incumbent proprietor or union of incumbent proprietors, and the incumbent proprietors could delegate or introduce other agents conforming to regulations as subjects of investment, construction or asset management, to achieve mutual participation in the implementation of urban regeneration projects"; therefore the investors and developers usually join regeneration projects through delegation by proprietors. Property-right configurations after regeneration are further regulated by the Shanghai Regeneration Planning Land Implementation Details , which suppress the purely profit-seeking activities of property construction and transactions by proprietors through urban regeneration projects: "for projects planned for commercial and offices usages and jointly developed by incumbent proprietors, the incumbent proprietors should hold no less than 50% of the property; for those independently developed by incumbent proprietors, the incumbent proprietors should hold no less than 60% of the property."

178 *Critical elements and future development*

9.2.5 *Property-right boundary adjustments for plots and property-right time limit*

Whether or not the property-right boundaries of the plot are eligible for adjustment, as well as the regulations on setting and alterations of property-right time limits, affects the market appeal of the implementation of urban regeneration projects and influences the choice of implementation models. The Shanghai Urban Regeneration Implementation Measures regulate that "in the same neighborhood, boundary adjustments such as splits and merges can be performed on regeneration plots conforming to relevant regulations". The Technical Requirements of Shanghai Urban Regeneration Planning (Trials) (2015) further states that boundary adjustments of plots in the same neighborhood are allowed, on condition that the stakeholders have reached a consensus. For property-right time limits, the Shanghai Urban Regeneration Implementation Measures stipulate that "concession time limit can be reset if implemented through demolition and reconstruction; concession time limit should remain consistent with the original concession contract if implemented via land transfers or expansions without involving function changes; the concession time limit for the additional function part shall not exceed the maximum nationally-regulated concession time limit for the corresponding function, if involving function alterations. Incumbent proprietors or their union shall pay the land concession fee for the remaining time limit, which is calculated on the basis of the differences between the market price for land use right under the new usage and under the previous usage". The Shenzhen Urban Regeneration Measures include similar requirements, such as that "for projects involving function alteration, the land use time limit shall be derived as the remainder of deducting the actual time consumed in the original function". The Guangzhou Urban Regeneration Measures stipulate that "for urban regeneration projects implemented through demolition and reconstruction, the concession time limit of land use right shall not exceed the maximum concession time limit of corresponding land use. For those implemented by land transfers or expansions not involving function alteration, the concession time limit shall be consistent with the original land concession contract; if involving function alteration, the concession time limit shall not exceed the maximum concession time limit of the land with the corresponding function." Specifically, for industrial land use, the conventional 50-year concession time limit for industrial land consolidated the control of numerous inefficient or even abandoned pieces of industrial land in the hands of some enterprise proprietors not eligible for effective "market releasing" and redevelopment (Tang, 2015). Plots of industrial property rights are usually large, thus splitting the plot for property-right alterations ensures the mobility, flexibility, and operability of the regeneration and reuse of factories, while the risk of overly complicated splits would cause the fragmentation and disorder of property rights and introduce administrative risks. Therefore, in different construction phases of different cities, the policy tendencies and administrative regulations on the property-right time limit, property-right splitting and boundary adjustment of industrial land tend to differ (Table 9.1)

Table 9.1 Comparison of Policies to Activate Industrial Land across Various Cities (before 2015)

City or Province	Land Concession Time Limit	Land/Building Split	Land/Building Leasing	Construction Indemnity	Complementary Facility Construction	Land Revocation	Land/Building Circulation	Other
Beijing	Shortening concession time limit, generally not above 20 years	–	Direct leasing, with 10-year time limit	–	–	Inefficient land use	Conditional circulation	Factory construction in place
Shanghai	20 years/ flexible 10–50 years	Forbidding integral or split concessions	Leasing encouraged	Contract fulfillment indemnity	7% devoted to complementary facility construction	Possible land revocation if construction overdue	Diverted circulation, where qualification of the taker has to be reviewed	Purchase or customization of commercial buildings encouraged; project land concession with plans
Shenzhen	Flexible time limit	–	–	–	–	–	Possible arrangement the ratio of reservation and sales; appreciation revenues of concessions have to be submitted to the administration	Joint review of commerce and investment attraction projects

(Continued)

Table 9.1 (Continued)

City or Province	Land Concession Time Limit	Land/Building Split	Land/Building Leasing	Construction Indemnity	Complementary Facility Construction	Land Revocation	Land/Building Circulation	Other
Hangzhou	30 years maximum, 6 years of probation require before concession	Factory building could be conceded by building or floor	–	–	No more than 7% of land for complements	–	–	Industrial land development encouraged; floor area ratio of industrial land no less than 1.2; standardized factories not less than 1.8
Guangzhou	–	–	–	–	7% (single projects), 14% (building);15% (land)	–	–	Forbidding the construction of complete residential sets
Hunan	Five tiers of concession time limit (10–50 years)	–	Supply from leasing as the norm; supply from concession as special cases	–	–	–	–	Promotion of the standardized factories model
Qingdao/Linyi/ Zhongshan	Flexible time limit; maximum 20 years, with a maximum 20-year extension (Linyi) (Qingdao)	Function transformation applications allowed after splitting	–	–	–	–	–	Admission approbations for industrial building development (Zhongshan)

Sources: Tang Y (2015). Study on Strategies to Revitalize the Old Industrial Land: Dealing with the "New Normal" Economy and "Stock Land" Development. *Reform of Economic System*, 4: 102–108.

9.3 Function regulations in urban regeneration institutional innovation

The regulations on land-use (function) alterations in the urban regeneration institutions mostly involve whether statutory plans are adjusted, and the equitable distribution and reasonable dispensation of land appreciation revenues after alteration. The practices of altering land use through revisions of regulatory planning need to conform to planning management and control regulations; other new procedural requirements and regulations on the disposal of appreciation revenues are breaches and reforms of current planning management.

9.3.1 Function alteration and land-use control in regulatory planning

In Guangzhou and Shanghai, the function alteration of urban regeneration plots normally has to follow established procedures under which land use in the regulatory plans has to be changed before the land can be redeveloped and reused. The Guangzhou Urban Regeneration Measures require that "after the revision and approval of urban regeneration regional plans by the leading municipal urban regeneration organization, if adjustments to regulatory plans are involved, municipal urban regeneration departments or district governments shall revise the argumentation reports, propose opinions on planning and apply for regulatory plans adjustments, and then inform the municipal planning committee office and submit the materials to the municipal planning committee for review and to the municipal government for approval". The Shanghai Urban Regeneration Implementation Measures require that "the land use in urban regeneration projects shall be determined based on approved regulatory plans". The Shanghai Implementation Measures of Urban Regeneration Planning (Trials) require that for urban regenerations "involving adjustments to regulatory plans, the district planning and land resources departments shall explicate the planning adjustment requirements based on regional assessment reports, design tasks for formulating regulatory plans, and concurrently report to the municipal Planning and Land Resources Department. When regional assessment reports received replies from the district governments, and are recorded and approved by the municipal urban regeneration leadership group office, the municipal Planning and Land Resources Department shall concurrently complete the reviewing or recording of the planning task design, and initiate the regulatory plan adjustment." Alteration of land use by revising and adjusting regulatory plans is a long process involving complicated procedures, which to some extent increases the cost of projects, discouraging market participation. Thus, the Implementation Details of Urban Regeneration Measures of Shenzhen regulated that "the approval of urban renewal unit plans shall be viewed as the completion of the formulation and revision of corresponding content in statutory plan, and approved urban renewal unit plans are the legal basis for relevant administrative permissions", which reduced the cumbersome procedures and cost of adjusting old plans, facilitated project implementation, and improved market appeal. However, it also caused the breach of reasonable regulations in statutory plans and created construction problems in some projects, and as a result

182 *Critical elements and future development*

Shenzhen regulated that the core contents of statutory plans must be followed and its compulsory contents must not be changed. Thereafter, city-wide coordination began to prevent the loss of control in regeneration and to tackle the lack of complementary facilities supply caused by over-relaxation of control.

9.3.2 Land price measures in function alterations

"Inventory land premium payment" is a system for distribution of interest that specifically addresses the increase in revenue generated by land-use alterations. According to the Shenzhen Urban Regeneration Measures, "urban regeneration projects of the function alteration category alters building functions in part or in full, but do not change the subject and time limit of land use rights, and should perverse the original primary structure". The measures stipulate that "upon approval of function alterations, the municipal Planning and Land Resources Department shall conclude supplementary contracts to the land use rights concession contract, or conclude land use right concession contracts in complement; and subjects of the land use rights shall pay land prices in adherence to pertinent regulations". The Shanghai Urban Regeneration Measures stipulate that "the method of inventory land premium payment is applicable to regenerations initiated by incumbent proprietors or their unions that add construction volume or alter functions". The Guangzhou Old Factories Regeneration Implementation Measures regulated that "the functional alterations to old factories shall conform to regulatory plans. Projects altering functions of old factory buildings in principle shall not increase building areas, and when the addition of attached facilities is necessary to consummate the functions of the buildings, planning permission documents should be acquired and land concession fee needs to be paid in compensation following pertinent regulations". Land premium payment procedures, relevant derivation standards, methods and requirements are listed in the urban regeneration policies of the three cities. Through the promulgation of a series of independent land price policies, including the Rules for Calculating Land Plot Prices in Shenzhen (Trial) (2013), Shenzhen laid down requirements for land price compensation and the distribution of land appreciation revenues, among which the government possesses a small number of shares under the current regulations, and the proprietors and developers have the vast majority of shares, in order to encourage the urban regeneration market.

9.3.3 Land-use flexibility and compatibility regulations

Establishing land-use compatibilities and some flexible land uses is an effective way of reducing frequent statutory plan adjustments due to function alterations in the urban regeneration process, on which both Shanghai and Shenzhen have made institutional experiments and innovations. The Shanghai Urban Regeneration Implementation Measures regulate that "under the conditions of conforming to regional development orientation and pertinent planning and land requirements, land use compatibility and transformation are permitted, and reasonable composite and intensive configuration of public facilities are encouraged". Addressing land-use compatibility and alterations, the Technical Requirements on Urban

Regeneration Planning of Shanghai (Trials) (2015) stipulated that "public welfare facilities may be established in compatibility or mixed with other land uses, following the mixed land use guidance published in the Technical Standards of Regulatory Planning of Shanghai, and reasonable mixed distribution of public welfare facilities is encouraged; residential land may be partially or fully converted to public welfare facilities land or affordable housing (dormitories, talent apartments, etc.) land; commercial land and offices land are mutually convertible under the condition of alignment with regional planning orientation; and non-residential land may not be converted to residential". The Land Implementation Details of Shanghai Urban Regeneration Planning (Trials) (Draft Opinion Survey) regulates that "historical buildings eligible for protection and preservation after feature preservation requirements, when reused for function optimization, may have land-use properties converted according to actual conditions through corresponding argumentation procedures". In Shenzhen, the urban regeneration measures stipulate that "according to pertinent requirements of affordable housing construction and industrial building construction, a certain proportion of policy-based housing may be constructed in demolition and reconstruction projects"; "auxiliary facilities may be constructed in supplement in function alterations projects, which would be adjusted for the requirements of eliminating security risks, improving infrastructure and public services amenities, and conforming to the requirements of urban planning, environmental protection, and architectural design, energy saving and fire safety."

9.4 Volume regulations in urban regeneration institutional innovation

Increasing the floor area ratio (volume) has become a regular method of advancing the implementation of urban regeneration, yet a lack of regulations on the volume upper limits and the pre-conditions of floor area ratio increases would damage urban spatial capacity, due to the intensive construction and overload of old and dilapidated public facilities. In Shenzhen, market-driven urban regenerations are mostly demolition and reconstruction, and the ever-increasing compensation-to-demolition ratio has ultimately transformed into floor area ratio and construction increments, which has led to the continuous densification of urban spaces in Shenzhen and further population clustering. The urban regeneration institutions therefore have to coordinate construction of large areas and maintain public interest by setting reasonable upper limits for floor area ratios, and the floor area ratio reward and transfer mechanism, while also realizing revenue sharing through reasonable distribution mechanisms.

9.4.1 Floor area ratio reward and transfer

The reward measures, where the magnitude of the permitted floor area ratio increase is derived based on how much the urban regeneration project contributes to the "extra" public interests of urban construction, is common in the planning management of developed countries, but still in the exploratory phase in China.

184 *Critical elements and future development*

The administrative documents and technical codes relevant to regulatory planning published by the cities usually involve regulations and innovations on floor area ratio reward, and these rules also apply to urban regeneration projects. The Shanghai Urban Regeneration Implementation Measures stipulate that "those providing public facilities and public open spaces for the region following the requirements of urban regeneration regional assessments are entitled to rewards of appropriate building areas, on the basis of the building volume of the original land plot to encourage economical and intensive land use. Those identifying more objects for feature protections (preserving historical building) are entitled to building area rewards." The 2018 Review of Regulations on the Floor Area Ratio of Shenzhen Urban Renewal Unit Planning included specific floor area ratio reward regulations: ① in development and construction land, the building area of policy-based housing, including talent accommodation, affordable housing, talent apartments, and innovative industry buildings, with the exception of the part explicitly regulated to be calculated in the basic building area, are included in the reward area; ② in development and construction land, the building area of attached public facilities, transportation facilities, and municipal facilities fulfilled following effective planning and regulations is included in the rewarded area; ③ as required by approved statutory plans, within important transportation and public spaces in renewal units, once the projection area of the ground-level passages, underground passages and hanging corridors, established following review and approval, that are unconditionally open to the public 24/7 and whose construction responsibilities and cost are undertaken by the implementor, the area is rewarded; and ④ within the range of demolitions in urban regenerations, those who preserve historical buildings deemed worthy of preservation by the government are awarded 1.5 times the sum of the building areas of preserved buildings and projection areas of preserved structures. The Review of Regulations on the Floor Area Ratio of Urban Renewal Unit Planning of Shenzhen also regulated the "transferred volume" in Urban Renewal Units in Shenzhen, i.e., the floor area requirements within Urban Renewal Units transferable to construction and development.

9.4.2 Floor area ratio limits and revenue distribution

To prevent excessive growth of urban construction volume during regeneration, cities usually explicitly restrict the upper limit of floor area ratio increment or rewards. In recent years, floor area ratio in the urban regeneration of Shenzhen has continued to grow, and it is common for regeneration projects within the original special economic zone to reach a floor area ratio of more than 10, with ultra-high residential complexes and 200–300 m ultra-high office blocks springing up even in areas conducive to regeneration beyond the original special economic zone (Zhao, 2013). Shenzhen regulated that the sum of floor area ratio rewards should not exceed 30% of the basic floor area in normal circumstances, and organized the upper limit of urban regeneration by zoning. In 2017, the intensity zoning in the Shenzhen Standards and Principles of Urban Planning was revised, yet intensity levels one and two zones beyond the original special economic zone were expanded, essentially raising the development intensity upper

Critical elements and future development 185

limit and regeneration operational space in areas beyond the original special economic zone. The Shanghai Land Implementation Details for Urban Regeneration Planning (Trials) (Draft Opinion Survey) also regulated the "aggregate volume balance of regeneration units and plot floor area ratio rewards". The added construction volume and corresponding appreciation of revenues should not be the exclusive preserve of the developers or original proprietors, and urban regeneration policies would also address such scenarios. For example, the Implementation Measures of Old Village Regeneration of Guangzhou stipulated that "in old village renovation projects, the surplus between the planned building (land) area and the building (land) area in reviewed and approved implementation plans shall be shared by the municipal government, the district government and the village collective in a ratio of 4:3:3". However, generally, the current fiscal and taxation systems in China are unable to support pathways and mechanisms in cities that effectively revert spatial appreciation revenues to government budgets; the current revenue sharing in urban regenerations is limited to the scope of the projects, the equitable distribution of spatial revenues being to a large extent not yet feasible (Zou, 2017).

9.5 Future trends in urban regeneration institution innovations in China

Beyond the three aspects of critical institutional regulations discussed in detail above, the urban regeneration institution system in Chinese cities in the future is likely to focus on objective guidance, procedural revisions, subject determination, interest definition, and diversified mechanisms.

9.5.1 Objective guidance

The establishment of clear regeneration objectives and value orientations is a beacon for urban regeneration institutions to lead regeneration construction, as well as a value cornerstone by which government and society can assess regeneration decisions in the process of regeneration. The Shanghai Urban Regeneration Implementation Measures defines urban regeneration as construction activities that sustainably improve urban spatial configurations and functions in the built-up areas of Shanghai, and "should adhere to the people-oriented principle, activate the metropolitan vigor, pay attention to regional coordination, motivate social subjects, facilitate regional function development and public services consummation, and realize coordinated and sustainable organic regeneration"; the objectives of urban regeneration are to "consummate urban functions, strengthen urban vigor, and promote innovation and development; consummate public services amenities, improve community services standards; strengthen historical preservation, highlight humanitarian culture and improve urban charisma; improve the ecology and environment and strengthen green building and ecological community construction; consummate slow-traffic systems, facilitate the commutation of citizens and promote low-carbon lifestyle; increase public open spaces and promote citizen communications; and improve urban infrastructure and urban security, and safeguard the lives of the citizens". The Guangzhou Urban Regeneration Measures also propose urban regeneration objectives and value orientations as: public interest promotion and public facilities consummation; promoting industrial restructuring, upgrading and transformation; continuation of historical and cultural heritage; and shaping characteristic urban appearance. The Shenzhen Urban Regeneration Measures state that the motivations and objectives of urban regenerations are "to further consummate urban functions, optimize industrial structures, improve living conditions, facilitate the economical and intensive use of land, energy and resources, and promote the sustainable social and economic development". The urban regeneration of Shenzhen prioritize "public welfare", emphasizing that complementary public facilities have to be arranged as a priority within Urban Renewal Units and revenue sharing must be realized through measures including floor area rewards and transfers (Ao and Huang, 2017). Promoting industrial development is also a core objective of the urban regeneration of Shenzhen, as the city has issued a series of motivational policies for old industrial areas, including permits for additional constructions, function alterations and time-limit extensions, and trials of composite urban regenerations centered on comprehensive renovations. However, conventional urban renewal unit planning in Shenzhen was founded on "plots" that are scattered spatially, therefore industry-oriented coordination of urban renewal unit planning on the regional level is indispensable (Fan, Sheng and Zhao, 2015).

9.5.2 Procedural revisions

The institutional construction of urban regeneration, a special category of urban construction, first has to design anew the entire regeneration procedure to realize efficient and clear regeneration "procedural revisions". A clear working procedure and the setting of relevant requirements are prerequisites and foundations to help urban regeneration actors to efficiently design the works of regeneration projects and advance the project schedule following procedures, before ultimately achieving fulfillment of the project and subsequent maintenance.

The book *Regenerating Urban Land: A Practitioner's Guide to Leveraging Private Investment* (Amirtahmasebi et al., 2016) concisely divided urban regeneration into four phases: scoping – planning – financing – implementation (Table 9.2):

(1) *The scoping phase.* Understand the history and unique "DNA" of the city through investigations to provide an analytical foundation for strategic decisions of urban regeneration;
(2) *The planning phase.* Establish long-term planning vision and planning principles through planning, and promote the coordination among the government, the private sectors and the residents through effective planning frameworks in combination with the supervision procedures;
(3) *The financing phase.* Large-scale urban regeneration projects are relatively complicated, with few cities possessing enough resources to finance the implementation of urban regenerations, thus the cost of urban regeneration,

as well as risks and technologies, have to be shared between the government and private sectors;
(4) *The implementation phase.* The implementation phase needs to convert long-term regeneration visions into financial, contract and institutional relationships between the public and private sectors. This phase also includes the construction of robust institutions and feasible and sustainable organizations, fulfilled through cooperation among multiple government departments. (Amirtahmasebi et al., 2016)

Table 9.2 Toolbox for Urban Regeneration Management

	Phase	Content	
1	Scoping	Micro Level	Setting a Vision; Geography; Growth Dynamics; Asset Mapping; Market Analysis; Physical Survey; Obstacles to Growth; Potential Range of Costs of the Project and Sources of Funding; Community Mapping and Local Dynamics; Socioeconomic Considerations
		Macro Level (Data)	Economic Sectors; Economic Data; Socioeconomic and Demographic Data; Physical Analysis; Assets/Networks/Social Media Mapping; Infrastructure; Growth Dynamics; Housing; Fiscal Analysis; Political Analysis; Market Assessment and State of the Private Sector Institution; Historical Analysis; Best Practice; Institutions
2	Planning	Planning Systems and Tools	Tool: Planning Framework (Framework Plan; Planning Process; Planning Regulations) Tool: Master Planning (Feasibility Studies; Strategic Framework; Physical and Spatial Elements) Tool: Developing Design Standards
		Creating a Planning Process	Tool: Setting the Scene Tool: Defining the Implementation Process and Institutional Arrangements Tool: Partnering Arrangements with the Private Sector Tool: Defining Early Wins
3	Financing	Municipal Finance Tools	Capital Investment Planning Intergovernmental Transfers
		Land-Specific Financial and Regulatory Tools	Public Land (Sale or Long-Term Lease; Land Swaps; "In-Kind" Payments; Equity Contribution toward a Joint Venture) Private land (Financial tools: Non-capital/capital markets; Regulatory Tools: Policy/fiscal)

(Continued)

Table 9.2 (Continued)

	Phase	Content	
4	Implementation	Political Leadership	Developing a Strong Vision; Managing the Tension between Shortand Long-Term Horizons; Creating Democratic, Transparent, Open, and Fair Processes; Selling the Vision; Setting Priorities and Allocating Scarce Resources; Galvanizing Coalitions and Public–Private Partnerships; Leveraging Capital; Being Tenacious; Managing Succession and Legacy
		Public- and Private-Sector Roles and Inter-Relationships	Public Land Position; Profit Participation; Competitive Process; Infrastructure Commitments and Funding Responsibility; Transparency and Protecting the Public Interest; Regulatory Process and Certainty; Changes in Conditions
		Mitigating Risk Project Phasing	Framework for Assessing Risk

Source: Amirtahmasebi et al. (2016). *Regenerating Urban Land: A Practitioner's Guide to Leveraging Private Investment*. World Bank Publications.

In reality, the above four phases may be implemented all together or in a different order. Currently, the administration and management of urban regenerations are much more detailed: more attention is paid to the economy, society, and culture of the city, as well as the feasibility of regeneration projects, in the scoping phase; the combination of planning and legislation and collaborations with the private sector are emphasized in the planning phase; the realization of diverse government funding channels and financial supervision tools occurs in the financing phase; and attention is focused on public–private relationships, implementation risks, and procedures in the implementation phase.

Different urban regeneration procedure designs have the same advantages and disadvantages, but the specific effects work differently in practice as regards the different initiating actors and types of regeneration project. In summary, current urban regeneration institutional design in China usually includes in its procedure five major phases: establishment of the regeneration project and planning phase; status evaluation and compilation phase (or as part of the project establishment phase); regeneration unit/area planning formulation phase; project review and approval, and construction management phase; and project implementation and revenue-sharing phase. Shanghai proposed a "full life-cycle" working procedure, with the emphasis on urban regeneration, including early planning and negotiation and late implementation. In the trial regeneration projects with a "regional assessment – implementation planning – full life-cycle management" procedure, the strict management and control of the government effectively normalized the implementation of urban regeneration projects, but also raised the transaction costs and dampened the enthusiasm of market and social participation, due to the complicated procedures for adjusting regulatory planning, the extensive but trivial processes of urban regeneration negotiations, and the lack of effective communication platforms between government, implementors, regeneration subjects, and other stakeholders. In Shenzhen, procedures for large-scale residence demolition projects in current urban regeneration are[4]: ① in the early phase of the project, the proprietors initiate urban regeneration and select a developer before announcing the project, the core issue being reaching consensus over demolition compensation; ② in the project establishment phase, after the inclusion of the project into the urban renewal plan, the proprietors and the developer have to organize special urban renewal planning and obtain government review and approval, the key being determining technical planning indicators and land involving public interest; ③ in the project implementation phase, after following regeneration regulations, the implementor is responsible for investing in and leading the demolition, land expropriation, compensation and construction work, as well as land premium payment; and ④ in the project revenue distribution phase, after land price compensation payment and resettlement housing allocation in accordance with the initial agreements have been completed, the developer acquires the sales revenues from the commercial housing and the complementary affordable housing that is constructed according to the regulations. In the process, the proprietors have the right to initiate regeneration and select developers, which protects the interest and the rights of proprietors to participate in regeneration; and the right to formulate urban renewal plans and the surplus of appreciation revenue mostly belong to the developing party, which greatly encourages market participation (Su, Hu and Li, 2018). Yet this "government-less" procedural design also imposes challenges on the constraints of urban construction order and the integral adjustment and control of regeneration planning.

9.5.3 Subject determination

The stakeholders and project interveners in urban regeneration activities are diverse, and it is vital to determine the operating subject through institutional design, the key to determining the leadership of regeneration projects and operational mechanisms. The subjects of an urban regeneration operation can be individual or mixed (such as between the government and enterprises, and between proprietors and enterprises). In the past, against the background of China's rapid urbanization, urban regeneration was powerfully supported by land finances, with the government and developers forming "growth machines" to rapidly propel urban renovations and improve spatial appearances through "campaign-style" regeneration of demolitions and reconstructions (Zhang, 2017).

If urban regenerations are simply divided into the three categories of "government led", "society led", and "market led", according to which force is leading, then the different types have extremely different regeneration methods and models of interest distribution. "Government-led" urban regeneration has been practiced for a long time in China, as the government has implemented resident settlement, re-planning, and redevelopment of regeneration plots, taking full control of the cost, progress, and planning of regeneration with the support of vested public power. "Society-led" urban regeneration emphasizes quality improvement and effect enhancement of plot construction through spontaneous renovation by the "proprietors", therefore the resolution of funding source problems, the consensus of stakeholders, long-term regeneration and maintenance, and cost control are prerequisites for the effective operation of society-led regeneration. Society-led urban regeneration projects are not yet mainstream in China, but with the advocacy, leadership, and demonstration of the new activities of community empowerment and minor renovations, this category of regeneration practice is becoming more and more important and widespread. "Market-led" urban regeneration epitomized by developers has long been the normal model of urban redevelopment, supported by the strength of powerful market capital injection, yet having the common shortcoming of the blind pursuit of profit by the developers.

The integral institutional design of urban regeneration also tends to divide responsibilities and rights between the government, society (proprietors) and the market (developers). In the urban regeneration of Guangzhou, the government has played a more significant role, having experienced the shortcomings of market operations. The urban regeneration of Shenzhen tends to establish the role of government as that of "night watchman", with a referee–athlete relationship forming between the government and the enterprises and proprietors, where the government undertakes the responsibility of making the rules and supervising implementation; hence the proprietors and the development enterprises are responsible for the specific items of regeneration projects, advance the construction and fulfillment of urban regeneration projects, and benefit under regeneration rules formulated by the government (Su, Hu and Li, 2018).

9.5.4 Interest definition

Institutional arrangements on property rights, function, and volume in the construction of urban regeneration institutions involve the definition of relevant interests in urban regeneration projects. These are the rules that define rights and responsibilities, and revenue distributions in detail. The setting out of urban regeneration project procedures, especially negotiation procedures, also defines the possibilities and extent of conflicts of interest between the various parties in the process of regeneration, as well as the stages and composition of the subjects of the competition for interest. In urban regeneration systems under strong government leadership, the scope for interest competition by the various sides is relatively small, while in the "government-guided" urban regeneration systems epitomized by Shenzhen, competition between the parties has become an important method of reaching a definition of interest.

The urban regeneration of Shenzhen employs the multiple models of comprehensive renewal, function alteration, and demolition and reconstruction in parallel, and emphasizes the protection and indemnity of the rights and interests of original proprietors. The implementation of the majority of regeneration projects requires the unanimous agreement of the original proprietor (usually more than 2/3), which is beneficial in resolving conflicts at the outset of project construction and avoiding the possibility of violent disagreements over the preservation of rights in the later demolition proceedings, by distributing interests and responsibilities among the parties in advance. However, due to a lack of clear demolition compensation standards, plenty of argument over demolition compensation between the proprietors and the developers can occur. In the past, the original proprietors would often be at a disadvantage as a result of unequal rights and information, but at present, the market temptation of appreciating properties and the ample protection of the interests of the original proprietors by the regeneration institutions has caused unprecedented inflation of a risk-taking mentality in some proprietors, who may strive for more compensation by rushing illegal construction. Constant recurrences of exorbitant demands and layered overcharges mires urban regeneration in the dilemma of "unable to demolish, unaffordable compensation, and stagnating operations", causing societal questioning of the justice and equality of regeneration revenue distribution. Moreover, the government entrusts proprietors and developers with the right to formulate Urban Renewal Unit plan – regeneration special planning reviewed and approved by the government could "replace" the original statutory planning, which reflects the characteristics of the institutional design requiring three-way gaming between government, developer, and proprietors (Su, Hu and Li, 2018).

9.5.5 Diversified mechanisms

Diversified regeneration operation mechanisms should be intentionally developed and nurtured in the process of institution construction, for example mechanisms to reform urban regeneration-oriented land management, innovative regeneration models, public participation, and the establishment of community planner institutions.

Shenzhen has promoted land management institutional reform by urban regeneration through policy coordination, and has made policy innovations on land concession methods, differential land price standards, and linkages between land price and floor area ratio (Ao and Huang, 2017). Having permitted proprietors to initiate self-renewal and decreed that land-use rights in self-renewal projects do need to be delegated through "bidding, auctions and listing" methods, Shenzhen has substantially encouraged the original proprietors in the direction of spontaneous regenerations (Feng, Li and Yu, 2019). Government document No.78 stated that the "three olds" renewal of Guangdong province had made six major breakthroughs on land resources policies: first, procedural simplification for completion of land expropriation; second, permission to complete registration of historically informally used land based on the status quo; third, permission to supply land through agreed concession; fourth, permission to revert land profits to support land users' development and renovation work; fifth, procedural simplification for transforming collective-owned construction land to state-owned construction land; and sixth, preferential policies over regeneration of corners, exclaves, and sandwiched land. Moreover, from the perspective of the construction of the community planner institution, good practice in Shanghai's Yangpu District is to become an important component of overall urban regeneration institutional systems. The regeneration of communities needs to bridge top-down development requirements and bottom-up development demands by using

192 *Critical elements and future development*

community planners to advance the implementation of community planning. It is suggested that for government-led integral regional regenerations and public space regenerations, community planners could be selected by the government or undertaken by third-party organizations; for regeneration projects implemented by proprietors, the government should step back to coordination and supervision roles, and the community planners can be selected by proprietors or undertaken by third-party organizations (Kuang, 2017).

9.6 Suggestions for urban regeneration institution innovation in China

In summary, the experiences of Guangzhou, Shenzhen, and Shanghai suggest the following procedures for developing urban regeneration institutions in other cities in China (Table 9.3).

(1) Build standardized drawings and information databases: collecting comprehensive information through investigation of inventory land resources in urban built-up areas, and establish the locations, ranges, sizes, and ownerships of the areas where urban regeneration is necessary, for the establishment of a database to be used in regeneration management.
(2) Overall guidance: determining the overall idea, integral objectives, major principles, classifications, and coordinated construction requirements of urban regeneration through macroscopic special regeneration planning, and microscopic short-to-mid-term regeneration planning. Actively bridging the urban master plan and zoned planning at municipal and district levels, and formulating urban regeneration special plans connected with statutory planning.
(3) Spatial management and control: providing spatial management, control, and guidance to regeneration projects through regulatory planning and complementary policy tools. The key points of spatial management and control are: the determination of key indicators including density, intensity, and height; complementary construction regulations on affordable housing and public interest land; completing the list of traffic, municipal, and public service facilities; and the potential development motivating measures including floor area rewards and transfer.
(4) Institutional innovations: in combination with the construction status of relevant policies and legislation in the cities, promoting urban regeneration institution construction in steps, phases, and order of difficulty, while easing the pressures placed upon the urban regeneration process by current institutions and mechanisms, and gradually formulating legal documents on urban regeneration.
(5) Project trials: under the premise of clear policy ideas, performing project trials by selecting representative sites, conducting practices on project implementation and regeneration mechanisms, continually summarizing problems and experiences in the trials, examining and optimizing urban regeneration institutional designs, and facilitating adjustments and completion.

Table 9.3 Implementation Steps for Urban Regeneration Institution Innovations

No.	Implementation Steps	Main Content	Specific Points
1	Drawings and Information Database (Regeneration Database)	Warehousing of fundamental data	Collecting basic information on regeneration land including overall size, spatial layout, land ownerships, and construction status to be included in databases
2	Overall Guidance	Overall Objectives and Requirements	Establishing overall objectives, principles, and coordinated construction requirements through macroscopic regeneration special planning and short-to-mid-term regeneration planning
3	Spatial Management and Control	Planning and Design/Policy Tools	Providing spatial management, control, and guidance through regulatory planning and complementary policy tools on regeneration projects, including development intensities, policy-based housing supplies, public elements list, development motivations, etc.
4	Institutional Innovations	Policy/Mechanism/Organization	Providing policy supports and implementation pathways through institution supplies and reasonable breaches of current institutional and mechanical barriers
5	Project Trials	Trials and Practices with Multiple Subjects, Types, and Models	Conducting trial projects by selecting representative sites; examining, feeding back, and optimizing regeneration institution designs through urban regeneration practices
6	Deepening and Promotion	Comprehensive Promotion of Success Experiences	Promoting wider spread of the experiences accumulated in the trials and other investigations

Sources: compiled by the authors.

(6) Deepening and promotion: summarizing the successes accumulated in trials and other relevant investigations, promoting them comprehensively on a larger scale, and perfecting urban regeneration institutional and system design.

The establishment and innovation of complementary institutions, including land institutions, planning management, financial and taxation institutions, and supervision and maintenance, are powerful indemnities in the implementation of urban regeneration, as breach points of reform are needed to accompany regeneration practices. These could refine the technical requirements on urban regeneration in different cities in terms of policy tools, following the above institution construction steps, and explore different categories of regeneration models and paths, such as government led, public–private partnership, market led, and spontaneous regenerations in project implementations. Before the large-scale promotion of regeneration policies and integral policies, trials in representative regions could help to effectively avoid the risks associated with reform, explore collaborative working platforms between government, proprietors, and the market, introduce bold innovations on critical property-right adjustment problems, interest division, and development models, thus exploiting strengths and avoiding shortcomings in a continuous process of feedback, revision, and perfection of regeneration institutional systems.

Notes

1 According to existing regulations, the property-right time limit for industrial land after acquisition is usually 50 years, yet in the present time with increasingly frequent industrial transformation and upgrading, more flexible industrial land property-right time limits of between 10 and 15 years have become the new tendency in policy reforms.
2 According to land administration regulations in China, when the use of certain land is adjusted, the right attached to the new land use can only be achieved by bidding, auction, and listing.
3 Tao R, Wang R. (2014). "Urban Villages" Redevelopment and Land System Reform: Pearl River Delta Experience. *International Economic Review*, 3:28.
4 Su H, Hu Z, Li R. (2018) Pros and Cons and Demolition and Reconstruction Mode Urban Renewal. *Planners*, 6: 123–128.

References

Amirtahmasebi R, Orloff M, Wahba S. et al. (2016). *Regenerating Urban Land: A Practitioner's Guide to Leveraging Private Investment*. Washington, DC: World Bank Publications.

Ao Q P. (2017). *Study on Urban Renewal of Public-Private Partnership—In the Perspective of Taiwan*. Chongqing:Chongqing University.

Ao G X, Huang Y. (2017). Urban Regeneration: Innovation in Urban Construction – Fashion of Innovation Leads Urban Regeneration and Construction, Boosting an Urban Metamorphosis. *Shenzhen Special Zone Daily*, May 19, 2017 (A07).

Cao H, Chu C. (1990). *Urban Construction in Contemporary China*. Beijing: China Social Sciences Press.

Cabinet Office of Cabinet Public Relations Office. (2004). *Basic Policies for Urban Renaissance*. Available at: http://japan.kantei.go.jp/policy/tosi/kettei/040416kihon_e.html [Accessed May 12, 2018].

Chen C, (2016). "Walking in Shanghai 2016—Micro Regeneration Plan of Urban Community Space". *Public Art*, 4:5–9.

Chen Y X. (2018). *Public Welfare Priority, Mutual Construction and Sharing – Interpretations of the Technical Requirements of the Urban Regenerations of Shanghai*. Available at: http://www.shgtj.gov.cn/bmzx/zcjd/201804/t20180410_828592.html [Accessed April 2, 2018].

Ding F, Wu J. (2017). The Evolution of The Concept of Urban Regeneration and the Practice Connotation in Today's Society. *Urban Planning Forum*, 6:95–103.

Dong M, Chen T, Wang L. (2009). Development Course and Policy Evolution of Urban Renewal in Western Cities. *Human Geography*, 10:42–46.

Fan H, Sheng M, Zhao X Y. (2015). Built Up Area Renovation: Meilin Area, Shenzhen. *Planners*, 11:111–115.

Fan W Q (2017). The Reason for The Unimaginably Fast Old Urban Area Renovations is Reformation and Power Concession. *Daily Sunshine*, February 15, 2017 (A04).

Feng X J. (2017). "Demolition Maps" and "Compensation Prices" Determined in Enning Road. *Yangcheng Evening News*, May 14, 2008.

Feng J, Li S N, Yu H X. (2019). Officials at The Prefectural Planning and Land Resources Committee Introduce the Five Major Policy Breaches in the Urban Regeneration Measures of Shenzhen Prefecture: Bidding, Auctions, and Listing Not Required for Land Concession in Urban Regeneration Projects. *Shenzhen Special Zone Daily*, November 13, 2019 (A06).

Gao S Q. (2016). *Enlightenment of Land Division and Consolidation in Japan on Urban Renewal in China. 2016 China Urban Planning Annual Conference Proceedings*. Shenyang, China.

Ge Y, Guan Y, Nie M Y. (2017). The Evolution Character and Innovation Research of Urban Regeneration Policy in Shanghai. *Shanghai Urban Planning Review*, 10:23–28.

Geng Y L. (2015). The Way Out of Urban Renewal in Shenzhen City (1). *Housing & Real Estate*, 3:58–62.

Hong Kong Development Bureau. (2011). *Urban Renewal Strategy*. Available at: https://www.ura.org.hk/f/page/1869/4861/URS_eng_2011.pdf [Accessed October 22, 2018].

Hu J X. (2000). Interpretation of Urban Renewal Ordinance. Taipei: *Build Magazine*.

Huang D Z. (2007). Transformation of Singapore's Central Area: From Slums to Global Commercial Hub (first half). *Beijing City Planning & Construction Review*, 11:102–104.

Huang C M. (2014). Ensuring Continuous Urban Regeneration by Learning from Singaporean Experiences. *Zhuhai Special Zone Daily*, April 27, 2014.

Information Office of Shanghai Municipality. (2015). Press *Conferences on Urban Regeneration Implementation Measures of Shanghai Municipality*. Available at: http://www.scio.gov.cn/xwfbh/gssxwfbh/fbh/Document/1432931/1432931.htm [Accessed March 22, 2018].

Jin G J, Dai J. (2010). Discussion on Taiwan Transfer of Development Right Institution. *Urban Planning International*, 8:104–109.

Kidokofio T. (2017). New Trends of Urban Development and Urban Renewal in Japan. *China Land*, 1:49–51.

Kong M L, Ma J, Du C L. (2018). Study on the Urban Reconstruction System of Japanese Cities. *Chinese Landscape Architecture*, 8:101–106.

Kuang X M. (2017). Research on the Difficulties and Countermeasures of Urban Renewal in Shanghai. *Scientific Development*, 3:32–39.

Lai S H, Wu J. (2013). Speed and Benefit: Guangzhou "Sanjiu" Redevelopment Strategies for New Urbanization. *Planners*, 29(5):36–41.

Lang W, Li X, Chen T T. (2017). Evaluating Sustainable Urban Renewal Approach in Hong Kong from a Social Perspective. *Urban Planning International*, 10:1–9.

Li T, Fang F. (2015). Research on the Development of Urban Renewal in Taiwan. *Journal of Jilin Jianzhu University*, 6:53–56.

Li Y L (2014). Several Frontier Issues in the Current Economic Situation. *Vision of Contemporary Social Sciences*, 11:33.

Liu G W, Yi Z Y, Liu D M, Wu W D. (2017). Comparable Research on the Mechanism of Urban Renewal in Mainland China, Hong Kong and Taiwan. *Construction Economics*, 4:82–85.

Liu X Y. (2014). First Domestic Urban Regeneration Organization Established, Boosting Urban Regeneration. *China Real Estate News*, June 2, (A02).

Liu X. (2009). Planning Institution and Property Rights in Urban Redevelopment: A Comparative Study Between Niucheshui In Singapore And Jinhuajie In Guangzhou. *City Planning Review*, 8:18–25.

Lu W M, Tang Y H. (2017). What Can We Learn from Hong Kong in Urban Renewal. *The Chinese Newspaper of Land and Resources*, November 1, 2017 (5).

Luo J. (2018). *Practical Explorations of the Urban Regeneration of Guangzhou. Conference of Compilation of "Three Olds" Renovations Policies of Guangdong Province and Interpretation of Practices of the Prefectures*. Shenzhen, China.

Ma L. (2010). The Urbanization Plight in Shenzhen City. *Faren Magazine*, 5:34–40.

Miao C S, Zou B, Zhang Y. (2018). Market-Oriented Development Under the Government Regulation in Urban Renewal: The New Idea for the 13th Five-year Plan of Urban Renewal in Shenzhen. *Urban Planning Forum*, 4:81–87.

National Bureau of Statistics of China. National Data (2018). Available at: http://data.stats.gov.cn/search.htm [Accessed October 22, 2018].

Niu T, Xie D X, Fan J H. (2016). The Historical and Cultural Protection of the Urban Village Reconstruction: A Case Study of Liede Village. *Urban Insight*, 4:132–140.

Planning and Land Resources Committee of Shenzhen. (2017). Interpretation Materials of *Provisional Measures on Strengthening and Improving the Implementation of Urban Regenerations*. Available at: http://pnr.sz.gov.cn/xxgk/ztzl/rdzt/csgx_zxcs/content/post_5842749.html [Accessed October 2, 2018].

Planning and Land Resources Committee of Shenzhen. (2018). Reports on the Status of Urban Regeneration of Shenzhen by the Municipal Planning and Land Resources Committee (*Shenzhen Planning and Land Resources [2018] No. 292*).

Shenzhen Special Zone Daily. (2017). *Comprehensive Acceleration and Efficiency Improvement of the Urban Regenerations of Shenzhen*. Available at: http://sztqb.sznews.com/html/2017-01/09/content_3704743.htm [Accessed March 22, 2018].

Shi Y. (2018). Gearing Type Urban Regeneration Strategy: Case on Otemachi Development in Tokyo, Japan. *Urban Planning International*. 8:132–138.

Song J. (2015). Discussion on Urban Renewal in Shenzhen. *Special Zone Economy*, 8:24–27.

State-owned Assets Supervision and Administration Commission, the People's Government of Guangdong Province. (2017). *Guangzhou Urban Regeneration Association Established*. Available at: http://zwgk.gd.gov.cn/758336165/201711/t20171117_731456.html [Accessed March 22, 2018].

Su H W, Hu Z, Li R. (2018). Pros and Cons of Demolition and Reconstruction Mode Urban Renewal. *Planners*, 6:123–128.

Su S. (2017). Research on the Development Process of Urban Renewal in Shanghai. *2017 China Urban Planning Annual Conference Proceedings*. Dongguan, China.

Tang Y. (2013). *Urban Renewal of Tawan in View of Property Rights Implementation Procedure and Inspiration on the Mainland*. Harbin: Harbin Institute of Technology.

Tang Y. (2015). Study on Strategies to Revitalize the Old Industrial Land: Dealing with the "New Normal" Economy and "Stock Land" Development. *Reform of Economic System*, 4:102–108.

Tang Z L. (2001). The Urban Planning System in Singapore. *City Planning Review*, 1:42–45.

Tian L, Yao Z H, Guo X, Yin W. (2015). Land Redevelopment Based on Property Right Configuration: Local Practice and Implications in the Context of New Urbanization. *City Planning Review*, 1:22–29.

Urban Regeneration Bureau of Guangzhou. (2016). *Recent Works of the Urban Regeneration Bureau of Guangzhou*. Available at: http://www.gz.gov.cn/550590033/8.1/201608/61f-4773cb8144a3ab95bbccda5fe8ac6.shtml [Accessed March22, 2018].

Urban Regeneration Bureau of Guangzhou. (2017). *2016 Work Summaries and 2017 Work Plans of the Urban Regeneration Bureau of Guangzhou Prefecture*. Available at: http://www.gzuro.gov.cn/csgxjxxgk/7.2/201701/953a1b13b76449dfadf0d9be29722e22.shtml [Accessed March 22, 2018].

Urban Regeneration Bureau of Guangzhou. (2018). *2016 Work Summaries and 2017 Work Plans of the Urban Regeneration Bureau of Guangzhou Prefecture*. Available at: http://www.gzuro.gov.cn/csgxjxxgk/7.2/201803/690cde20218241c2acc7ad36a9b16405.shtml [Accessed March 22, 2018].

Wang C Q, Sha Y J, Wei J J. (2012). An Introduction to Urban Planning and Development of Singapore. *Shanghai Urban Planning Review*, 3:136–143.

Wang S. (2017). Research on the Operating Mechanisms of Growth Alliances in Urban Regenerations: Case Studies Based on Guangzhou. *City*, 12:47–58.

References

Wang S F, Shen S Q. (2015). From "Three-Old" Reconstruction to Urban Renewal—Thinking around the Newly-established Urban Renewal Bureau in Guangzhou. *Urban Planning Forum*, 3:22–27.

Wang S F, Bouhouch L, Wu K Q. (2017). Experience and Prospects of Urban Renewal in Guangzhou. *Urban and Rural Planning*, 12:80–87.

Wang S Y. (2018). Refection on the "Three-Old" Reconstruction Policy and Exploration of Urban Renewal Direction in Guangzhou. *Land and Resources Information*, 5:51–56.

Wang Y. (2013). *The Comparative Study of the Urban Renewal Based on the Land System Differences--Taking Mainland China and Taiwan as Example*. Nanjing: Nanjing University.

Wen X L. (2017). Switching to the Slum Regeneration Path, Shenzhen Resolves Strife Over Urban Regeneration Interests. *China Real Estate News*, May 1, 2017 (2).

Wu J L. (2014). New Journey of Economic Reform. *China Economy & Informatization*, 12:14–18.

Wu L. (1994). *The Old City of Beijing and its Juer Hutong Neighbourhood*. Beijing: China Architecture & Building Press.

Wu Z, Zhou S. (2005). Solutions to the Renovation of Urban Village: Balancing the Interests among the Municipal Management, Urban Development, and Inhabitants – a Case Study of Wenchong Community in Guangzhou. *Urban Studies*, 2:48–53.

Wu Z, Fu X. (2008). *References for the Urban Regeneration in China from the Renewal Mode of Urban-Village of Liede, Guangzhou. China Urban Planning Annual Conference Proceedings*.

Xie Y C, Costa F J. (1993). Urban Planning in Socialist China: Theory and Practice. *Cities*, 10(2):103–104.

Xu Q. (2017). "Real Expo" Opens, with Urban Regeneration under the Spotlight. *Shenzhen Special Zone Daily*, 2017-8-23(A05). Available at: http://sztqb.sznews.com/PC/content/201708/23/c153029.html [Accessed March 22, 2018].

Yang L, Yuan Q F, Qiu J S, Zheng J R. (2012). First Probing of the Difficulty of Regenerating "Urban Villages" (Old Villages) in the Pearl River Delta. *Modern Urban Research*, 11:25–31.

Yang Y R. (2013). Financialization, Urban Planning and Double Movement: Exploring the Conflicts of "Urban Renewal Taipei Style". *Urban Planning International*, 8:27–36.

Yao Z H, Tian L. (2017). Transition of Pattern and Modes of Governance for Urban Renewal in Guangzhou since the 21st Century. *Shanghai Urban Planning Review*, 5:29–34.

Yin N Y, Wang H Y. (2016). Study on the Urban Renewal Model under the Multi-coordination: A Case Study of Urs in Taipei. *Jiangsu Urban Planning*, 9:8–13.

Yin Q. (2013). *The Review Process of Hong Kong's Urban Renewal Strategy and Its Inspiration for the Renewal of the Old Cities in the Mainland. China Urban Planning Annual Conference. Urban Era, Collaborative Planning: 2013 China Urban Planning Annual Conference Proceedings*. Qingdao: Qingdao Publishing House.

Yu H X, Gu X Y, Li F Y. (2017). A Study on the Implementation Strategy and Mechanism of Urban Renewal—A Case Study of "West Bund" Urban Renewal. *Housing Science*, 37(10):18–23.

Yu H Y, Wen H. (2016). Urban Regeneration in Japan: Integrated by State-level Policies. *Urban Environment Design*, 8:288–291.

Zhai B, Wu M. (2009). Urban Regeneration and its Realities in Urban China. *Urban Planning Forum*, 2:75–82.

Zhang C. (2017). Shenzhen Establishes Urban Regeneration Committee. *Shenzhen Special Zone Daily*, 2017-8-1(A04).

Zhang J. (1996). Exploring the Small-scale Transformation and Renovation of Urban Historic conservation area. *City Planning Review*, 1996(4):14–17.

Zhang J. (1999). Discuss of Small Scale Urban Reconstruction based on Community. *Urban Planning Forum*, 3:64–66.

Zhang L, Liu Q. (2017). 616 Projects Listed in Urban Regeneration of Shenzhen, Involving 48.92 km^2 of Land. Available at: http://www.sznews.com/news/content/2017-08/23/content_17090728.htm [Accessed March 22, 2018].

Zhang X Y, Zhang A L. (2018). Experience and Inspiration of Transfer of Development Rights During Urban Renewal in Taiwan. *City Planning Review*, 2:91–96.

Zhao R Y. (2013). Thought Over Negotiation Mechanism of Urban Renewal in Shenzhen. *Urban Development Studies*, 8:118–121.

Zhong C. (2017). To Solve the Problems in Urban Renewal with Policy Update - Reflections on the "Forced Sale" System of Land in Hong Kong. *China Land*, 5:27–30.

Zhuang S Q. (2015a). Conservative and Intensive Land Use in Shanghai under the "New Normal". *Shanghai Land & Resources*, 3:1–8.

Zhuang S Q (2015b). New Exploration of Shanghai Urban Regeneration. *Shanghai Urban Planning Review*, 5:10–12.

Zhu Z Y, Song G. (2017). "Micro-Renovation" Becomes Reality: Reviewing the Renovation of Yongqing District of Enning Road. *Architecture Technique*, 11:66–75.

Zou B. (2017). Practices, Effects, and Challenges of the Inventory Development Pattern: The Assessments and Extended Thoughts of Urban Renewal Implementation in Shenzhen. *City Planning Review*, 1:89–94.

Index

Page numbers in **bold** indicate tables, page numbers in *italic* indicate figures and page numbers followed by n indicate notes.

affordable housing 8, 51, **66**, 92, 99–100, 103, 107n3, **118**, **120**, 124–125, **146**, **147**, 149, 160, 175, 183–184, 189, 192
Annual Program 58, 70, 72, *74–75*, 86, 143, **144**, **147**

Bantian change of use 35, 65, **66**, 74, 118, **133**, 140n21, 147
Bao'an 104, 148

Caojiadu 52
Caoyang New Village **126**, 149, **151**
Changning 52, 81, **126**–**127**, **129**, 138
Chen Zhanxiang 2
Colorful Community program 43
community planner 43, **66**, 115–116, 130, 191–192
comprehensive renewal 31, **46**, 48–49, 57, 64, 72–75, 94, 108–111, 143, **144**, 154, 158, 170n16, 176, 190
comprehensive renovation 35, 49–50, 54–57, 60, *65*, **66**, 78, 98, 103, 109–110, 114, 117–118, **120**–**121**, 124, 139n7, 147, 159–160, 163–165, 170n14, 186

D. C. North 5
demolition and reconstruction 1–2, 35, 37, 49–51, 54–57, 60, *65*, **66**, 69, **70**, 74–75, 78–79, 84–85, 86n1, 98–101, 103, 111, 114–118, 122, 139n10, 146–148, 159, 161, 164–165, 168, 170n13, 170n18, 174, 177–178, 183, 190, 194n4, 197
development intensity 9, 40, 47, 62n5, 88, 90–91, 96, 131, 159, 164, 172, 184
Discounting Factor 106

East Siwenli 52
emptying cages and changing the birds (teng long huan niao) 32

Enning Road 113–114, 139n5

Floor Area Adjusted **98**
function 1, **2**, 6, 9, 15, 20, 21, 38–39, **42**, 49–50, 53–54, 57, 60, 62n8, 65, 67–68, 75, 88, **89**, **90**, 99–100, 103, 104, **105**, **110**, 114, 122, **132**, 134, 137, 143, 149, 153, 155–159, 161, 164, 166, 170n20, 173–174, 178, **180**, 181–183, 185–186, 190
Futian Shuiwei LM Youth Community 124

Hengsha urban village 109
Huadu **89**, **95**, 156

ID Town 124
informal 5, 8, 33–34, 54, 174–175
innovative industrial building 99–100
Intensity Zoning 96–98, 107n2

Jing'an 52, **127**, **129**, 135, **150**–**151**

land expropriation 27, **46**, 95, **112**, **144**, 176, 189, 191
land premium payment 94–95, 153, 173, 176, 182, 189
Liede Village 31, 110–113, 153
life-cycle management 55, 65, 76, 104, 188
Liwan 30, 111, 113, 139n2, 143, 156
Longgang 104, 117, **120**, 125, **148**
Lujiazui 53, 149, **150**
Luohu 70, 87n5, **119**, 125, 147, **148**, 164

micro regeneration 9, 39, 43, **46**, 48–49, 53, 57, 62n8, 64, **66**, 73, 83, 92, 108–111, 113–115, 125, 130, 140n20, 140n22, 143, **144**, 154, 166, 168

Index 201

Nanshan **120**, 125, **148**, 164
new normal 3, **180**
No.228 Neighborhood **127**, 130–131, **132**

Panyu **89**, 138, 156
Pearl River Delta 3
Pengpu Town 135
policy-based housing 99–100, 146, 160, 183–184
property right 1–2, 8, 9, 21, 23–27, 46–47, 52, **81**, *85*, **106**, **120**, 140n20, 142, 152, 154, 156–157, 159–160, 171n35, 172–173, 175, 177–178, 190, 194
public elements list 104–105, 132, 166, **193**
Pudong 53, **126–127**, **129**, 130, 138, **150–151**
Putuo 52, **126**, **129**, 130, **151**

regeneration database (drawings and information database) 61, **66**, 72, *74*, 81–83, 86, 87n10, 155–156, 175, **193**
regional assessment 39, 44–45, 53, 55, 58, 60, 65–66, 72, 76, 80, 81, **82**, 86, 104, 108, 126, 130, 165–166, 181, 188

spatial management 104–106
Special Urban Regeneration Plan 54, 57–58, 65–66, 77–78, 98

Tangxia Village 115
three olds (old towns, old villages, and old factories/industrial lands) 7, 29–33, 35, 40–49, 56, 62n3, 63n9, 68, 77–78, 82–83, 87n6, 87n10, 95, 107n1, 108–109, 141–143, 152–155, 158, 169n1, 169n8, 175–176, 191
365 slum clearances program 37–38, 40
Tianzifang 38

20,000 households 130–131, 149, 151

urban regeneration area 57, 58, 66, 88, 105, 145
Urban Regeneration Unit 35, 50–51, 54, 58, 63n10, 65, **66**, 77, 80, **82**, 84, 86, 104, 122, 126, 131, **132**, 146–147, 149, 159, 166, 170n20
Urban Renewal Unit 17–18, 58, 65, *66*, 71, 74–75, 77–78, 79–81, 84–85, 86n1, 102, 104, 106, 117, 122–123, 139n9

volume 3, 8–9, 52, *55*, 71, 78, 124, 131, 140n21, 156, 159, 163, 167, 172, 174, 183–185, 190

Walking in Shanghai 166
West Bund 131, 134–135, *136*
Wu Liangyong 3

Xintiandi 38
Xuhui 52, **127**, **129**, 131, 134–135, *136*, **150–151**
Xujiahui 51–53, **129**, **150**, **151**

Yangmei New Village 122–123, 139n9
Yangpu **127**, **129**, 130, 133, 137, 139n15, 149, **150–151**, 191
Yangtze River Delta 3
Yantian 122–123, 139n9
Ye Min 116
Yongqing area 114
Yongqingfang 155
Yuexiu 29, 111, 114, 143, 155–156

Zengcheng **70**, **90**, **95**, 156
Zhangjiang **127**, 152
Zhang Jie 3

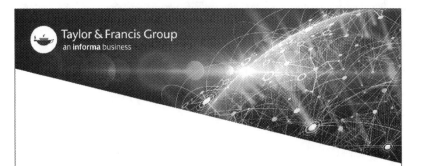

Printed in the United States
by Baker & Taylor Publisher Services